Reichsrock

Reichsrock

The International Web of White-Power and Neo-Nazi Hate Music

KIRSTEN DYCK

Rutgers University Press

New Brunswick, New Jersey, and London

Library of Congress Cataloging-in-Publication Data

Names: Dyck, Kirsten, 1983- author.

Title: Reichsrock : the international web of white-power and Neo-Nazi hate music / Kirsten Dyck.
Description: New Brunswick, New Jersey : Rutgers University Press, [2016] | ©2016 | Includes bibliographical references and index.
Identifiers: LCCN 2016003234| ISBN 9780813574714 (hardcover : alk. paper) | ISBN 9780813574707 (pbk. : alk. paper) | ISBN 9780813574721 (e-book (epub)) | ISBN 9780813574738 (e-book (web pdf))
Subjects: LCSH: Heavy metal (Music)—Social aspects. | Heavy metal (Music)—Political aspects. | Punk rock music—Social aspects. | Punk rock music—Political aspects. | White supremacy movements. | Neo-Nazism. | Hate groups.
Classification: LCC ML3918.R63 D87 2016 | DDC 306.4/842—dc23
LC record available at http://lccn.loc.gov/2016003234
A British Cataloging-in-Publication record for this book is available from the British Library.

Visit our website: http://rutgerspress.rutgers.edu

Manufactured in the United States of America

For my parents, Arthur and Suzanne Dyck, who have helped me to edit more drafts of this book than I reasonably should have asked them to read

Contents

Acknowledgments

This book was made possible (in part) by funds granted to the author through a 2014 Cummings Foundation Fellowship at the Jack, Joseph and Morton Mandel Center for Advanced Holocaust Studies of the United States Holocaust Memorial Museum. The statements made and views expressed, however, are solely the responsibility of the author. I am also grateful to the Emerging Scholars Program at the Mandel Center for Advanced Holocaust Studies for its support in the preparation of the manuscript and of the book proposal. I appreciate, in particular, the help of Steven Feldman from the Mandel Center, who helped me to revise my work and to connect with interested publishers.

This book was also supported through a 2011–2012 Fulbright grant from the German-American Fulbright Commission, as well as the former "Music, Conflict and the State" research group at Georg-August-Universität Göttingen, which hosted me during my tenure as a Fulbright fellow. Many thanks both to Fulbright and to the members of the research group. In addition, I am thankful for the help of both the Auschwitz Jewish Center in Oświęcim, Poland and the Museum of Jewish Heritage in New York City for jointly awarding me a 2011 Auschwitz Jewish Center Fellowship. I owe an immense debt of gratitude to each of these institutions for their backing and encouragement.

Also, thank you to Marlie Wasserman and the other staff members at Rutgers University Press who believed in me, invested in my project, had patience with me, and helped me to turn my manuscript into a book. Their support especially includes soliciting feedback from anonymous peer reviewers, to whom I am grateful for comments that have helped me to strengthen this book immeasurably.

I am also thankful for the guidance and research support I received from my doctoral dissertation committee in the Department of American Studies at Washington State University—my dissertation supervisor, C. Richard

King, and committee members, David J. Leonard and John Streamas. Furthermore, I am beholden to my Fulbright project supervisor, M. J. Grant, not only for helping me to revise drafts of my work before, during, and after the period of my Fulbright grant, but also for helping me to network with European scholars who were working on the subject of white-power music. I also appreciate the assistance of the mentors who helped me with the initial stages of this research project while I was a master's student at York University, especially my supervisor, Robert Simms, as well as Robert Witmer and Robert van der Bliek.

Finally, I am grateful to the friends and relatives who have offered me emotional support and revision assistance with this project. Most importantly, I appreciate the help of my parents, Arthur and Suzanne Dyck, without whom none of this would have been possible. Also, a big thank you to Alex Parrish, who helped me to revise many preliminary drafts of this manuscript, as well as to John Niblett, who helped with the revision of the final draft. I deeply appreciate the hard work of all of these individuals.

Reichsrock

What Is White-Power Music?

On September 24, 1993, thirty-six-year-old Ian Stuart Donaldson died of injuries he had sustained the previous day in a Derbyshire, England car accident.[1] Donaldson, considered the founding father of neo-Nazi rock music, had spent more than a decade working as an activist for the European white-power movement.[2] At the beginning of Donaldson's career, no such thing as "hate rock" and no coherent genre of contemporary "white-power music" existed. Today, online white-power music retailers like Micetrap Distribution, Label 56, and OPOS Records sell thousands of racist albums and concert videos. Many of these products pay tribute to Donaldson and his work. White-power music has developed into a global commodity that now expresses ideologies as diverse as Russian neo-Nazism, Brazilian white-nationalist separatism, and German nativism. The advent of readily accessible Internet technology has allowed pro-white racist groups from around the world to communicate more freely with one another than they did in earlier decades, marketing their music to sympathetic individuals who in previous generations might never have made contact with organized white-power activism, thereby facilitating the spread of white-power music to audiences that might not have discovered it otherwise.

Despite the influence of the Internet, white-power music and its complex ideologies still remain largely unknown in the English-language mainstream. Many readers of this book will have had little contact with white-power music due to the socially taboo, underground, niche-market, and occasionally even illegal nature of the genre in many areas. Some may even have been unaware of its existence. It is crucial, then, to address a number of important questions in order to introduce readers to this music and to explain its international appeal. How, when, and why did white-power music develop as a coherent genre of music in different geographical areas? How do white-power musicians in various places construct the racial categories of "insider" and "outsider" that are crucial both to racist ideology in general and to various localized racial hierarchies in particular? How do white-power musicians and fans in different areas interact with one another philosophically, intellectually, physically, digitally, and musically? How do outsiders to the movement react to white-power music? Perhaps most importantly, how do white-power musicians' ideas reflect mainstream European-descended racial hierarchies today, and how does white-power music affect the societies around it? In answering these questions, I will explore how white-power music crosses and transcends boundaries such as national borders, language barriers, cultural differences, and historical divergences.

First, it is important to explain what I mean when I refer to the genre of music known as "white-power music." While scholars have used many different terms to refer to the overtly racist music that emanates from neo-Nazi and white-power circles in western countries, for the purposes of this book, I have chosen to use white-power music because the idea of "power" or "empowerment" creates a clear distinction between the music of blatantly pro-racist groups and music that might inadvertently express racist goals, as could be the case with "white-supremacist music." The term white-power music also encompasses non–rock 'n' roll subgenres, such as hate folk and hard bass, which do not fall under the category of "hate rock," another term I initially considered. White-power musicians often prefer to call this "white-nationalist music," but some musicians whose work deserves consideration in a book on this genre— for example, Landser and other German neo-Nazi bands who have followed the hard-line ideology of the original Third Reich in viewing Poles and other Slavic groups as ethnically inferior to Germans—do not subscribe to the idea that all European-descended peoples should band together to form one coherent "white nation." Thus, I use the term white-power music, with the caveat that authors with other research agendas might choose differently.

White-power music actually represents an umbrella category that encompasses many local music scenes and various types of pro–white racist music from around the world. Some of these scenes have little interaction with one another, and some participants may disagree with others about key ideological tenets. In other cases, members of scenes in different countries maintain close business and personal ties because they have deep affinities for each other. Scholars sometimes disagree about which groups, individuals, and scenes to consider within the purview of white-power music, but for the purposes of this book, I define white-power music as any music produced and distributed by individuals who are actively trying to advance what they view as a white-power or pro–white racist agenda.

White-power ideology tends to involve belief in Jewish world conspiracy theories, opposition to national governments and international power structures like the United Nations or the World Bank, and hostility toward sexual minorities and visibly non-white individuals. Nonetheless, it is important to remember that the constellation of white-power beliefs aligns itself differently in each white-power believer. This means that while the ideologies of some core white-power musicians overlap with one another, some do not. The only unifying ideology for all groups across the genre seems to be a shared belief in a Jewish world conspiracy that threatens to breed the white race to extinction via biological race-mixing and intermarriage with partners from non-white ethnic groups; most other aspects of white-power ideology are subject to discussion and disagreement among and between different white-power groups and believers. In other words, the world of white-power music today involves conversations among many different racist groups and individuals, not all of whom agree with one another's interpretations of white-power ideology.

Strictly speaking, then, white-power music is not a "scene" or a "movement" in the same way that the Seattle grunge music scene of the early 1990s was a scene or the 1968 student movements were movements. In fact, it can be difficult to define what the social structure of white-power music really *is*, because existing terms seem inadequate. Christian Dornbusch and Jan Raabe have suggested that the term "white-power music network" might be appropriate here, but they caution that the term network carries its own set of scholarly baggage, which may make this term difficult to use as well. In concert with Dornbusch and Raabe, I propose the term "web" instead, in the hope that it will evoke the intricate sorts of brittle links and fissures that have defined white-power music since its inception.[3] This is not to argue that all members of movements or scenes hold homogeneous worldviews, but rather to point to the structural differences between social constellations with clear geographical or philosophical centers and those that lack them. While the term web is likely to prove as unsatisfactory as its predecessors, it does denote an interconnected system of groups and individuals who may agree with one another on a few key points and work together when necessary, but who sometimes also maintain separate spheres of influence and differ in important regards.

Uses and Effects of White-Power Music on Fans

Regardless of socio-historical and geographical variations within pro-white racism across different countries and localities, white-power music performs several important roles for pro-white racist groups and white-power believers worldwide. Aside from generating money for white-power organizations, the white-power music industry can also disseminate ideology, voice the movement's fantasies, and facilitate social bonding rituals. It is important to mention these social functions of music in general and white-power music in particular in order to demonstrate why white-power adherents bother to make music at all.

Musicians and fans of white-power music often tend to focus on creating community and building interpersonal relationships among European-descended individuals who might otherwise feel isolated. Several prominent figures in the world of white-power music have stated explicitly that they have used music's community-building potential to unite racist sympathizers. For example, William Pierce—the late founder of the US neo-Nazi organization the National Alliance and the former owner of the white-power music label Resistance Records—discussed the role of music in white-power recruiting before he died, writing, "Through music I want to give [people] more awareness and a better understanding of what needs to be done. Music is truly a mass medium which reaches and influences everyone, not just those who are already politically committed."[4] As Pierce's remark illustrates, a primary goal of Resistance Records was not just to entertain listeners or even necessarily just to earn a financial profit, but also to recruit new members for hate-based organizations. The same has also been true for many other white-power music producers, distributors, and musicians.

How effective white-power music actually is as a recruiting tool for organized hate groups is, of course, open for debate; statistics are difficult to obtain, because most white-power organizations do not publicize their membership rosters or other data. A long-term, interview-based research study on young participants in German right-wing extremist scenes by the *Deutsche Jugendinstitut* (German youth institute) found *"dass (. . .) Musik keine initiatorische Rolle hatte"* (that [. . .] music had no initiatory role [in recruitment]).[5] Anecdotal remarks from white-power music fans who post messages to the Stormfront white-power forums on the Internet tend to belie the certainty expressed in the *Deutsche Jugendinstitut* report, expressing how white-power music in general and Ian Stuart Donaldson's band Skrewdriver in particular facilitated many individuals' introductions to white-power beliefs and activism. One Stormfront user, for instance, wrote in 2013 that "It was I.S.D. [Ian Stuart Donaldson] and Skrewdriver that made me start questioning European politics and made me realize how sick it is. Great inspiration to so many Europeans," and another stated in 2014 that "A Skrewdriver record is what led me to read [Adolf Hitler's 1925 manifesto] *Mein Kampf* eventually."[6] Whatever the case, it is clear that William Pierce and other prominent and long-standing members of white-power communities worldwide have *intended* for their involvement with the white-power music industry to recruit new members into their organizations, and that many members of white-power scenes worldwide *believe* the music should serve that purpose.

White-power music's role in the cultures of various white-power scenes worldwide does not end, of course, after the initial recruitment phase of an adherent's experience with white-power groups. An important part of white-power music's role as a social organizing tool is its ability to provide adherents with "safe" contexts—what Pete Simi and Robert Futrell call "free spaces"—in which they can act out values that may run counter to those of the mainstream.[7] In other words, white-power music can provide the fantasy of a world in which the movement's values are already common currency. Concerts are obvious settings for these safe havens because of their face-to-face, community-building potential, but even the experiences of reading movement-related materials online and listening to recordings can make white-power believers feel less alone and more connected to a group of fellow sympathizers.[8] This aspect of music in social movements is particularly important to individuals like white-power activists, for whom group membership bears a heavy social stigma in most western countries. Free spaces allow adherents to enact their values in situations that minimize opposing opinions, creating miniature versions of their ideal societies for short periods of time and helping to facilitate white-power identity formation. Free spaces can also help established white-power believers to teach new members of their groups about white-power ideology without subjecting them to tedious lectures or speeches.[9] The white-power music web thus provides opportunities for developing and living not only white-power ideals but also entire identities based on racist ideologies. In this way, white-power music can help to sustain the movement by cultivating new generations of racist activists.

According to anti-racist scholars like Simi and Futrell as well as to prominent participants in the world of white-power music, then, music may help to keep white-power believers centered in their racist worldviews; this group-building and ideology-reinforcing potential is an important part of music's role in nearly any belief community, and helps to explain why every human society in the world today makes some form of music. In fact, music's effects on human behavior actually go even beyond these strictly social functions. While clinical research on music psychology remains in its infancy, investigations have already shown that music can influence the human autonomic nervous system—which controls bodily functions including sexual arousal, breathing, digestion, heart rate, and perspiration—and that music has an especially pronounced effect on how and when the human endocrine system, which controls hormone levels, releases the pleasure hormone dopamine and the stress hormone cortisol into the body's bloodstream.[10] When someone listens to a piece of music that he or she enjoys, he or she therefore experiences actual sensations of physical pleasure—although, of course, the same piece of music might engender the opposite physical reaction in a listener who prefers other types of music.

What this means for the study of white-power music and other forms of musical propaganda is twofold. First, white-power music does not have the power simply to "brainwash" unsympathetic listeners into believing in white-power ideologies, because listening to music that one dislikes actually tends to produce physical stress reactions. Second and equally, however, for some individuals—for instance, those who experience white-power music in the context of enjoyable social interactions with friends and loved ones, those who already agree with the political messages they hear in the lyrics to white-power songs, or even those who simply like the sound of the music—white-power music can have a powerful effect on physical and social experiences of the world.

Noting these physical effects and social uses of music helps to explain why people make and listen to political propaganda music in general and to white-power music in particular. Music affects our bodies, including our brains, in important and measurable ways. As a phenomenon with the power to influence how we interact with other people and how we feel within ourselves, music can function as an important tool for manipulating others' behavior, even though it clearly is not an unlimited or fail-safe tool. White-power racists have adopted music as a propaganda strategy and as a social bonding mechanism for many of the same reasons and in many of the same ways as other groups have done historically, including, of course, the Third Reich and other violently racist totalitarian regimes, but also left-wing, anti-racist, and anti-authoritarian protest movements, such as the Civil Rights and anti–Vietnam War protest movements in the United States in the 1960s. Music is a medium that can, in at least some circumstances, attract new adherents to white-power ideologies, help existing believers maintain social ties with one another over long periods of time, and link believers in similar ideologies over long distances. For the purposes of this book, those long-distance linkages are critically important to understanding how the white-power music web operates not only in its localized, scene-based forms, but also in an international and transnational context.

Examining White-Power Music as an International and Transnational Phenomenon

The white-power music web, as previously mentioned, is a "structure" that lacks a clear geographical center. It consists of scenes and organizations scattered throughout the world, connected by many different types of digital and interpersonal ties. However, many of the key scholarly sources on white-power music thus far treat the genre as if the white-power music scenes in the authors' home countries constitute the core or even the entirety of the white-power music web. Focusing on local or national white-power music scenes, of course, allows scholars to provide rich and valuable descriptions of white-power beliefs and practices in particular areas, but it can sometimes also leave readers with the mistaken impression that violently pro-white music is the province of one particular group in one specific area, rather than the product of long-standing, large-scale, transnational power imbalances that it really is. This book represents the first in-depth study of white-power music as a transnational rather than simply a localized phenomenon, helping to explain why racist political groups still continue to find support across the European-descended world during what is often mistakenly referred to in popular media as a "post-racial" era.[11] With the exception Anton Shekhovtsov and Paul Jackson's edited volume *White Power Music: Scenes of Extreme-Right Cultural Resistance*—which includes one of my own articles—the vast majority of the book-length scholarly writing on white-power music in English and German thus far focuses only on white-power music scenes in individual countries, spending little time exploring the international linkages among white-power musicians worldwide. Even in the Shekhovtsov and Jackson book, the individual chapters are mainly isolated national studies, most of which trace few comparisons or connections with one another. My study will add to this conversation by drawing these disparate conversations together, as well as by adding discussions of white-power music scenes in places like South America and Russia, which have received almost no attention from scholars who write in the genre's two main research languages of English and German. By acknowledging the links among racist ideologies and racist hate groups in various western cultures, I hope that this book will provide scholars of white-power music with a stronger sense of the international white-power music web as a whole.

Contemporary white supremacy and its previous iterations have been fundamental elements of European-descended societies for centuries, even though many people living in Europe and its former settler colonies today would prefer to believe that racism no longer affects their societies in significant ways. Ignoring racism's continuing influence will do nothing to explain how or why individuals become involved in white-power hate groups, nor will it help to determine why those groups develop in the first place. Understandably, many readers may find white-power musicians' inflammatory rhetoric to be offensive. Readers may wish to dismiss the fans and practitioners of this music as idiots or antisocial lunatics. However, these reductionist views explain neither the attraction the music holds for its fans nor the influence it continues to exert over significant numbers of people. The white-power music web has grown rapidly since its birth in late-1970s England; this fact alone seems to suggest that western culture has not outgrown its racist, colonialist, or even genocidal tendencies. "Political correctness" and anti-hate-speech legislation may demand that the most overtly violent racist expressions be purged from public discourse, but one should not confuse superficial suppression of dialogue with the far lengthier and more difficult process of moving past such ideas in the public (sub)consciousness. It is for these reasons that this topic remains salient decades after many people wish or even believe the influence of violent racism essentially to have disappeared from most western societies. In fact, understanding why people play white-power music and how it influences its fans and practitioners is now particularly pressing, given the recent electoral successes of openly racist political parties in many countries that produce significant numbers of white-power musicians—parties such as Greece's embattled Chrysí Avgí (golden dawn) and Germany's Nationaldemokratische Partei Deutschlands or NPD (national democratic party of Germany), which have both sponsored concerts of racist music at their political rallies and knowingly endorsed white-power musicians like Franke Rennicke and Giorgos Germenis for national political office.

In this book, I focus on how white-power music unites contemporary racism and popular culture in countries like Greece and Germany by discussing how musicians employ particular ideas of race, nation, and history to separate themselves from their supposed "enemies." This does not mean, of course, that the tropes I focus on here are the *only* important ones in the genre of white-power music. Some of the genre's most important rhetorical constructs receive little attention in this book; gender and religion, for instance, appear peripherally in my discussions of other themes in white-power music, but will have to wait for in-depth treatment in later projects. It seems to me that in order to understand concepts such as gender and religion in white-power music, one must first examine how white-power musicians construct their ideas of racial identity, enmity, in-group history, and belonging in particular, localized ways. It is because I view geographies, collective memory, nationalism, and racial identity as the key themes around which other genre tropes revolve that I have chosen to focus on them instead of on other worthy candidates.

White-power nationalism and racial identity connect directly with notions of nationalism, patriotism, and racial identity across the mainstream West today. In fact, contemporary white-power racism stems from a centuries-long history of white-supremacist western colonialism, exploitation, globalization, and genocide. One of the goals of this project is to explore the connections between seemingly non-racist elements of mainstream ideology and blatantly racist aspects of white-power philosophy. This is a vital aspect of this work, because white-power groups often appear in mainstream portrayals as extremist or fringe entities that have nothing in common with the racially tolerant mainstream. The mainstream, in this conception, does not hate, because only evil bigots espouse racist ideologies. Upon examining white-power music in its socio-historical context, however, it becomes clear that white-power music actually draws much of its explanatory power from its relationship to mainstream, systemic racism across the European-descended world. Far from being a fringe phenomenon, contemporary racism flourishes in the very structures that support western life. This book establishes links between mainstream and white-power racism in various places in order to argue why white-power groups matter. If white-power musicians truly were just extremists who had nothing to say to the rest of society, their actions would impact few lives; it is their ability to strike sympathetic chords with supposedly non-racist individuals that gives them influence and necessitates this study. This is not to say that the majority of contemporary Westerners listen to or espouse the ideologies expressed in white-power music, but rather to say that white-power musicians and fans are exploring ideas that appear more often in mainstream western socio-political discourse than many people who consider themselves non-racist would prefer to acknowledge.

Because white-power music is one of the most visible yet under-studied elements of contemporary white-power propaganda, and because white-power ideology represents archetypal racism for many Westerners today, an in-depth discussion of how and why this genre developed in different places can aid in understanding racism itself in those places, both among white-power believers and in the mainstream. White-power constructs of race are inseparable from the widespread mainstream racism that pervades Europe and its former colonies. In fact, the types of racial hierarchies that flourish in countries as disparate as Russia, Australia, and Chile today are connected to one another through the histories of European colonialism and nationalism, although they also bear distinctly local characteristics and emphases. The white-power music web, when examined as a specifically international phenomenon, provides a convenient lens for studying the links between fringe and mainstream racism in different places. By discussing what white-power musicians and fans have to say about race, nation, history, and place, this book will explore how the public face of overt racism responds and adapts to changes in the mainstream rhetoric of race, nation, and collective memory.

Rather than proceeding in a strictly chronological fashion, I have organized the chapters of this book by region. I will begin with a chapter on white-power music's origins in Britain, and will then follow the genre's expansion into continental Western Europe, Eastern Europe, and European-descended communities outside the European continent. I have chosen this structure because white-power music scenes have developed differently in different places, often in response to specific historical circumstances in particular countries and regions. Many white-power music scenes have maintained close ties with scenes in other countries, shaping other scenes' trajectories in important ways. Still, their shared characteristics often cannot erase the overwhelming impact of localized ethnic conflicts, differing experiences with the Third Reich, and the division between East and West during the Cold War era. All white-power musicians are, by definition, worried about maintaining the power and purity of white populations (however they might choose to define white), but their specific concerns can differ widely. Regional variations mean that a country-by-country history of white-power music makes more sense than a strictly linear account. This does not mean, of course, that white-power music scenes in specific countries are isolated entities, and the histories I present here will in fact note important points of contact among musicians and fans from various regions. What it does mean is that regional scenes are often different enough from one another to necessitate specific attention to local histories as well as to the development of white-power music as an international phenomenon.

Sources and Methods

I explore three main types of primary sources in this book: first, white-power songs and albums; second, white-power music magazines, particularly the British *Blood & Honour* and the now-defunct, US-based *Resistance*; and third, online discussions from white-power Internet forums, especially the Stormfront community. I analyze these sources for meaningful patterns related to race, nationalism, collective memory, and local and global pro–white racist identities. For the most part, I have chosen not to draw on a fourth potential type of source material—direct quotations of lyrics to white-power songs—because, due to the secretive and transitory nature of most white-power bands and labels, determining who owns the copyright to white-power albums, songs, and lyrics is often nearly impossible, placing authors who reprint white-power song lyrics or album imagery in dubious legal territory.

Most of the music I choose to discuss in this book comes from prominent white-power bands like Skrewdriver, Bound for Glory, Squadron, Graveland, RaHoWa, Landser, Dirlewanger, and Sokyra Peruna. As such, many of these songs seem to be relatively popular with fans of white-power music, although few sales figures or charts exist that might prove this statistically. When I discuss bands that generally receive less attention from white-power music fans, it is because they either distill tropes and trends that run through white-power music into particularly clear examples or have had historical impacts disproportionate to the size of their audience bases.

In some respects, white-power music is more difficult to study than other types of music. Sales figures, market demographics, and other key statistics are typically unavailable. The few statistics that do exist are quoted *ad nauseam* in scholarly and journalistic work about white-power music, even when they are years or even decades old. Practitioners, fans, marketers, and distributors of white-power music are often reluctant to speak with scholars and journalists, whom they tend to view as enemies. Few libraries and archives collect white-power albums or music magazines. Internet sources on white-power music can come and go without warning, as when, in June 2012, the German government suddenly shut down the German-hosted neo-Nazi Internet forum Thiazi—home to the most comprehensive discography of white-power music then available—before I could finish saving this discographic information for my future research. In some cases, white-power music researchers must use sources that scholars would normally regard as unreliable, such as anonymous websites that are full of spelling errors, grammatical mistakes, and factual inaccuracies; in other cases, the best information available comes from anti-racist watchdog groups, which have been known to distort facts about white-power activism in order to secure private donations and government funding.[12] In this book, I attempt to balance the need for reliable sources with the reality of the sources that are actually available, and to evaluate and cross-check dubious sources whenever possible. Still, when dealing with a genre of music that is semi-legal in some countries and illegal in others, this can be a difficult process. I do not knowingly report erroneous information here, but I ask for the reader's patience if evidence comes to light suggesting that I have used inaccurate material.

Some scholars of white-power movements and white-power music, such as Mattias Gardell, Pete Simi, Robert Futrell, and Benjamin Teitelbaum, have conducted fieldwork among white-power believers, activists, and musicians, attending concerts and analyzing how people relate to one another in the relative safety of white-power venues. The performance aesthetics and in-person group dynamics of white-power concerts and other gatherings are crucial aspects of white-power music to study. However, in this book, I focus not on the faces that white-power musicians and fans present to each other, but on the aspects of themselves that they choose to broadcast to the outside world. I examine the music, lyrics, and publications that emerge from the white-power music web, rather than focusing on white-power believers' relationships with one another. For this reason, this book does not include the types of ethnographic performance analysis that appear, for instance, in Simi and Futrell's *American Swastika*. Rather, this book relies on published primary and secondary texts about white-power music in order to construct histories of white-power music scenes in various countries and to explore how white-power musicians and fans discuss their world in the materials they publish.

I use my analysis of published materials from white-power musicians and fans in this book to argue that one must understand white-power music as an international genre because one must understand contemporary white-power racism—along with the older forms of racism and white supremacy that have preceded it—as a global phenomenon. A key goal of this book is to argue that the kinds of racism that appear in the lyrics to white-power songs are descended from the kinds of racism that have justified the genocide and exploitation of Europe's racial others for centuries. I explore how white-power musicians' ideologies descend directly from older types of racism and relate to racism that mainstream, "non-racist" populations in European-descended societies continue to tolerate. I hope that this analysis will serve as an intervention into the scholarly literature on white-power music, influencing other scholars to explore the links among mainstream and extremist white-power racism across time and historical borders as well.

2

The History of
White-Power Music
in Britain

Contemporary white-power movements did not invent racist music. History is rife with examples of people using music to advance ideas of ethnic conflict and violence—for instance, in the Third Reich itself and in the US antebellum South.[1] Despite the existence of a long history of racist music, however, white-power music in its current incarnation is a relatively new phenomenon. It got its start in late-1970s England, when members of the mod-descended skinhead subculture adopted a variant of punk music known as "oi!" and began espousing racist ideologies and forging connections with right-wing and neo-Nazi political organizations. Because this early period in Britain was crucial to the formation of white-power music as a contemporary genre, this chapter will focus exclusively on the history of white-power music in Britain, making Britain the only country to warrant its own chapter in this book. Not only did British musicians found the genre of contemporary white-power music, they also drove its early development, providing the genre with many of its "classic" bands. This chapter will explore why white-power music arose in 1970s Britain, how it developed, how it influenced the growth of white-power and neo-Nazi music scenes elsewhere in the world, and how it continues to affect the white-power music web today. In particular, this history will focus on the towering figure of Ian Stuart Donaldson and his band Skrewdriver, by all accounts the most famous white-power musicians in the world. The goal of this chapter will be to situate the seminal British white-power music scene within the international white-power music web and within late-twentieth-century history in order to provide a basis for the histories of white-power music in other countries, which will appear in subsequent chapters.

To explain why white-power music originated in England during the late 1970s, it is important to discuss the social conditions to which Ian Stuart Donaldson and other early British white-power musicians were responding when they first began to compose and perform overtly racist music. England, of course, had a long history as a brutal and even genocidal colonizer of non-European peoples, but expressions of overt interpersonal racism such as racially motivated violence and obvious racial slurs had become increasingly taboo among mainstream Britons during the post–World War II era. A decrease in public displays of obvious racial bigotry, however, did not mean that racist attitudes simply withered away and died there during the postwar period, just as racism did not merely cease to exist among the many other European-descended populations who adopted social norms of racial tolerance during this period. When the British economy entered a depression in 1973, economic insecurity exacerbated long-standing but often latent xenophobic attitudes among some demographics in British society. Of course, not everyone there responded to the recession with racism; for instance, some of the young Britons who felt the negative impact of the 1973–1975 depression turned to left-wing and antiauthoritarian movements instead. This spurred pop culture trends such as 1970s British punk music and produced songs like the Sex Pistols' sarcastic 1977 "God Save the Queen," which equated the British monarchy with the World War II–era fascists and suggested that England would have no future if it continued to support Queen Elizabeth II and her family. Another faction of British citizens, however, placed direct blame for their problems not on the monarchy or the fragility of the world capitalist market, but rather on non-white immigrants to the British Isles, paradoxically viewing these immigrants as unwanted competition for employment *and* as lazy freeloaders who had come to Britain solely to abuse the country's already overtaxed net of social services.

Ian Stuart Donaldson, of course, was one of those discontented Britons. Born in 1957 in Poulton-le-Fylde, Lancashire, near the city of Manchester, Donaldson formed his first band—a Rolling Stones cover band called the Tumbling Dice—in 1975. In addition to the Rolling Stones, his early influences included the British punk scene of the 1970s, especially the Sex Pistols, who themselves had recorded a 1978 song called "Belsen Was a Gas," intended to provoke outrage among the mainstream British population by seeming to celebrate the Nazi concentration camp Bergen-Belsen.[2] By 1976, the Tumbling Dice had morphed into a punk band that took its name from Donaldson's personal nickname, Skrewdriver, and recorded a non-racist album called *All Skrewed Up* on London's Chiswick Records in 1977. Chiswick, however, became increasingly uncomfortable with the violence that tended to accompany Skrewdriver gigs. Donaldson protested in a 1982 interview that Skrewdriver had never been associated with unprovoked violence, saying, "There has never been any violence at a Skrewdriver gig. The only time there is trouble is when the police come barging into our gigs and try to stop them. Or when supporters are going home after the gigs and they bump into large gangs of big mouthed Blacks."[3] In fact, though, even according to white-power sources, the band had actually earned a London-wide gig ban in the late 1970s due to fights and riots that had erupted at concerts, leading to the breakup of the group in 1979.[4] Donaldson moved back to the Manchester area and began to get involved with the local skinhead scene, as well as with right-wing political organizations such as the National Front.[5]

Donaldson did not return to London until 1982, but at that point, he re-formed Skrewdriver with a new skinhead lineup and began to play gigs again. Rumors circulated in London about the increasingly racist orientation of the group's politics. Late in 1982—at about the time he and his band met and began performing with another racist punk band that would become one of the longest-running and most important forces in the worldwide white-power music web, the Islington-based group Brutal Attack—Donaldson addressed these speculations by giving an onstage Hitler salute to a crowd at London's 100 Club, one of Skrewdriver's most frequent venues.[6] In the words of Paul Jackson, a writer for the British anti-racist magazine *Searchlight*, this was Donaldson's "notorious political 'coming out' moment" as a neo-Nazi.[7] Other British skinhead bands had played music with racist lyrical overtones prior to 1982, and a number of skinhead musicians and fans had been involved in street-level racist violence, but Donaldson's onstage Hitler salute marked the point at which racist skinhead bands first began to associate themselves openly with the world of organized white-power and neo-Nazi political groups such as the British National Party, the British Movement, the National Front, and even the US-based Ku Klux Klan.[8] Skrewdriver's second album, 1984's *Hail the New Dawn*, left no doubt that Donaldson's 1982 onstage Hitler salute had been serious; songs like "Europe Awake" and "Free My Land" featured overtly racist lyrical themes, signaling the band's transition from a punk band with right-wing leanings to a genuine neo-Nazi musical group. Today, Donaldson holds near-legendary status in white-power circles, and is regarded as the godfather of white-power music.

Oi! punk music, Donaldson's genre—named for a popular Cockney greeting that signaled the genre's self-conscious working-class attitude—coalesced around the skinhead subculture of the 1970s.[9] Skinhead style originated from the 1960s British mod subculture as a non-racist expression of proletarian identity. As mainstream mod style became increasingly commercialized over the course of the 1960s, a breakaway group of mods began to imitate both the dress codes and the musical style of the Jamaican "rude boys," a lower-class Kingston subculture that sported stylized suits and listened to ska and reggae music.[10] These early British "skinheads" of the 1960s—so named because their short-cropped hairstyles signaled a rejection of the long-haired hippie look—drew on Jamaican popular culture in fashioning their own backlash to the 1960s hippie movement. Skinhead fashion caricatured a masculine British working-class appearance with its short hair, button-up and polo shirts, rolled-up blue jeans, suspenders, and work boots, positioning these items of dress in conscious opposition to the flowing, bohemian couture of the Woodstock generation, which was fashionable at the time.[11]

These early skinheads listened to Jamaican musicians like Desmond Dekker and often attended the same concerts and clubs as Afro-Caribbean youths. Some 1960s skinhead crews boasted non-white members, as many later non-racist and anti-racist skinhead groups have continued to do. However, other groups, particularly in the late 1960s, began to engage in violent attacks such as the "Paki bashing" of South Asian immigrants and the "queer bashing" not just of homosexuals, but also of any males who did not seem to fit stereotypical definitions of working-class hyper-machismo.[12]

In the early 1970s, as the hippie movement declined in popularity, all but a small minority of the 1960s British skinhead scene dissipated. Racism and other forms of socio-political radicalization among the remaining skinheads became more apparent during this era, largely due to the financial difficulties that many working-class skinheads faced as a result of the floundering British economy of the 1970s. Some individuals among the hard-core remnants of the 1960s skinhead movement even began to involve themselves with ultra-right-wing and neo-Nazi political groups in Britain, particularly the National Front and the British Movement.[13] Had the skinhead movement actually died out in the mid-1970s, as it appeared at the time that it might do, the politicization of these remaining skinheads would likely have seemed an insignificant development. However, the influence of punk rock in the mid-1970s changed the fate of the skinhead subculture.

Punk music, pioneered by US bands such as the MC5, the New York Dolls, and Iggy Pop and the Stooges, had taken root in cities like Detroit and New York as early as the late 1960s. In the mid-1970s, punk began to appear in England as well. Punk's working-class, anti-hippie aesthetic stood in opposition to the acid-drenched jam sessions of California-based bands like the Grateful Dead and the Jefferson Airplane, promoting punchy, three-minute songs with catchy tunes and memorable choruses. Punk also abandoned the hippie movement's purportedly bourgeois long hair and bohemian clothing for a do-it-yourself ethos of safety-pinned second-hand apparel and sado-masochist leather couture, attempting to shock outsiders by deploying symbols that violated many different social taboos. Even punk bands that claimed to be non-racist or politically neutral, such as the Sex Pistols, Siouxie and the Banshees, and the Ramones, occasionally appeared in public sporting swastikas and singing non-condemnatory songs about Bergen-Belsen and *Blitzkrieg*.[14] This confrontational and transgressive symbolism appealed to the nihilistic and anti-hippie elements of the skinhead subculture, inspiring a group of young British skinheads like Ian Stuart Donaldson to form their own punk bands. Their new, punk-derived form of skinhead music revitalized the dying skinhead scene in the late 1970s with a punk subgenre called "street punk" or "oi!," which removed many of the overt rhythmic markers of punk's ska and reggae progenitors in favor of a more rhythmically simplistic sound.

The schism between oi! and the ska-and-reggae-derived British skinhead rock music of the 1960s opened a rift in the skinhead movement. Growing numbers of racist oi! fans began to clash with anti-racist—or at least non-racist—skinheads. To be clear, racist skinheads have always represented a minority within the overall skinhead movement, and many contemporary oi! bands remain anti-racist, despite the fact that popular media occasionally portray all skinheads and oi! bands as racists. However, this numerical imbalance did not always seem obvious to the warring British skinhead factions who used music as a battleground for the political orientation of the skinhead movement in the late 1970s and early 1980s. Anti-racist oi! bands like Sham '69 found that their racist and non-racist fans often got into bloody fights at concerts. Even by denouncing racism publicly, such bands could not necessarily prevent significant racist followings from continuing to attend their concerts.[15]

Musical style was not the only difference between the newly politicized "second-wave" or "revival" skinheads of the mid-1970s and the less political skinheads of the 1960s. Fashion, like music, became a site of conflict among skinheads in the late 1970s and 1980s. In response to the self-consciously transgressive influence of punk fashion, many revival skinheads began to enhance the aggressive and militaristic aspects of the skinhead appearance. They began wearing taller work and military boots—as high as twenty eyelets—as well as military-surplus bomber jackets. Many also shaved their hair instead of merely cropping it short, and some began to sport tattoos on body parts that were easily visible even when the bearer was fully clothed, such as hands, necks, and faces. Although this division was not universal—some racist skinheads also maintained the older look, and some anti-racist skinheads changed to the militarized revival style—the general trend was toward a split between anti-racist skinhead fans of reggae-based skinhead music wearing 1960s-era skinhead clothing and racist skinhead fans of punk-based skinhead music tending toward the more aggressive second-wave militaristic look.[16]

As the skinhead movement divided along the lines of music, politics, and fashion, its internal disputes started to spill over into British public life. In particular, the frequent violence that accompanied skinhead gigs caught the mainstream public's attention. For instance, at a July 3, 1981 concert by several non-racist oi! bands at the Hambrough Tavern in the Little India section of London's Southall suburb—a venue that previously had been sued for barring non-white patrons from entry, although some non-white fans did attend the July 3, 1981 gig—racist oi! fans handed out racially charged leaflets and reportedly committed several serious assaults on elderly members of the sizeable local immigrant community outside the venue. Rumors of racist violence at the Hambrough Tavern gig infuriated the locals, who had already experienced an escalating pattern of violence surrounding other skinhead concerts in the area; in fact, an anti-racist schoolteacher, Blair Peach, had actually died in a violent clash between the Anti-Nazi League and the racist National Front in the same area in 1979.[17] An incensed group of about 400 South Asian youths gathered outside the tavern to protest the July 3, 1981 concert, and when skinheads attacked onlookers with bricks and clubs, chanting slogans like "Sieg Heil" and "Kill the Pakis," the protesters threw gasoline bombs into the venue in retaliation.[18] As a result of the ensuing riot, the Hambrough Tavern burned to the ground, and at least 120 people, including 61 police officers, sustained serious injuries.[19] The public furor over this incident quickly led embarrassed mainstream record labels to begin discontinuing oi! records from their catalogues.

One such record was the contentious May 1981 oi! compilation album *Strength Thru Oi!*, which originally appeared on Decca Records, a label that also carried a number of major international stars like the Rolling Stones, Louis Armstrong, Patsy Cline, and Bing Crosby. The cover of the *Strength Thru Oi!* album featured a photograph of the archetypal second-wave skinhead Nicola Vicenzio "Nicky" Crane, the North Kent organizer for the overtly neo-Nazi British Movement. The album's producers had airbrushed Crane's Nazi tattoos out of the photo. The album had already drawn public criticism because its title seemed to reference the name of the Third Reich's leisure program *Kraft durch Freude*, usually translated into English as strength through joy. In the wake of the Southall riot, Decca withdrew *Strength Thru Oi!* and announced that it would no longer handle any other oi! bands or albums. Other mainstream labels, record shops, and concert venues followed suit.[20] After the summer of 1981, if members of the British oi! scene wanted to express racist sentiments, they had to do so without the help of the mainstream music industry. Some racist oi! bands, like London Branch, decided to split up in response to the pressure, while others, like the version of Ian Stuart Donaldson's band Skrewdriver that re-formed in 1982, became increasingly militant in their racism and their extreme-right-wing activism.[21]

Right-wing oi! musicians needed a new production and distribution infrastructure if they hoped to keep their scene alive in the immediate post–Southall riot period. Into this void stepped Donaldson, who had become the Blackpool and Fylde organizer for the racist Young National Front organization while he was back living in the Manchester area between 1979 and 1982. Donaldson had already helped to set up the white-power music organization Rock Against Communism (RAC) as a branch of the Young National Front in 1979.[22] RAC's organizers chose the organization's name to counter the left-wing Rock Against Racism association, which had been coordinating anti-racist rock concerts in Britain since 1976. By late 1982, just months after the Southall riot and the *Strength Thru Oi!* debacle, and around the same time that Donaldson publicly "outed" himself as a neo-Nazi, RAC was holding regular gigs and distributing the skinhead albums that mainstream record stores would no longer sell. RAC quickly became so influential among fans and practitioners of racist music that members of white-power music scenes today continue to use the acronym "RAC" to refer not just to the Rock Against Communism organization, but also to the bands and even to the seminal *sound* that emanated from 1980s Britain, which has been adopted by many different musicians outside Britain in the interim. In some instances, musicians and fans still use RAC as a designation for white-power music overall.

The National Front also set up its own record label, White Noise Records, producing as its inaugural release a 1983 Skrewdriver single that featured the songs "Smash the IRA [Irish Republican Army]," "Shove the Dove," and Donaldson's particularly seminal anthem "White Power." In 1986, the National Front even began to publish a skinzine—a type of self-published skinhead fan magazine usually featuring photocopier-style production quality and low circulation numbers—called *White Noise.*[23]

Despite these investments in early white-power music, the National Front was in trouble as an organization. Its membership roster had been declining in numbers since the mid-1970s, and leaders had been using the proceeds from White Noise Records to keep the parent organization afloat.[24] A worse development, at least from the perspective of the National Front's supporters in the early-1980s white-power music scene, was the fact that many members of the organization had begun attempting to garner a greater support base among the mainstream populus by distancing themselves from overt racism.

Frustrated with the National Front's new political direction and its lack of influence, Donaldson and *Strength Thru Oi!*'s Nicky Crane—a Skrewdriver roadie starting in 1984 and the artist for several of Skrewdriver's album covers—spearheaded a new white-power music organization in 1987 called Blood & Honour. They chose this name because it translated directly to the German phrase *Blut und Ehre*, a slogan that had been etched into the blades of standard-issue Hitler Youth knives known as *Hitler-Jugend-Fahrtenmesser*—"Hitler Youth journey knives," hunting and pocket knives issued to members of the violently racist Third Reich children's organization the Hitler Youth. Donaldson and Crane took Blood & Honour's logo, alternately known as the triskelion, "rolling sevens," or left-facing three-armed swastika, from the

South African white-separatist, pro-apartheid paramilitary organization the Afrikaner Weerstandsbeweging (Afrikaans resistance movement). Blood & Honour leaders promised to remain independent of the infighting that often occurred among English right-wing political groups.[25] Blood & Honour's primary focus was the glossy magazine *Blood & Honour*, but the group also organized and promoted concerts. Donaldson and Crane brought with them several prominent white-power bands as founding members of Blood & Honour, including not only Donaldson's own band, Skrewdriver, but also Brutal Attack, Sudden Impact, Squadron, Skullhead, and No Remorse. Several of these groups, alongside Skrewdriver and Brutal Attack, have become premier bands of the white-power music canon in their own right.[26] Skrewdriver continued to record albums during this period, releasing a number of singles and a string of late-1980s albums that included *Blood & Honour* in 1985, *White Rider* in 1987, *After the Fire* in 1988, and *Warlord* in 1989.

Because the mainstream music industry was increasingly turning its back on racist music, in the late 1980s, these founding Blood & Honour bands wanted to use their organization to help struggling white-power artists find recording labels, music stores, and concert venues that were willing to work with them. They knew that staging Blood & Honour gigs was no longer an easy feat; the violence and organized opposition that had dogged even ostensibly non-political oi! concerts since before the July 1981 Southall riot continued to plague Donaldson and his colleagues in the late 1980s.

One glaring example was a 1989 Blood & Honour concert in London dubbed the "Main Event," which was supposed to feature Skrewdriver, Brutal Attack, Sudden Impact, No Remorse, and Squadron, as well as other bands like Vengeance and Bunker 84. Blood & Honour touted the concert as the biggest white-power skinhead gig ever, advertised internationally, and sold more than a thousand tickets. However, under pressure from anti-racist activists, a concerned group of local authorities and venue owners figured out which concert hall Blood & Honour had booked for the gig and convinced the owner to cancel the venue reservation, leaving disappointed fans on the streets to clash violently with anti-racist protesters and local police.[27] Blood & Honour lost respect from many of its would-be concertgoers as a result of the fiasco, making the failed Main Event one of the last large white-power concerts that organizers dared to advertise publicly in Britain. In fact, debacles such as the Main Event drove white-power concert organizers to implement increasingly strict measures for preventing anti-racists and law enforcement officials from crashing events, a strategy that provided safety for those who attended gigs regularly, but which also meant that concerts became less accessible to potential new recruits as contact points for learning about white-power ideology, befriending white-power activists, and joining white-power groups.

Blood & Honour also had another problem, although this one was easier to solve. Its split from the National Front and White Noise Records had not been amicable. Blood & Honour bands like Skrewdriver, Skullhead, and Brutal Attack could no longer rely on White Noise Records to produce their albums. They needed to find a new label. After 1987, British Blood & Honour bands released some of their records through the British label Link Records—the only British company that knowingly worked with neo-Nazi bands in the era immediately after the Southall riot—but far more regularly, they chose the Rock-O-Rama Records label in the West German town of Brühl, near Köln in Nordrhein-Westfalen.[28] Donaldson admitted to a British newsmagazine in 1988 that his association with Rock-O-Rama was not only helping him to build the white-power music scene in Britain, but had also actually put him into contact with former members of Hitler's SS who still lived in Germany, with whom he discussed "our common goal, getting rid of Britain's uninvited guests."[29] Skrewdriver began to tour West Germany and Scandinavia in the late 1980s, and Donaldson even received money from Rock-O-Rama's owner, Herbert Egoldt, to recruit other bands for Rock-O-Rama and its associated distributor, Independent Schallplatten Versand (independent record distribution).[30]

For Donaldson, this juncture in the late 1980s and early 1990s was the pinnacle of his white-power music career. His international fan base was growing, and he began to experiment with side bands such as the rockabilly-and-country-inspired Klansmen and the racist heavy metal group White Diamond, releasing a solo album called *No Turning Back* in 1989, as well as two Klansmen records—*Rebel with a Cause* and *Rock 'n' Roll Patriots*—in the same year. It was also at this point, though, that Donaldson began to show signs of dissatisfaction with the movement he had built. He played increasingly fewer concerts and seemed to be withdrawing himself from the movement. He even handed over most of his responsibilities with Blood & Honour to someone else, a skinhead named Neil Parish, who was convicted of nearly forty separate crimes during his tenure in the white-power movement.[31]

The reasons for Donaldson's gradual disaffection were numerous, but his experiences with various European prison systems seem to have been prominent. On December 11, 1985, he assaulted an elderly black man at King's Cross Station in London, for which he served a twelve-month sentence at Wayland Prison in Norfolk.[32] He was incarcerated again in 1990; in September of that year, Skrewdriver played at a German reunification celebration concert in the former East German city of Cottbus, Brandenburg, which was soon to become a white-power stronghold. The gig descended into rioting and landed Donaldson in Berlin's Moabit Prison along with five other Skrewdriver associates, including Skrewdriver drummer John Bellany, Jr. (a.k.a. John Burnley), the older brother of No Remorse frontman Paul Bellany (a.k.a. Paul Burnley) and the son of the famous Scottish painter John Bellany, Sr.; Skrewdriver bassist Jonathan "Smiley/Icky" Hickson, formerly of the white-power band Lionheart; and Skrewdriver's new lead guitarist, Stephen "Stigger" Calladine, also the lead guitarist for Donaldson's metal band White Diamond and the brother of Donaldson's girlfriend, Diane Calladine. Authorities released Donaldson after a few days, but some of the six remained there for a full month. On returning to England ahead of his bandmates, Donaldson put together an impromptu band, which he called Ian Stuart and Rough Justice, to record a six-track mini-LP which Rock-O-Rama released in 1992 under the title *Justice for the Cottbus Six*.[33] Donaldson continued after his release to issue aggrandizing statements about his willingness to sacrifice for his white-power beliefs, but he told friends privately that he had no desire to return to prison again.[34]

Another event that contributed to Donaldson's disaffection from the British white-power music scene came in July 1992, when his former right-hand man, the violent street brawler Nicky Crane, admitted on live national television that he had been leading a secret double life as a homosexual. Crane had hidden his sexuality from his violently homophobic white-power associates by working as a security guard and insisting that his only connections with London's gay subculture were work-related. In reality, throughout his period of activism with the National Front and Blood & Honour groups, Crane had been a regular in London's gay clubs, and had even acted in several amateur gay porn films, graphic stills of which are now available on the Internet.[35] On December 8, 1993, the year after Crane's on-air confession and just months after Donaldson's own death, Crane died of an AIDS-related illness.

Donaldson viewed Crane's on-air revelation as the worst betrayal of his life, saying,

> I feel more betrayed by him than probably anybody else, because he was the head of our security. I actually used to stick up for him when people used to say that he was queer, because he convinced me that he wasn't. I always used to ask him why he worked at these gay clubs, telling him that he'd get a bad name. He used to say that it was the security firm that he used to work with, that they used to give him the job there. I accepted him at face value, as he was a Nationalist. I was fooled the same as everybody else. Perhaps more than everybody else. I felt I was betrayed by him and I want nothing to do with him whatsoever. He's dug his own grave as far as I'm concerned.[36]

Donaldson's shock at Crane's homosexuality was genuine, but in retrospect, perhaps he was naïve to have been surprised. Researchers have often noted that the presence of closeted homosexuals can be surprisingly common in masculinist, homophobic extremist movements. In fact, Johann Hari, a homosexual journalist with the London news giant *The Guardian*, published a December 2002 article about how he had made a project of seducing homophobic male neo-Nazis and Islamist fundamentalists. Hari pointed out that the head of Hitler's paramilitary *Sturmabteilung* or "Brownshirts," Ernst Röhm, was homosexual—a fact confirmed by Richard Plant, a leading historian of homosexuals in the Holocaust, who adds that Hitler seems even to have condoned Röhm's sexuality up to a point—and that many male homosexuals have actually enjoyed the ultra-macho atmospheres of some Nazi, neo-Nazi, and Islamic fundamentalist groups.[37] Other notorious homosexual neo-Nazis have included the American terrorist and transsexual Pete Langan, a Timothy McVeigh associate who belonged to the same Aryan Republican Army cell as white-power musicians Scott Stedeford and Kevin McCarthy of the band Day of the Sword, and who, along with Stedeford, McCarthy, and others, participated in a string of bank robberies and other heists that helped to fund white-power crimes, including, in all likelihood, McVeigh's 1995 bombing of the Murrah Federal Building in Oklahoma City.[38] Knowledge of homosexual Nazis and neo-Nazis other than just Nicky Crane, of course, would hardly have consoled Donaldson.

In addition to the revelation that Nicky Crane was gay, the year 1992 held other disappointments for Donaldson. On March 13, 1992, a car accident killed Brian and Darren Sheeley, Paul Cassey, and Jason Oakes, four of the five members of the Welsh white-power band Violent Storm.[39] The band had been on the way to the airport to play at a large white-power concert which was to take place in Valencia, Spain the next day.[40] Shortly after the accident, anti-racists in Violent Storm's hometown of Cardiff emblazoned the outside of the band's favorite pub with graffiti reading "FOUR DOWN ONE TO GO."[41] There was some small comfort for Donaldson and the white-power music world, however, in the fact that Violent Storm's only surviving member, the nightclub bouncer and bodybuilder Nigel "Billy" Bartlett, went on to found the band Celtic Warrior—named after a Violent Storm album—which quickly became one of the most active and famous bands in white-power music, performing regularly in small mining villages across Wales, as well as touring and recording internationally.[42]

Another 1992 setback for Donaldson was a large concert that Blood & Honour tried to organize in conjunction with No Remorse frontman Paul Burnley and the British Movement. The gig featured Skrewdriver, No Remorse, Skullhead, and one of the star acts of the 1990s Swedish white-power music scene, the band Dirlewanger, which was named after Dr. Oskar Paul Dirlewanger, the German commander of a World War II–era SS penal unit that committed a number of notorious Nazi war crimes. Everything went according to plan with concert preparations until anti-fascist groups discovered the location of the concert's pre-arranged redirection point, where audience members were supposed to meet at the last minute in order to learn the true venue for the concert from a Blood & Honour representative positioned at the spot. At the redirection point for this concert—Waterloo Station in London—anti-racist protesters succeeded in wreaking such havoc with the skinheads who arrived at the station that area police, in addition to making a number of violent arrests, actually had to evacuate the entire station. Most of the would-be concertgoers, including dozens who had traveled from abroad to attend the gig, never arrived at the pub in southeast London where the concert took place. Donaldson and his bandmates blamed the debacle on Burnley, who had posted only one redirection agent to Waterloo Station—an agent who was arrested almost instantly upon arrival.[43] Blood & Honour leaders found themselves particularly humiliated as the mainstream press began dubbing the fracas at the redirection point "The Battle of Waterloo."[44]

Blood & Honour's embarrassment, however, was good news for other groups who wanted to control Britain's white-power music scene and thereby harness the music's earning power for their own activism. The most aggressive of these was the Combat 18, or C18, terrorist group, under the leadership of Paul "Charlie" Sargent. The "18" in the organization's name was white-power numerical code for Adolf Hitler, referencing the fact that "A" is the first letter of the Latin alphabet and "H" is the eighth. Sargent and C18 duped a struggling Neil Parish into handing Blood & Honour's assets to them, and then smeared Parish's name to Donaldson and other prominent Blood & Honour members while Parish was behind bars for illegal possession of CS gas, the chemical irritant that allows riot-control tear gas to incapacitate its subjects.[45]

After Donaldson's death in September 1993, C18 also used a disgruntled former No Remorse band member named Will Browning to pursue command of the *Blood & Honour* magazine, which Paul Burnley and the British Movement controlled. Browning even hijacked Burnley's band, releasing a provocative, ultra-racist, Burnley-less No Remorse album called *Barbecue in Rostock*—an album title that referred to a violent race riot in the former East German city of Rostock in August 1992, during which hundreds of rioters, cheered on by thousands of bystanders, attacked and burned down a refugee hostel while chanting racist slogans.[46] Burnley, who quickly went to work on new band projects such as No Fear, responded by printing a highly publicized 1997 No Remorse farewell article in the big-name US white-power music magazine *Resistance* as an attempt to dash public support for Browning's No Remorse.[47] Browning's No Remorse nonetheless continued to release albums until 2006, some of which have received positive reviews from white-power music fans. For instance, one Stormfront user, who was clearly unaware of the bitter feud that had recently taken place over No Remorse, Blood & Honour, and Combat 18, posted this 2007 review of the 2005 No Remorse album *Oi! Monkey*:

Good album. Has a hard driving guitar sound, and quite nasty, racist lyrics. I don't know the history of this band, but I do know there was both an older NR [No Remorse] and a newer. I believe there's separate singers in each incarnation, as well as other sound differences primarily related to production, with the newer CDs having a heavier, beefier sound. [. . .] I've heard this band, and RAC in general, criticized for being simplistic, repetitive, and boring. My response is: simplistic, maybe; repetitive, probably; but boring, no. I grew up listening to AC/DC and Bad Company, both of which were able to create much with a very basic formula. I think the same thing applies here.[48]

This fan obviously likes not only the robust sound of the later No Remorse albums like *Oi! Monkey* as well as the particularly violent brand of racism that the post–Burnley No Remorse expressed in its song lyrics. This review also provides a cogent response to listeners who criticize No Remorse's musical ability, pointing out that many of the most famous bands in the mainstream rock 'n' roll canon have produced interesting work despite lacking the versatility to play in multiple genres. Nonetheless, fans who know more about the history of the British white-power music scene tend to express resentment over the rift that Browning and Burnley caused in their struggle for control of Blood & Honour, which created a schism in the British white-power music movement that actually seems to have stalled the scene's forward momentum.[49]

At the center of the Burnley-vs.-C18 feud was the image that Ian Stuart Donaldson had left behind when he died after his car accident on September 24, 1993. Despite his gradual decrease in performances and retreat from direct involvement in the day-to-day operations of the Blood & Honour organization, Donaldson had recorded prolifically in the early 1990s. Stephen Calladine's facility as a guitarist had allowed Donaldson and Skrewdriver to increase their stylistic range into genres of music with which they had not previously experimented, such as acoustic ballads. In addition to Donaldson's solo albums *Slay the Beast* (1990) and *Patriot* (1991)—as well as the Skrewdriver albums *The Strong Survive* (1990), *Live and Kicking* (1991), *Freedom What Freedom* (1992), *Hail Victory* (released in 1994, after Donaldson's death), and *Live at Waterloo* (also released posthumously, in 1995)—Donaldson and Calladine released two acoustic albums as the duo Ian Stuart & Stigger, entitled *Patriotic Ballads* (1991) and *Patriotic Ballads II—Our Time Will Come* (1992). During this period, Donaldson also recorded the 1991 album *Fetch the Rope* with his rockabilly band the Klansmen, along with *The Reaper* (1991) and *The Power & the Glory* (1992) with his heavy metal group White Diamond.

Then, on September 23, 1993, Donaldson's designated driver lost control of his vehicle on the A38 highway after leaving a pub in Burton-upon-Trent and heading to Heanor, half an hour away on the other side of the British town of Derby. The car spun out and crashed into a ditch, making impact primarily on the left-hand side of the vehicle. One of Donaldson's friends, Stephen "Boo" Flint, sat next to the left-hand window in the back seat, and was killed on impact. Donaldson, who had been riding in the left-hand front passenger seat—and who had reportedly tried to grab the steering wheel when he first saw that the driver was losing control—was rushed to a Nottingham hospital, but never regained consciousness from the head injuries he sustained in the accident. He died the next morning, September 24, 1993.[50] An independent investigator discovered that a nail in one of the rear tires of Donaldson's car had caused a slow air leak, and that the front shock absorber was also leaking. Derby coroner Peter Ashworth told the press, "All we can say is that because of the car's two defects the car became less easy to control."[51]

Official reports failed to ascertain how or why Donaldson's car had incurred those two defects, but many of Donaldson's fans have since alleged that Britain's Security Services had sabotaged the car as a way of trying to eliminate a prominent critic of their purportedly Jewish-controlled government. By suggesting that government-directed foul play caused Donaldson's fatal accident, many white-power sources argue that Donaldson was actually a martyr who chose to die for his beliefs rather than stay silent. This accusation features prominently, for example, in the 1997 song "60 Sekunden für Ian Stuart" (60 seconds for Ian Stuart) by the German band Staatsfeind (enemy of the state).[52] A biography of Donaldson that still appeared on the C18 website as of early 2016 even alleges that in the months leading up to his death, Donaldson had suspected some sort of government interference with his car, telephone, and mail. The writer states,

> I believe he [Donaldson] was murdered because:
> a) His car had previously been tampered with.
> b) His death was a carbon copy of Violent Storm.
> c) The threat he had become.
> d) The police and press coverup.
> e) He was about to play the biggest ever festival in Europe.
> f) The date of the "accident" coincided precisely to the 1939 Nazi law forbidding Jews from owning a wireless and listening to music on the radio. Retorsion served ice cold by the Diaspora.
> g) Ian informed C18 members that he believed he was about to be killed. He was right! [...]

If our enemies even contemplated victory by murdering Ian they were deeply misguided. Ian is now a legend, a martyr, a hero, an idol and by killing him they have made him immortal. Ian's deeds shall reverberate through time and his songs shall echo throughout eternity. Ian Stuart Donaldson will never be forgotten, a true Aryan son. His fire still rages in our hearts. Through his music and his deeds he will remain a great inspiration to many people. We will continue his fight to win a brand new day![53]

This Donaldson biographer constructs Donaldson as a murdered saint of the white-power cause, and then clearly employs Donaldson's image in order to legitimize C18's own activities. By claiming that Donaldson had been close enough to C18 leaders to confide in them—*only* in them—about the government tampering, this C18 writer uses the Donaldson ethos to suggest that fans of Donaldson's music should regard C18 as the heirs to Donaldson's political legacy. The C18 biography itself, however, undercuts its argument for government sabotage by describing Donaldson's car earlier in the biography, calling it a "semi-reliable automobile that just about managed to get him from A to B" as a way of arguing that Donaldson was willing to sacrifice luxury and financial stability for his political ideals. The biographer fails to address the fact that this "semi-reliable automobile" may not actually have *needed* government interference in order to put its occupants in danger.

Of course, the government-sabotage hypothesis is a non-falsifiable conspiracy theory; in other words, there is no way to prove that government agents did *not* damage the shock absorber or plant the nail in the tire of Donaldson's car prior to the fatal accident. Because disproving deliberate government tampering with Donaldson's vehicle is impossible, white-power activists with a variety of different political agendas have been able to use Donaldson's supposed martyrdom as a tool to help them justify their actions and muster support for their causes. Donaldson was to provide white-power music movements from late 1993 onward with the image of a flawless racist activist whose memory could raise support from musical and political groups the world over. Sweeping away Donaldson's inconvenient late-life wavering, white-power musicians and far-right political organizations constructed him as the central saint of white-power music. Some of Donaldson's fans placed a makeshift monument bearing a Norse life rune at the scene of his fatal car crash, and after anti-racist activists destroyed this memorial, his supporters replaced it with a more permanent version which they fixed into the ground with concrete. It became a site of pilgrimage.[54]

Tributes to Donaldson and Skrewdriver began to appear everywhere in white-power music circles. An international pantheon of 1990s white-power bands contributed to a 1996 double album of Skrewdriver covers entitled *A Tribute to Ian Stuart and the Glory of Skrewdriver: The Flame that Never Dies*. On Brutal Attack's 1998 album *White Pride, White Passion*, the band's much-celebrated lead singer, Ken McLellan, released one of white-power music's best-known anthems, a ballad called "Always Near," which suggested that

Donaldson's spirit was urging McLellan to continue his white-power activism. The "Swedish Madonna of the far right," a female singer named Saga, released three full albums between 2000 and 2002 comprised exclusively of Skrewdriver covers.[55] In 2004 and 2005, the German white-power music distributor MolokoPlus Versand also released *another* two-disc series of international Skrewdriver tribute covers.

In addition to such tribute songs and albums, white-power musicians and fans have paid homage to Donaldson in other ways. Donaldson tribute concerts and festivals have taken place regularly in various countries since Donaldson's death. Large, Internet-based white-power music retailers often have whole Skrewdriver sections in their catalogues, with some, like the US-based Micetrap Distribution, still listing Skrewdriver albums and paraphernalia among their top sellers. Even years after Donaldson's death, white-power music magazines have frequently printed tributes to him, like this fan letter from *Blood & Honour* in 2000:

> I was honoured in 1984 to finally meet Ian Stuart, at a pub in West London. Me a nobody meeting a man I classed a hero and idol. But I didn't find a man who was a big head, nasty, foul mouthed and awash with jewelry as sadly most idols turn out, but I shook hands with a man who was very humble, polite, and after a few pints—very humorous. [...] His music and lyrics reached white youth the world over and he started a backlash against a society that dictates what we believe in as evil. Blood & Honour in any way, shape or form continues and will continue to do so whatever ZOG [the Zionist Occupation Government one-world Jewish conspiracy theory] throws at us! Ian showed the way, started a worldwide resistance and gave a defiant two-fingered salute [an offensive hand gesture in British culture] to the "one world" conspirators.[56]

Likewise, Stormfront users often praise Donaldson in broad terms, expressing sentiments such as, "Ian Stuart Donaldson [...] is responsible for the solidarity that exists among European nationalists."[57] In short, Ian Stuart Donaldson hero worship has become common in the white-power music universe over the past two decades. As Paul Jackson argues, adulation of Donaldson functions as something upon which nearly all white-power musicians and fans seem to agree, regardless of their disagreements about almost everything else.[58] Even though this idealized version of Donaldson does not correspond exactly with the history of Donaldson's later life, it does turn Donaldson into a central organizing figure around whom white-power musicians and fans can shape their movement.

The fact that Donaldson was becoming the central figure in the white-power canon was obvious to most members of the movement almost as soon as he had died. Also obvious was the fact that his memory would be a money-maker for white-power music labels. The growth-oriented C18 therefore set about attempting to corral Donaldson's lucrative image for its own purposes. Will Browning set up a record label in January 1994 under the aegis of the C18-controlled Blood & Honour, and in order to harness the Donaldson mythos, he named his new label ISD Records after Donaldson's initials. Browning had little interest in sales; ISD initially sold limited numbers of records because it marketed only through *Blood & Honour* and other skinzines. Still, ISD turned a profit, and over the course of 1995 and 1996, investments in sound equipment allowed the label to set up a studio that circumvented the risk of renting time in non-white-power-controlled professional recording studios. The label produced more than twenty individual albums and pressed 35,000 CDs between 1994 and 1996, earning an estimated £100,000 per year during this peak period.[59]

Then Sargent and Browning were arrested in January 1995 for publishing a C18 magazine that included illegal content such as death threats, hit lists, and bomb-building plans. Several big-name British white-power bands—particularly English Rose and Squadron, whose guitarist, Brad Hollanby, had butted heads with Browning and the C18 leadership—seized C18's brief moment of vulnerability as a chance to voice their disapproval of C18. Other bands joined in, complaining that ISD Records was taking too big a cut of its artists' profits. With growing support from other white-power musicians, Squadron and English Rose—a band that had seen several members spend time in jail for attacking the staff of an Indian restaurant—spearheaded a group of bands who stopped working with C18 and ISD Records and began to cooperate again with the British Movement.[60] Several members of the white-power band Legion of St. George, including Stephen Swingfen, Gary Smith, and Simon Dutton, started their own section of Blood & Honour, drawing on the expertise of Jamie Hunter, a white-power activist who had previously worked on the magazine of the Blood & Honour Scottish Highlander division.[61] Several prominent members of the scene quickly followed them, including Stephen Calladine, Chingford Attack member Mick Dunn, and Chris Hipkin, who eventually became the driving force behind the new *Blood & Honour* magazine.[62] It was a sign of worse things to come for the C18-controlled Blood & Honour and for ISD Records.

Before the Burnley-vs.-C18 feud was over, both sides had assembled international supporters to help their causes. ISD and the C18-run Blood & Honour allied themselves with the white-power music label Ragnarock Records in Sweden—which got its name by blending the Norse pagan word for "apocalypse," *Ragnarök*, with the term rock 'n' roll—and with NS88 (short for National Socialist *heil Hitler*, because "H" is the eighth letter of the Latin alphabet), a white-power mail-order company run from Denmark by the racist German expatriate Marcel Schilf. Burnley's non-C18-controlled Blood &

Honour group, along with the English-Rose-and-Squadron faction, forged connections with Resistance Records in the United States—the label that had printed Burnley's No Remorse farewell article in its magazine—as well as with leading Ragnarock competitor Nordland (north land) Records in Sweden. The conflict became increasingly violent, largely due to the volatile Will Browning. Browning and other members of C18 assaulted several individuals who had sided with Resistance and Nordland, and even attempted to kill the skinhead shop owner Pers "Pajen" Johansen in Gothenburg, Sweden after mistakenly assuming that Johansen was running Nordland Records. After a failed mail-bombing campaign sent Browning and several other prominent members of C18 to prison, Burnley and the Resistance/Nordland axis emerged victorious from the struggle—but not before most of the fight and all of the unity had leeched out of the British white-power music scene. The C18-controlled Blood & Honour continued to stage its own concerts, while Burnley operated a separate Blood & Honour organization with a different web address.[63]

Finally, Will Browning's Blood & Honour associates—tired of dealing with C18—ousted him and declared him a traitor.[64] Prominent Blood & Honour members, including Stephen Calladine, also pressured the organization into removing Paul Burnley from his position as editor of the badly mismanaged *Blood & Honour* magazine.[65] Burnley responded by refusing to turn over *Blood & Honour*'s mailing lists or staff computer to the new editors, but still failed to earn back his editorship.[66] Burnley eventually exited the white-power music scene and went to work in Britain's mainstream music and film industries under his real name, Paul Bellany, producing a 2010 documentary for BBC Two about his famous artist father entitled *Bellany: Fire in the Blood*, and also working on production crews for a number of well-known feature films including *Harry Potter and the Order of the Phoenix* and *The Bourne Ultimatum*. After *both* Browning and Burnley had lost control of Blood & Honour, Calladine and others had an easier time returning the organization to business as usual. Unfortunately for the involved parties, this reconciliation came too late to save the British white-power music scene from entering a downward slide. After the mid-1990s, the British white-power music scene that had launched the international white-power music web increasingly took a back seat to scenes and artists from elsewhere.

This did not mean, however, that the British white-power music scene was dead. In fact, the British-controlled Blood & Honour organization continued to grow and expand its reach into other countries. By the time issue 40 of *Blood & Honour* magazine appeared in 2009, Blood & Honour listed sixteen separate divisions within the United Kingdom, in addition to twenty-four non-UK divisions. The editors of *Blood & Honour* magazine, conscious of their status as international torchbearers of the early British white-power bands' historical influence, have waxed philosophical about the role of white-power music in several articles over the magazine's thirty-year run. An anonymous editorial entitled "What Are We?," taken from 2009's issue 42, is representative of this trend:

> We are […] a movement to secure national renaissance by people who feel themselves threatened with decline into decadence and death and are determined to live, and live greatly. We write and perform songs as instruments of mobilization. Our bands celebrate white consciousness and call for social change. […] The music of the resistance is about now. But it is intimately linked to generations of victory, suffering and struggle of our people and cultures, it derives its vitality from telling the truth right now and because of what it does right now for its people. […] Our music and plight is being sung and played in white nations all over the globe, thus both providing a universal basis of unity and, in particular, connecting with other patriotic struggles with a historical resonance. […] Our bands borrow and exchange musical styles and genres as they express affinity between conditions of marginalization and oppression. They syncretize skinhead, punk, ska, rockabilly and hardcore styles into their militant protest music, and moreover, most attribute their path to the influence of Skrewdriver. […] The distribution of LPs, cassettes, CDs, satellite and online media helps facilitate solidarity between our people and is giving hope on a global scale. […] We aim to give exposure to music that is created and performed by those immediately affected by political and leftwing oppression who are committed to using their music as a force for justice, change and rebirth.[67]

This editorial demonstrates several key characteristics of contemporary white-power discourse, including the idea that the white race has had a glorious history, but that racial and political enemies now threaten white people with racial extinction. The only solution to this problem, according to Blood & Honour and other white-power groups, is white-power activism. Crucially, the author of this editorial links white-power activism and the future of the white race with Blood & Honour's mandate as a white-power musical organization, attempting to solidify Blood & Honour's position by reminding the reader, first, that white-power bands from across the world trace their lineage back to Blood & Honour's founding band, Skrewdriver, and, second, that the increasingly international web of white-power musicians requires an international parent organization like Blood & Honour to keep itself afloat.

Of course, Blood & Honour has not remained in operation through statements of ideology alone. Its bands and fans have stayed active as well, both musically and in terms of white-power violence, sometimes in ways that have overlapped with mainstream culture and the mainstream music industry in Europe. *Blood & Honour* writer Ed Winchester brags that while in Helsinki for a white-power concert in 1999, he and members of Stephen Calladine's post-Skrewdriver band, Warlord, assaulted a Finnish MTV presenter who had insulted skinheads on television.[68] In 2000, the Blood & Honour–affiliated London band Legion of St. George—named not only for the third-century Palestinian Christian martyr St. George, who purportedly slew a dragon, but also for the 1970s British ultra-nationalist group the League of St. George—found a receptive disc jockey who remixed one of the band's albums, *In Defence of the Realm*, along with a song called "White Preservation Society" from their album *Shadows of the Empire*. The DJ played this set for clubbers at mainstream London discos. However, to the chagrin of the band's singer, Simon Dutton, "it seems not one of these disco zombies [clubgoers] has had the brains to discern the message in our music."[69] A white-power drum corps called Reich Force formed in the East Midlands area, and when anti-racists barred them from using their practice hall, they staged weekly impromptu concerts at public locations in their hometown, including the train station waiting room.[70] Dozens of British white-power bands such as these have continued to play at gigs both at home in Britain and overseas, as well as to release new white-power albums and maintain contacts with white-power musicians in other countries.

Blood & Honour still holds about ten gigs a year in Britain, although observers suggest that these concerts function mostly as social gatherings for aging skinheads rather than as recruiting events for the next generation of British neo-Nazi activists.[71] Many racist Britons now worry more about the threat of Islamist terrorism and the recent European migrant crisis than they do about Jewish world conspiracies, and neo-Nazi organizations like the British Movement have largely given way to radical anti-Muslim associations like the violent English Defence League.[72] A recent alliance of anti–Blood & Honour organizations formed out of several British white-power and neo-Nazi groups such as British Freedom Fighters, Racial Volunteer Force, and the UK chapter of the American organization Volksfront; however, this alliance—which referred to itself as Unity—splintered due to infighting in 2012, shattering not only Unity itself, but also one of the British white-power music scene's longest-running and most-lauded bands, Avalon, whose lead singer, Graham "Grumpy" Thompson, had originally been one of the key figures in the Unity movement. Many key British bands, including Brutal Attack, Legion of St. George, and Celtic Warrior, had continued to express vocal support for and play gigs with the original Blood & Honour throughout its period of conflict with Unity.[73] Nonetheless, old-school white-power groups like Blood & Honour, having learned to fear police and anti-racist interference from their experiences with failed large-scale gigs in the 1990s, guard the details of their concerts carefully, preventing many interested newcomers and casual supporters from attending. It would be a mistake to declare British white-power music a thing of the past; big-name British white-power bands like Brutal Attack and Whitelaw continue to play to three- and four-digit crowds internationally and to elicit positive fan response. Still, the British white-power music scene of the 2010s appears to be a shell of what it was in the 1980s and early 1990s.

The continued viability of the British white-power music scene demonstrates that white-power music remains an important part of organized white-power and neo-Nazi culture even after three decades. Analyses suggesting that virulent racism is a historical anachronism which will necessarily die out over time miss the important ways in which white-power beliefs and activism help some individuals to express frustration with contemporary social circumstances they feel powerless to change. The long tenure of white-power music in Britain illustrates that white-power music is not simply the relic of a long-ago time when overt racism was acceptable in the British mainstream. Rather, it represents a new incarnation of fluid and influential racist ideologies that have adapted to changing socio-historical circumstances for centuries. Examining British white-power music's trajectory over the past three decades illustrates just how strongly some individuals continue to cling to violently racist beliefs.

Exploring British white-power music is also important because British white-power musicians, particularly in the early years of the genre, helped to spread white-power music to other countries, affecting groups and individuals far beyond their shores. The next three chapters will take the history of white-power music away from Britain—first to Western Europe, then to Eastern Europe, and finally to the Americas and Australia—but it is important to remember that these histories of white-power music outside Britain have affected white-power music in Britain too. Although the focus of these chapters will shift away from the seminal British scene, examining historical trends, figures, and events that might seem to have little to do with Britain, white-power music is an interconnected web of groups and individuals who communicate with one another and influence one another's music. In turning to the histories of white-power music scenes in Western Europe, I aim not to suggest that the British scene is isolated from scenes elsewhere, but rather that it has helped to inspire them.

3

The History of White-Power Music in Continental Western Europe

Largely due to the efforts of early British white-power musicians like Ian Stuart Donaldson, white-power music spread to the European continent shortly after it initially developed in Britain. It appeared first in Germany, a product of Donaldson's close relationships with Rock-O-Rama Records and German white-power activists. From there, scenes quickly began to arise in other Western European countries, blossoming especially during a short window in the 1990s when Internet communication had become widely available to the mainstream public and law enforcement agencies had not yet begun devoting serious resources to curtailing the genre's proliferation. These scenes have developed into far more than simple shadows of their British progenitor; in recent years, the German scene in particular seems even to have usurped much of the British scene's former dominance. Moreover, some of the white-power music that has evolved in continental Western Europe, such as the Norwegian National Socialist black metal (NSBM) of the early 1990s, has produced fundamental shifts in the *sound* of white-power music worldwide. White-power ideological movements from outside Britain, like German neo-Nazism and Scandinavian racist paganism, have contributed important new concepts to the ideological canons of white-power musicians in Britain and elsewhere.

This chapter will focus on white-power music scenes from Western Europe, with the aim of explaining why they arose and how they have affected the development of white-power music as an international genre. Like the previous chapter's history of British white-power music, each of the studies of white-power music scenes from individual countries that appear in this chapter will begin by discussing the socio-historical circumstances that have helped to foster the development of white-power music in those places in the late twentieth and early twenty-first centuries. After establishing *why* white-power music developed in key continental Western European countries during the late twentieth century, these studies will then explain what happened as white-power music scenes evolved in each country, outlining key ways in which white-power musicians from some countries have influenced scenes elsewhere.

Due to space limitations, this history must focus on the most important and influential white-power music scenes that have arisen in continental Western Europe thus far, leaving smaller and less influential scenes for later treatment. While white-power musicians do exist in places like the Low Countries, Austria, Denmark, Finland, Ireland, Portugal, and Switzerland, they have been fewer and less influential than those in any of the countries included here except Norway, which receives special treatment because the Norwegian NSBM scene has had an impact on worldwide white-power music disproportionate to its numerical size. I have chosen not to focus on smaller white-power music scenes because the larger and/or more influential scenes that I *have* chosen to examine—those from Germany, Sweden, Norway, France, Spain, and Italy—provide such fertile material for discussion. I arrange the interconnected histories in this chapter by region, focusing first on white-power music scenes from Northwestern Europe, then moving on to explore white-power music in key Western Mediterranean countries. As with the previous chapter, the purpose of this survey is not to provide a comprehensive history of white-power music in the region, but rather to highlight the most important musicians, events, and trends in the genre's evolution, and to explain how the development of white-power music in Western Europe responds to the wider history of Western Europe today.

Germany

I begin with a discussion of white-power music in Germany for two reasons: first, as the historical seat of the Third Reich, Germany functions as a spiritual home for most white-power and neo-Nazi musicians today; and second, contemporary Germany is the physical home of the world's numerically largest white-power music scene. The first stirrings of white-power music appeared in West Germany at approximately the same time as they arose in Britain. Through the Rock-O-Rama Records connection and through white-power music fans in the British military, which had troops stationed in West Germany, the British skinhead subculture arrived in West Germany in the early 1980s.[1] There, the racist skinhead subculture dominated the skinhead scene of the early and mid-1980s. English bands like Skrewdriver were popular with these early racist skinheads in Germany, but a growing sense of nationalism also prompted members of the community to begin forming their own bands to express a particularly German racist worldview as well.[2] In the early 1980s, a number of bands emerged from the ranks, such as the Böhse Onkelz (evil unclez) from Frankfurt am Main; Endstufe (final stage, referring to the genocidal Nazi final solution) from Bremen; Vortex from Hameln in Niedersachsen; Oberste Heeresleitung or OHL (high command) from Leverkusen in Nordrhein-Westfalen; Cotzbrocken (a misspelling of the German slang word *Kotzbrocken*, for asshole or, more literally, piece of vomit) from Köln; Springstoifel (spring devil, misspelled from the similar-sounding German Springsteufel to signal the band's allegiance to oi! punk music) from Mainz; and Kraft durch Froide (Strength through Joy, another reference both to oi! punk and to the Third Reich leisure program *Kraft durch Freude*) from Berlin.[3] These bands' musical style, similar to that of the English racist skinhead bands at the time, was generally oi! punk.[4]

At first, bands such as these did not espouse open neo-Nazism, expressing in the lyrics to their songs mainstream xenophobic trends and the stereotypically masculine gender tropes of the skinhead movement, but making no references to the Third Reich or to neo-Nazi imagery.[5] The Böhse Onkelz song "Türken Raus" (Turks out), for instance, argues for expelling Turkish immigrants from Germany, but never espouses overt neo-Nazism. Other early German racist punk bands were less popular than the Böhse Onkelz, but clearer in their political orientation, such as Cotzbrocken, which titled its 1981 debut album *Jedem das Seine . . .* after the famous German proverb *Jedem das Seine*, or 'to each his own [fate],' which appeared instead of the more typical concentration camp slogan *Arbeit macht frei* (work makes one free) on the gates to the Nazi concentration camp Buchenwald, near Weimar.[6]

As the 1980s wore on, German white-power bands began to express an increasingly radical neo-Nazi political worldview, deploying the symbolism of the Third Reich more blatantly. New bands appeared, like Kruppstahl (Krupp steel) from Augsburg in Bayern, Voll die Guten or VdG (fully the good ones or fully the good guys) from Oberhausen in Nordrhein-Westfalen, Sturmtrupp (storm troop) from Neuburg an der Donau in Bayern, Commando Pernod from Hamburg, and Noie Werte (a conscious misspelling of the German *neue Werte*, or new values) from Stuttgart in Baden-Württemberg. Such groups gradually adopted new sonic material, particularly hard rock and heavy metal, to complement their newfound adoration for Third Reich figures like Adolf Hitler and Rudolf Hess.[7] The band Saccara—named for an ancient

Egyptian necropolis—was founded in 1986 in Meppen, Niedersachsen under the leadership of Daniel "Gigi" Giese, and represented the first foray of actual long-haired heavy metal musicians into a German white-power and neo-Nazi music scene which, in its early years, was dominated by skinheads.[8] Giese later became a notorious member of white-power bands like Stahlgewitter (steel storm) and Gigi & die braunen Stadtmusikanten (Gigi & the brown town-musicians, a band name that refers to the Brothers Grimm folktale "Die Bremer Stadtmusikanten"—"The Bremen Town Musicians"—as well as to the symbolic brown uniform color of Hitler's Sturmabteilung paramilitary group, now the official color of Germany's ultra-right-wing NPD political party).[9] By 1987, the German white-power music scene had expanded its range of musical styles even further; that year, the prolific and influential acoustic ultra-right-wing singer/songwriter Frank Rennicke from Braunschweig, Niedersachsen released his first album.[10]

In the early years of the German white-power music scene, members adopted the appearance of British second-wave skinheads relatively wholesale. However, as the scene developed, racist groups in Germany and elsewhere in continental Europe added to that militant skinhead couture, adapting it for their own purposes. As well as wardrobe staples from the British racist skinhead movement, such as work or combat boots, T-shirts, polo shirts, jeans, and military-style jackets, German white-power skinheads in the 1990s and 2000s began wearing pro-Arab symbols, such as the black-and-white Palestinian keffiyeh or kufiya scarf, in solidarity with the Palestinian struggle against Israel, Jews, and Zionism.[11] Also popular among the extreme right wing in Germany is clothing from the mainstream British sportswear and streetwear company Lonsdale, which has tried unsuccessfully to distance itself from its neo-Nazi following, but has the unfortunate luck to contain the consecutive letters "NSDA" in the middle of its brand name, so that when customers wear unzipped jackets over T-shirts and sweatshirts emblazoned with the Lonsdale brand name, the only letters of the name that others can see from under the jacket are NSDA—very similar to the official initials of Hitler's Nazi party, the NSDAP, Nationalsozialistische Deutsche Arbeiterpartei, or National Socialist German Workers' Party.[12]

The Lonsdale company might not appreciate its accidental re-branding as a clothing label of the far right, but other firms, including the particularly successful Thor Steinar, have appealed to white-power activists in Germany and elsewhere in continental Europe by marketing products specifically geared toward pro-white racist demographics. In fact, Thor Steinar took as its logo two rune signs intertwined in a way that resembled the double-sig-rune insignia of Hitler's SS, although the company was quickly forced to change that logo in order to continue doing business in Germany. It does still sell clothing that bears Norwegian flags and slogans such as "Nordic company," "Viking roots," and "100% pure Viking blood."[13] The brand, dubbed "Hollister for Neo Nazis" by Samantha Payne of the *International Business Times*, has been part of a larger trend away from the aggressive-looking second-wave skinhead appearance in ultra-right-wing German fashion since about the turn of the millennium.

Normalization—the attempt to blend in with mainstream fashion trends as a way of trying to attract followers to racist movements who might not respond well to the aggressive second-wave skinhead look—has in fact been increasingly common among white-power and neo-Nazi groups worldwide over the past two decades.[14] The extreme right wing in Germany and its neighboring countries seems to be at the forefront of this trend, led by the so-called nipsters, short for Nazi hipsters, of the early 2010s. Nipster fashion mirrors mainstream hipster fashion trends, which, in the early years of the nipster trend, included skinny jeans, tote bags, and "uppercut" hairstyles that left hair a few inches long on top but shaved on the sides, resembling a cross between the shaved head of skinhead couture and the longer, more carefully groomed and gelled look popular among men in Nazi Germany. Because of this normalization, observers at right-wing rallies and concerts in Germany now note that participants are more difficult to distinguish from mainstream populations and even from extreme-left-wing activists on the basis of appearance alone.[15]

Contemporary German nipsters, with their penchant for normalization, bear some similarities to the white-power musicians and fans of previous decades. For example, the entire white-power music web began in the late 1970s and early 1980s as an attempt to make hard-line racist ideologies seem interesting and relevant to young audiences by presenting them through the vehicle of youth culture. Yet the white-power and neo-Nazi musicians of the 1980s and early 1990s strove to stand out rather than to fit in, a mark of their increasingly radical politics. Late-1980s German white-power musicians, like Frank Rennicke and Daniel Giese, demonstrated an ever more neo-Nazi political orientation and a growing willingness to express this orientation publicly.[16] The number of white-power and neo-Nazi concerts boomed in the late 1980s and early 1990s, and neo-Nazi symbols like swastika flags began appearing openly onstage to accompany Hitler salutes from the performers.[17] The period from 1989 to 1993 represented the peak time when German white-power musicians recorded and publicly performed songs expressing *explicit* violence, anti-Semitism, racism, and neo-Nazism.[18]

This overt neo-Nazism and violent rhetoric brought the German white-power music scene into increasing conflict with its national government. Since the end of World War II, racial hatred and the legacy of the Third Reich have been contentious social issues in Germany. The embarrassment of the Nuremberg trials and the occupation of Germany by the former Allied powers—not to mention the division of the country into East and West for more than

forty years or the ever-growing sense of genuine anger in most German public discourse over the racist violence and widespread destruction caused by
the government of the Third Reich—mean that representatives of the German government, with the exception of a few ultra-right-wing NPD officials,
now typically repudiate the government of the Third Reich and support legal
sanctions against expressions of blatant racial hatred, especially direct calls to
violence and glorifications of the country's Nazi past. Even those early German
racist bands that avoided overt neo-Nazi symbolism drew unwanted international attention and outrage to the small but vocal ultra-racist faction among
the West German populace, humiliating Germany on the world stage.

As would become routine for racist bands in the post-1990 reunified Germany, therefore, the West German government began to censor many of these
early bands' expressions of racist ideology, using provisions in the German
Constitution that allow officials to outlaw materials they view as threats to
the democratic system or to young people. For example, the German government placed the 1984 Böhse Onkelz album *Der Nette Mann* (the nice man)
on an index of banned, "youth-compromising" music, and prosecuted Böhse
Onkelz band members in 1990 for the racist sentiments they had expressed on
the album.[19] The Böhse Onkelz had actually written only two blatantly racist
songs, and the group began to distance itself from its early racist sentiments
as early as 1985–1986; several members have even denounced hardcore neo-
Nazis in public in the intervening years.[20] Band members have apologized for
their former stance and now claim that the intolerant rhetoric of their early
years was thoughtless youthful rebellion, not a concerted attempt to promote political ideology; for example, bassist Stephan Weidner told reporters in 2003 that "I have done things in the past that could be interpreted as
being fascist. There's nothing that can be prettified about this," although he
also grumbled, "But now that I'm 38 years old, do I still have to justify what
I did as a 16-year-old[?]"[21] Having forsworn racism and xenophobia, the
group later became a mainstay of German rock music and has enjoyed a successful, long-running career on the German pop charts. Still, the influence of
songs like "Türken Raus" helped to inspire a generation of young German
musicians to begin playing white-power music that *did* express overt and
unapologetic neo-Nazism.

In fact, after the Böhse Onkelz, the German white-power music scene grew
rapidly. Bands like Radikahl (bald radical) and Störkraft (destructive force)
released music that was far more politically radical and lyrically explicit than
anything the Böhse Onkelz ever released, influencing many other racist bands
that sprang up in the late 1980s and early 1990s. For instance, in the words of
one of Stormfront's most prolific CD reviewers, a Dutch user who calls himself Ju-87 after the serial number of the German Junkers Ju-87 Stuka fighter
plane, "The albums that this band [Störkraft] made were the blueprints for the

entire German RAC/skinhead scene."[22] This particular review is, of course, hyperbolic; other German white-power musicians also played important roles in the development of racist music scenes in Germany. However, Störkraft and a handful of other early German white-power bands did catalyze much more widespread German involvement in the worldwide white-power music web in the following years.

Although this growing racist skinhead subculture and its accompanying music found receptive audiences in West Germany, it appealed in particular to angry youths from the former East Germany. When Germany reunited in 1990, the former East Germany was mired in economic problems that turned out to be worse than even the gloomiest of prognoses had estimated. The government agency tasked with privatizing the former East Germany's state-owned enterprises discovered that the sums of money needed to update infrastructure in the newly reunified Eastern states far exceeded their early expectations.[23] Former East Germans struggled to find jobs and other economic opportunities in their hometowns, even though the newly reunited German government was pouring resources into the economy of the former East from wealthy western states like Bayern and Baden-Württemberg. Large East German cities like Leipzig, Dresden, Halle, and Chemnitz had been in decay for decades—the iconic Frauenkirche church in Dresden's city center, for instance, had remained a pile of rubble since the Allied bombing of Dresden in February 1945—and their inner cities required immediate renovation.[24] Young people left the former East Germany in large numbers to find better jobs and opportunities in the West and abroad, leaving an aging and struggling population behind. The emotional catharsis of November 9, 1989 and the fall of the Berlin Wall gave way to a rift between the *Wessis* (westies, or citizens of the former West Germany) and *Ossis* (easties, or citizens of the former East).[25] Many former East Germans grew frustrated with the government's lack of progress in fixing local economies that often seemed to be getting worse rather than better as the 1990s wore on.

As had been the case in 1970s Britain, a small but vocal faction of young citizens of the former East Germany in the 1990s blamed their economic problems on Germany's rising tide of immigrants and refugees. Large numbers of laborers from Turkey and Southern Europe had been coming to Germany through a "guest worker" or *Gastarbeiter* program since the 1950s, and although these workers were originally supposed to return to their home countries after specified periods of work in Germany, many of them chose instead to apply for legal residency and remain in Germany permanently.[26] The German government also maintained a particularly welcoming policy toward refugees and political asylum-seekers, something many struggling former East Germans came to resent. In fact, a 2012 study revealed that even in the period before the 2015 European migrant crisis began, more than half of the people in the former East Germany *still* wanted the government to send foreigners back to their home countries in order to reduce competition for jobs in Germany.[27] In the same study, a quarter of Germans overall expressed the same sentiment.

The unexpected socioeconomic difficulties of the German reunification process exacerbated the xenophobia among some individuals in this demographic in the former East, providing a fertile environment for white-power music, typically referred to in Germany as *Rechtsrock*, or right-wing rock. In the first nine months of 1991 alone there were eighty separate attacks on buildings in which large numbers of non-white foreigners lived.[28] This wave of racist violence faded from the national headlines in the late 1990s, but the number of active white-power bands in Germany seems to have maintained itself or even grown in the intervening years. Between 1990 and 2003, about 380 German white-power bands released around 1,000 albums, including 86 in 2003 alone.[29] The former East Germany—and its provinces of Sachsen and Brandenburg in particular—still produces a vast per capita majority of Germany's white-power bands, although the densely populated states of the former West produce more bands numerically.[30]

Growing rosters of white-power bands and increasing numbers of white-power albums meant that more and more German white-power music began finding its way into the hands of listeners outside of organized white-power circles. By the early 1990s, the German government became increasingly concerned not only about violence and intolerance associated with white-power fans and concerts, but also with the fact that a few white-power and neo-Nazi bands were becoming household names among large numbers of German teenagers.[31] A May 1992 exposé on white-power music in the widely read national weekly newsmagazine *Der Spiegel* (the mirror), which appeared less than a year after an egregious terrorist attack on an apartment building reserved for asylum-seekers and temporary foreign workers in the city of Hoyerswerda, Sachsen, fomented a national discussion on the subject which increased pressure on the government to stem the proliferation of violently racist music.[32]

The fallout from the *Spiegel* article and the Hoyerswerda attack, followed by another large-scale assault on an asylum-seeker residence in Rostock, Mecklenburg-Vorpommern in August 1992—the one for which the British white-power musician Will Browning named the No Remorse album *Barbecue in Rostock*—precipitated a wave of investigations and criminal proceedings against white-power musicians in Germany. This new government attention made it effectively impossible for most white-power musicians to play and distribute racist music openly. Starting in late 1992, white-power songs appeared en masse on the government's index of "youth-compromising," banned music.[33] The country's Bundesamt für Verfassungsschutz (federal office for protection of the Constitution) was explicitly tasked with surveilling, investigating, and manipulating neo-Nazi groups.[34] Courts handed down a number of sentences for members of overtly neo-Nazi bands like Störkraft, Oi Dramz, Radikahl, Triebtäter (sexual offender), Tonstörung (sonic disturbance), Kraftschlag (forceful hit), Kroizfoier (a conscious misspelling of the similar-sounding German *Kreuzfeuer*, or cross fire), and Stuka (another reference to the German WWII Stuka fighter plane).[35] In February 1993, a German police raid on Rock-O-Rama Records' headquarters also led to the seizure of tens of thousands of white-power CDs, cassette tapes, and LPs.[36] This raid was part of the government's preparations for court hearings against Rock-O-Rama Records officials on forty counts of sedition over unconstitutional racist and neo-Nazi political sentiments expressed on the label's albums.[37]

The raid and the sedition trials signaled the end of the Rock-O-Rama Records era in white-power music, with owner Herbert Egoldt deciding to discontinue his dealings with white-power and neo-Nazi bands in order to avoid further legal problems.[38] Although white-power musicians met the increased government repression with frustration overall, some members of German white-power groups were actually happy to see Rock-O-Rama leave the white-power music scene, not only because Herbert Egoldt did not share their right-wing political views, but also because he had developed a reputation for short-changing the musicians who recorded with Rock-O-Rama.[39] In addition, listeners complained about Rock-O-Rama's low production quality on some albums. For instance, the Stormfront CD reviewer Ju-87 writes in an otherwise positive 2008 review of Brutal Attack's 1990 album *Steel Rolling On* that Rock-O-Rama's inferior production values had detracted from the quality of this and many other "classic" white-power albums: "Irritating is the overwhelming snare sound of the drums. It penetrates the whole sound. Sounds horrible. Lots of older (Rock-O-Rama) albums have that. [. . .] Very annoying. Nonetheless a good record."[40]

Still, many members of the German white-power music scene saw what had happened to Egoldt as a disaster, a warning of what might happen to others if they continued to produce and consume violently racist music in Germany. Many without deep connections to white-power music chose to sever ties with the scene when the risk of prosecution increased. Those members who remained involved in the scene, however, drew closer together and became increasingly radicalized, forming German divisions of both Blood & Honour and the Hammerskin Nation white-power skinhead network in 1994 for the purpose of promoting white-power music in Germany.[41]

White-power music, with its alluring taboo image, *still* remains massively popular among German teenagers in some areas of the country, particularly in the former East.[42] Nevertheless, leery of government repression after observing the fate of Rock-O-Rama Records, many white-power bands and labels began to display a newfound caution when writing lyrics and distributing music after 1993. Bands have increasingly chosen to hire attorneys to vet their song lyrics in order to ensure that they are not violating Germany's stringent laws on hate speech. Direct calls to violence and references to Jews as enemies of the white race—surefire triggers of swift government response—have dwindled from song lyrics since 1993, to be replaced by vague threats against "enemies" and effusive rhetoric about the love of nation and *Volk*.[43]

Other German white-power record labels quickly stepped into the void that Rock-O-Rama left behind, expanding the scene rather than diminishing its size as German authorities had hoped. The Düsseldorf-based company Funny Sounds, operated by former Störkraft band manager Torsten Lemmer—who has since exited the white-power movement and entered the world of mainstream business—produced white-power albums, along with a white-power music magazine called *Rock Nord* (rock north), which had a distribution of 17,000.[44] Di-Al Records of Erlangen, Bayern actually operated through Blood & Honour itself, and the "hatecore" (racist hardcore punk) label Hate Records was owned and operated out of Seibnitz, Sachsen by a known Hammerskins member, Mirko Hesse.[45] Hate Records in particular was so successful that it allowed the Hammerskins to finance a distribution system for white-power music and weapons along the Czech Republic's border with Germany, giving German white-power activists a nearby foreign location for purchasing illegal materials and even training in the use of firearms.[46] Smaller labels, such as Andreas Gängel's Endsieg-Verlag or ESV (final victory press), Ulrich Großman's DIM Records, the Walz brothers' Walzwerk (rolling mill) Records, and the Schaffelhuber brothers' Skull Records, found that they had an easier time competing in a white-power music market that no longer included Rock-O-Rama.[47] The German expatriate and C18 ally Marcel Schilf even founded a short-lived distribution company called NS Records and a related sublabel named NS88 Records in neighboring Denmark in the 1990s, taking advantage of more lenient hate speech laws in Denmark by using his Danish address to sell banned German records back to a largely German customer base.[48]

By 2003, in fact, a German white-power music scene that had once been dominated by Rock-O-Rama Records had splintered into more than thirty small white-power music labels and distribution companies.[49] New labels that appeared around the turn of the millennium included Pühses Liste (Pühse's list), founded in 2000 by extreme-right-wing NPD party official Jens Pühse; this label functioned for several years as one of the giant recording companies in German white-power music.[50] A Dresden-based label called OPOS Records—short for the English-language phrase "one people one struggle"—opened its doors in 2007, and, at the time of writing in 2016, still continues to market white-power heavy metal and punk music in Germany.[51] Besides formal businesses like Pühse's Liste and OPOS Records, many bands also chose to self-release their albums on cassette or CD, particularly when they wanted to record explicitly illegal neo-Nazi songs that even white-power labels were often afraid to distribute.[52]

None of this has escaped the German government's attention. Continuing the 1980s trend, the German police have continued to pursue members of the German white-power music scene, albeit without the vigor that many German anti-fascist groups call for. The government has persisted in indexing and censoring German white-power albums, including not only German but also important foreign releases like *In the Glare of Burning Churches* by Rob "Darken" Fudali's Polish one-man studio project Graveland, a Skrewdriver lyrics book entitled *The Ian Stuart Songbook*, and the Belgian band Kill Baby, Kill!'s *A Prophet Returns*, which refers to Adolf Hitler as a "prophet."[53] Banning white-power songs by placing them on the index, of course, does not stop recordings of the songs from reaching their intended audiences, although it does officially prevent distributors from selling them through mainstream channels and allow government officials to confiscate copies of the banned albums upon discovery. This does, in some cases, actually seem to restrict the number of copies of white-power albums that find their way into fans' CD collections, as the Stormfront CD reviewer Ju-87 grumbled in a 2006 review of the 1991 Noie Werte album *Kraft für Deutschland* (strength for Germany): "Digging up a mummy in your basement is a greater possibility than finding this banned disc."[54] However, for some fans of white-power music, albums that appear on the German government's index of banned songs are actually *more* desirable than others. Ju-87 himself wrote in a 2005 Stormfront review of the album *Das Eiserne Gebet* (the iron prayer) by Daniel Giese's band Stahlgewitter, "All Stahlgewitter CDs are banned in Deutschland [Germany], meaning that the lyrics are good."[55]

In 2000, the German government took the highly publicized step of raiding the homes of thirty Blood & Honour Deutschland members and banning Blood & Honour Deutschland as a criminal organization.[56] In retribution, the next week, Blood & Honour organized a concert in Germany featuring the US band Max Resist and the German white-power band Spreegeschwader (Spree fleet or Spree squadron, referring to Berlin's Spree River); the gig dissolved into a riot against the police in which forty-five police officers and sixteen concertgoers were injured.[57] German white-power musicians also retaliated against the Blood & Honour Deutschland ban by collaborating with several different German white-power recording labels to produce the 2004 album *Anpassung ist Feigheit: Lieder aus dem Untergrund* (adaptation is cowardice: songs from the underground), a CD that received mainstream media attention under the title *Projekt Schulhof* (project schoolyard).[58] This CD particularly angered the public because white-power activists handed out 50,000 free copies of it to German students outside public schools, sparking a number of copycat projects in Germany and abroad.[59] German white-power bands have complained to *Blood & Honour* about the increased police surveillance; for example, in 2002, one member of the German band D.S.T. (Deutsch Stolz und Treue, or German pride and loyalty) told the magazine, "After the banning of the B & H division Germany, concerts with 1000–2000 people are almost impossible. If there is a concert, the crowd is about 150–300 comrades. Sadly but truly, even these gigs are broken up by ZOG's keen boot lickers."[60]

German court proceedings against white-power musicians at the turn of the millennium did not stop with the ban of Blood & Honour Deutschland. The German white-power balladeer Frank Rennicke appeared before a court in Böblingen, Baden-Württemberg in November 2000 on charges of sedition and the dissemination of youth-harming materials for a 1987 song called "Das Heimatvertriebenen-Lied" (the song of those expelled from their homeland), which judge Werner Payer said was a call for anti-immigrant violence.[61] At issue was the fact that the song not only bemoaned the expulsion of ethnic Germans from the Sudetenland region of the former Czechoslovakia at the end of World War II, but also suggested that new immigrants to Germany were again robbing the German people of their homeland and should therefore be forced to leave. Unimpressed, Payer handed Rennicke a ten-month suspended prison sentence.[62] When Rennicke appealed the verdict in October 2002, a higher court in Stuttgart actually lengthened the suspended prison term from ten to seventeen months.[63] However, a federal court finally overturned the ruling in March 2008, mostly to prevent Rennicke from continuing to use the case for personal publicity.[64] Rennicke, presenting himself as a simple concerned citizen and father of six, responded with a move that some observers have suggested *"war offensichtlich [. . .] eine gezielte Zumutung"* (was obviously [. . .] a targeted insult) against the German government: accepting a nomination to run for president of Germany from the NPD in the 2009 federal election, during which he gained only the votes of the four NPD electors out of a possible 1224.[65]

Like Rennicke, other prominent German white-power musicians have also felt the impact of German government repression since 2000. In December 2003, a German court ruled the hugely popular white-power band Landser (foot soldier, an antiquated German term commonly used to refer to WWII-era German infantrymen) to be a criminal organization. The judge sentenced the band's lead singer, Michael "Lunikoff" Regener, to jail time beginning in 2005, handing down suspended sentences and community service requirements for Landser's bassist André Mörike and drummer Christian Wendorff, and also ordering the band not to regroup.[66] Landser songs had been associated with a number of violent crimes in Germany, including several instances in which perpetrators actually had sung the lyrics to Landser songs before or during the murders of non-white immigrants. For example, on February 13,

1999—a significant date in German white-power communities because it marked the fifty-fifth anniversary of the Allied firebombing of Dresden at the end of World War II, a bombing campaign that neo-Nazi groups often view as a foreign atrocity against the German people—witnesses in Cottbus, Brandenburg, less than ninety minutes' drive from Dresden, the same city in which Ian Stuart Donaldson and five of his Skrewdriver associates had been arrested nine years earlier, heard a group of young perpetrators sing the Landser song "Republik der Strolche" (republic of thugs) as they murdered the Algerian immigrant Farid Guendoul, also known as Omar Ben Noui.[67] Similarly, on June 10, 2000, perpetrators in Dessau, Sachsen-Anhalt were overheard singing excerpts from the Landser song "Afrika-Lied" (Africa song) directly before beating Mozambiquan immigrant Alberto Adriano so severely that he died in hospital after lying comatose for four days.[68]

Despite such violence—or perhaps partially due to it—Landser was by the turn of the millennium the most popular white-power band in Germany by far, and clearly one of the most popular groups in the international white-power music web overall. Estimates suggest that by the time of the trial, Landser had sold more than 100,000 albums.[69] Since Regener's release from prison in February 2008, he has also produced albums under other band names such as die Lunikoff Verschwörung (the Lunikoff conspiracy), but has softened the overtly neo-Nazi lyrics of his Landser days in order to avoid further legal problems. Fans, however, have been quick to commemorate Regener and his Landser bandmates with T-shirts and tribute albums.[70]

As in Britain, German white-power concert organizers have had to become increasingly cautious about releasing the details of their gigs ahead of time, announcing the true times and venues of concerts only to a few necessary individuals, and arranging for most attendees and sometimes even performers to meet just before concerts at pre-determined redirection points in order to avoid detection by police and anti-racist protesters.[71] One member of the German white-power band Sleipnir—named for the eight-legged horse of the god Odin in Scandinavian mythology—complained to *Blood & Honour*, "It has got very hard to play concerts in Germany. The Police suspect B & H [Blood & Honour] behind every gig and so many gigs are very small and secret. [. . .] People are smuggled into the scene by the state everywhere, the informers don't sleep."[72] Still, the German government, despite white-power musicians' protests of wanton persecution, has often been happier to compile statistics on white-power bands than actually to prosecute them. For example, the Bundesamt für Verfassungsschutz released a report in 2011 stating that there had been sixty-three right-wing extremist organizations and 25,000 right-wing extremists in Germany in 2010, 8,300 of whom—at least according to the report—had come to their extremist politics through white-power music.[73] Despite this implication that white-power musicians had been violating the

German Penal Code's statutes against neo-Nazi propaganda and incitement to hatred on a massive scale, German authorities had managed to thwart only four of the 128 known white-power gigs in Germany during that same year.[74] Members of the German white-power music scene report that concerts by US bands in Germany tend to draw particularly big crowds, sometimes in the four figures, and although organizing concerts on this scale is difficult, it certainly still takes place.[75]

Despite enormous pressure from police and anti-racist activists over the past twenty-five years, the German white-power music scene has remained the biggest in the world, and has produced far more white-power bands than any other country to date. Landser and the Böhse Onkelz have undoubtedly been the best-known German racist bands on the international market thus far, but within white-power circles, other German musicians are also popular. Beginning in the late 1990s, a growing German National Socialist black metal (NSBM) scene developed in response to the Norwegian NSBM scene of the early 1990s, spearheaded by bands like Absurd, Eugenik (eugenics), Totenburg (deadly castle), Bilskirnir (named after the hall of the Scandinavian god Thor), and Ulfhethnar (named, according to the band, after a group of Viking warriors who wore wolf coats). A few German musical groups such as Eneseess and das n'Socialist Soundsystem—both of which are side projects of the metal band Häretiker (heretic)—are even beginning to produce white-power rap and hip-hop.[76] This demonstrates that white-power musicians in the future may even manage to reformulate the racial connotations of a musical genre that most white-power groups until now have portrayed exclusively as a vehicle for race-mixing propaganda and anti-white hate speech.

Another new musical development among white-power circles in Central and Eastern Europe in the early 2010s is a form of electronic music called "hard bass," which mixes electronic music with political slogans that tend to express right-wing extremist themes.[77] Fans of hard bass are especially known for dancing to loud electronic music in public, sometimes chanting along to slogans that carry political messages, but sometimes dancing to music that has no lyrics at all or is sung in foreign languages like Russian, simply as a way of controlling public spaces like transit vehicles.[78] For a short time, this trend pervaded white-power hooligan scenes in both Germany and neighboring countries like the Czech Republic, where flash mobs posted online videos of themselves dancing in the streets and chanting, "We will bring Hardbass to your home. 14, 88," a reference not only to the neo-Nazi numerical code '88' for 'Heil Hitler,' but also to the '14 Words' slogan by late American neo-Nazi terrorist David Lane, which reads, "We must secure the existence of our people and a future for White Children."[79] Czech authorities noted, however, that reports of hard bass flash mobs had begun to decrease by late 2011, because, according to researcher Miroslav Mareš of Masaryk University in Brno, the unruly flash mobs had actually angered many "traditionalist" members of the far-right scene, who "viewed it as an ineffective and cause-discrediting form of propaganda."[80] In Germany, authorities pursued right-wing hard bass the same way they did other forms of white-power music that they deemed to violate hate speech laws.[81]

Clearly, German white-power and neo-Nazi musicians have proven themselves to be innovators in a number of the white-power music web's important subgenres. At the moment, German authorities are trying to determine whether white-power musicians may be at the forefront of neo-Nazi terrorism as well. This is a particularly pressing current issue in Germany because in November 2011, German officials uncovered a major white-power terrorist ring that had been responsible for a number of murders in Germany, all of which had previously seemed unconnected.[82] Evidence suddenly came to light demonstrating that between 2000 and 2006, neo-Nazi gunmen in several German cities had shot to death a total of nine behind-the-counter employees at various Döner shops—Turkish fast-food establishments particularly popular in Germany, with its high numbers of Turkish immigrants.[83] Beate Zschäpe, the sole survivor of the core group that carried out the murders, is still on trial in Germany. Her trial may reveal more information about the perpetrators' connections to white-power musicians and others in the German neo-Nazi movement. Beyond this, the terror spree and the prevalence of German white-power music demonstrate that some sectors of German society clearly still support neo-Nazi ideologies, propaganda, and even violence.

Especially interesting for this study is the fact that one German white-power band, Daniel "Gigi" Giese's group Gigi & die braunen Stadtmusikanten, had in 2010 produced a song called "Döner-Killer" on their *Adolf Hitler Lebt!* (Adolf Hitler lives!) album. The song's lyrics praised the perpetrator(s) of the Döner murders and included details of the attacks that were not yet known to police or the general public at the time of the album's release, such as the fact that nine victims had been killed and that the murders were connected to one another. Giese had already had a long history in German white-power music, having once served as a business partner in Nibelungen-Versand (Nibelung distribution, a name that references a mythical fifth-century Burgundian royal family), a white-power music distribution company that represented the main branch of the now-illegal Blood & Honour Deutschland organization.[84] He has also performed since 1986 with well-known racist bands including, as indicated previously, Saccara and Stahlgewitter, along with Goldhagens willige Speichellecker—a band name that translates directly as "Goldhagen's willing bootlickers," referring to the Jewish scholar Daniel Goldhagen's successful 1996 monograph *Hitler's Willing Executioners: Ordinary Germans and the Holocaust*, which was translated into German as *Hitlers willige Vollstrecker: Ganz gewöhnliche Deutsche und der Holocaust*, and which argued that ordinary

Germans were willing to perpetrate Holocaust atrocities out of deep-seated anti-Semitism. Giese has also been involved in other German white-power bands like Kahlkopf (bald head), In Tyrannos (under tyrants), and likely even the violently racist band project die Zillertaler Türkenjäger (the Zillertal [Ziller Valley, Austria] Turk hunters), a group whose lineup the German courts have tried and failed fully to ascertain for the purpose of prosecution.[85] In October 2012, the district court in Giese's hometown of Meppen, Niedersachsen found Giese guilty of incitement to hatred and endorsement of criminal activity for "Döner-Killer" and two other songs on the *Adolf Hitler Lebt!* album, sentencing him to a €600 fine and a seven-month suspended prison term.[86] When Giese appealed this verdict in 2013, a district court in Osnabrück not only confirmed the Meppen court's judgment, but also sentenced him to a second fine of €1000 for sedition and Holocaust denial expressed in the *Adolf Hitler Lebt!* song "Geschwür am After" (ulcer on the anus).[87] In March 2014, a higher appeals court in Oldenburg upheld the Osnabrück ruling.[88]

The fact that German white-power musicians support violent neo-Nazi ideologies and may even have links to individuals who commit real-world attacks illustrates why it is important to understand and analyze white-power music from German bands. In Britain, as the previous chapter demonstrated, the white-power music scene may have stagnated, at least for the time being. In Germany, government repression seems to have heightened rather than diminished the appeal of white-power music among some demographics. While the transitory and secretive nature of white-power musicians means that it is impossible to provide accurate statistics on the numbers of musicians and fans who participate in white-power music scenes at any given time (and this holds true for white-power musicians and fans everywhere, not just in Germany), many hundreds of German bands have sold their albums through white-power music retailers, performed at international concerts, provided interviews to white-power music magazines, and commented on white-power Internet forums. Their activism demonstrates that Nazi ideology is not just a remnant of the past for German society. The German white-power music scene holds a special place in the international web of white-power music, both for its size and for its claim to the history of the Third Reich. The German scene, like that in Britain, has significantly affected the international white-power music web. Yet white-power musicians from other places in Western Europe have influenced both the German and the British white-power music scenes as well.

Sweden

One of the white-power music scenes outside of Germany that has interacted most heavily with the German scene has been that in Sweden. In fact, in the 1990s, Sweden became a major hub of international white-power music, and although its size and significance have diminished since the turn of the millennium, this giant Swedish white-power music scene of the 1990s deserves consideration.

In order to understand the Swedish far right's relationship with neo-Nazism and white-power music today, it is important to appreciate how Sweden interacted with Germany's original Nazis during the World War II era. As a country, Sweden stayed neutral during the war, and even served as one of the few European havens for Jewish refugees during the Holocaust.[89] Official military neutrality did not preclude the existence of a small but vocal pro-Nazi demographic among the Swedish populace, however; for instance, a Swedish recording company called Tor (Swedish for Thor, one of the main gods of the Norse pagan pantheon) actually produced Swedish-language Nazi propaganda music during the Third Reich, despite the government's refusal to take sides.[90] Some individual Swedes also chose to volunteer for service in Hitler's army out of ideological conviction. A few of these former volunteers remained ideologically convinced Nazis even after the fall of the Third Reich. One in particular, Lars Magnus Westrup—who became a well-known radio personality in Franco's Spain when Hitler's defeat forced him to flee his homeland—returned to Sweden after Franco's death and used his radio experience to help found one the most important Swedish white-power record labels of the 1990s, Ragnarock Records.[91]

Sweden in the 1990s, like many other European countries, experienced a measurable upsurge in electoral support for right-wing politics. A populist party gained 6.7 percent of the national popular vote in 1991, and students occasionally turned up at public schools clad in Nazi uniforms during this period.[92] While the supporters of organized racism still represented a small minority of the overall Swedish population, this demographic was large enough in absolute numbers during the boom period of the late 1980s and early 1990s to foster the growth of one of the largest white-power and neo-Nazi music scenes in the world, at least for a few years.

The first large-scale white-power music organization to appear in Sweden in 1986 was Rock mot Kommunismen (rock against Communism), a Swedish branch of the British Rock Against Communism group. During the same period, two members of the Swedish white-power band Vit Aggression (white aggression), Göran Gustavsson and Peter Rindell, made contact with foreign racist groups like the British Movement in England and the Aryan Nations from the United States, working with Ian Stuart Donaldson to produce the Swedish-language neo-Nazi magazine *Vit Rebell* (white rebel), later renamed *Storm*. They affiliated *Storm* with the Swedish neo-Nazi group Vit Ariskt Motstånd (white aryan resistance), a branch of the US-based white-power organization White Aryan Resistance (WAR). Eventually, *Storm* became

Blod & Ära (blood & honor) a short-lived Swedish-language version of *Blood & Honour* magazine.[93]

Blod & Ära and *Vit Rebell* remained on the fringes of Swedish society, but not all Swedish white-power and ultra-nationalist groups were content to stay on the margins. Through a populist party official and record label owner named Bert Karlsson, the ultra-nationalist Viking-rock band Ultima Thule (Latin for true north) from Nyköping signed a contract with an EMI Records subsidiary called Marianne Records and placed several albums in the Swedish top 20 during the early 1990s, before EMI officials discovered that the band had neo-Nazi roots and dropped them from the label.[94] Prior to attaining national popularity, Ultima Thule had released a 1990 single entitled "Hurra för Nordens Länder" (hurrah for the north lands) on Rock-O-Rama Records and another single in 1991, "Havets Vargar" (sea wolves, referring to the Vikings) on the French racist label Rebelles Européens (European rebels). They may also have belonged to Swedish racist and neo-Nazi groups like Bevara Sverige Svenskt (keep Sweden Swedish), an organization which, in fact, may have sponsored the band's first album, although definitive evidence for this is difficult to produce.[95]

Ultima Thule have publicly disputed the charge that they are racist, and have avoided overtly racist sentiments in their music. Some scholars, such as Benjamin Teitelbaum, who has conducted fieldwork with the group, argue that Ultima Thule should not be classified as a white-power band, while others, like Anton Shekhovtsov, Stieg Larsson, Ugo Corte, and Bob Edwards, categorize Ultima Thule as a racist group without qualification.[96] The band's history of ultra-nationalism means that they *do* deserve consideration in studies of white-power music, but as a liminal case more like the Böhse Onkelz than as performers of blatant neo-Nazi music like Landser or Skrewdriver. While Ultima Thule's music may not praise Hitler or issue direct threats toward nonwhite immigrants, one must nonetheless consider the context for the music as well as what band members say to reporters. Even if band members themselves have had *no* interaction with white-power and neo-Nazi believers, Ultima Thule's music is clearly popular with hardcore racists and neo-Nazis; the US-based white-power recording company Label 56, for instance, praises Ultima Thule's career as a "fantastic journey" in a blog post about the band's decision to break up in 2012.[97]

Despite losing their mainstream recording contract with Marianne Records in the early 1990s, Ultima Thule earned enough money from their brief stint in the Swedish top 20 to purchase their own recording equipment, which they used to found their own record label, Ultima Thule Records.[98] They used this label to record notoriously racist white-power bands like Dirlewanger—which changed their overtly neo-Nazi name to Heroes and toned down the racism in their music in order to avoid public criticism—as well as the Jinx, Midgårds Söner (Midgard's sons, referring to the fact that Midgard is the world of humans in Scandinavian mythology), and the Viking-rock band Enhärjarna (a term for slain warriors in Scandinavian mythology).[99]

Ultima Thule broke up in 2012 after a thirty-year career, titling their farewell album *30-Åriga Kriget*, Swedish for Thirty Years' War, but the group's success—like that of the marginally racist Böhse Onkelz in Germany—showed *overt* racists and neo-Nazis just how profitable nationalist and even overtly racist music could be. Increasing numbers of Swedish record labels began to sell blatantly white-power and neo-Nazi music as the 1990s wore on. By 1996, at least twenty different Swedish companies like Last Resort, Nordland, Ragnarock, and Svea (Swede) Music were producing albums for more than fifty Swedish white-power bands like Midgårds Söner, Dirlewanger/ Heroes, Steelcapped Strength, Vit Aggression, Brigad Wotan (Wotan brigade or Odin brigade), Storm, Svastika (swastika), and Division S, along with foreign bands like Britain's No Remorse, Australia's Fortress, the US's Max Resist, and Finland's Mistreat.[100]

Nordland and Ragnarock—both of which became embroiled in the feud over Blood & Honour in Britain—were the largest of these labels. The founder of Ragnarock Records was, as discussed above, the old Nazi Lars Magnus Westrup, who had been an activist in Sven Olov Lindholm's Swedish Nazi movement during the Third Reich era.[101] Upon Westrup's death in 1995, long-time Norwegian neo-Nazi Erik Blücher (a.k.a. Max Hammer) took over the label. Blücher also owned and operated the English-language white-power music magazine *Blood & Honour Scandinavia*.[102] Ragnarock made about 900,000 SEK, or $138,000 US, per year, and Nordland made 400,000 SEK, or about $61,000 US, in its first year alone.[103] These record labels supplied Swedish white-power music fans, and also distributed to an international market.[104]

Nordland, like Ragnarock, was a major player in Swedish white-power music during the 1990s. The label produced its own white-power music magazine, *Nordland*, which initially appeared in a 7,000-copy run in January 1995 and was distributed free to students at some Swedish schools.[105] By its second issue, *Nordland* had increased its distribution to 15,000, and by 1996, it had improved its production quality and increased its initial page count from 20 to a symbolic 88.[106] Editors of *Nordland* included Midgårds Söner vocalist Patrick "Nitton" (nineteen) Asplund, who left the white-power movement in 1996, and Matti Sundquist, lead singer of Svastika and solo artist under the stage name Matti S.[107] In the pages of *Nordland*, Sundquist wrote of the motivation for his involvement in white-power music, saying, "I'm totally convinced that the music is the best way to awaken the young and to make them understand that they have a value, despite what the society and media states. [...] If Adolf Hitler, our spiritual leader, was alive today, I'm convinced that he would not run around in shoulder belt or riding trousers. Every era has its own strategy for the struggle and today our weapon is the music and our White skin our uniform."[108]

Yet despite Sundquist's optimism, as early as 1999, observers were noting that the Swedish white-power music scene seemed to have begun a downward slide.[109] The infighting that spilled over from the British Blood & Honour dispute caused problems for Swedish concert organizers by pitting Nordland and Ragnarock—along with their affiliated bands and fans—against one another. The Swedish scene's gradual deterioration has continued into the 2000s and 2010s, especially because the Internet has made white-power music less profitable by allowing fans to download music from one another or listen to music for free via sites and services like YouTube.[110]

Swedish authorities began to crack down on concerts in the mid-1990s too, although Sweden's hate speech laws are far less restrictive than Germany's.[111] Particularly disastrous was a Nordland-affiliated concert on January 3, 1998 in the town of Brottby, near Stockholm, which featured the Swedish bands Pluton Svea (Swedish platoon), Vit Aggression, and Svastika, as well as the prominent US band Max Resist. Police observers inside the concert watched audience members giving illegal Hitler salutes.[112] When Max Resist's lead singer, Shawn Sugg, responded in kind from the stage, police stormed the building and arrested 297 people, including Sugg himself, who was sentenced to a month in jail as a result. However, Sugg was back playing another concert in Sweden only six months later.[113]

A resentful Sugg spoke of the incident to a British television crew in 2006, downplaying the significance of his actions:

I played a gig in Stockholm one time and I got a little out of control. I made some hand motions that I guess weren't approved by the government. They wanted to keep me for further observation there. I had a little time in the jail there just for saluting. I think it's crazy. I make one little hand motion and, bang!, they wanted to give me two years in jail. [...] I was found guilty for a thought crime, because of what I think. I think skinheads like to do it [give the Hitler salute] because it's kind of a symbol of rebellion, it's a gesture that signals unity between us. When you give 'em the old "Sieg Heil," it's like they [the government] just become incensed. And it's just a hand motion, you know?[114]

However flippant Sugg may have been about the illegality of his onstage Nazi salute during this particular interview—an interview he gave to the film crew in the presence of the British white-power band Whitelaw and other prominent members of the international white-power music web—he admitted to the same crew in a private interview session that the taboo nature of white-power activism was one of racism's major attractions for him: "My lifestyle's an outlaw lifestyle because it's not accepted by the society or mainstream. Maybe that's one reason why I'm attracted to racial politics, because it's so extreme. I want to be extreme."[115]

Nor was Sugg alone in feeling the lure of the illicit. A 1997 joint study by the Swedish National Council for Crime Prevention and Sweden's Centre for Research in International Migration and Ethnic Relations found that 12 percent of Swedish school students between the ages of twelve and twenty—10 percent of girls and 15 percent of boys—listened to racist music "sometimes" or "often."[116]

Some of these Swedish fans of white-power music have become prominent white-power musicians in their own right. One in particular, a female devotee of Ian Stuart Donaldson and Skrewdriver who performs under the stage name Saga, rose in the 1990s to become a white-power celebrity often referred to in the popular press as the "Swedish Madonna of the far right."[117] Originally the lead singer for an otherwise all-male white-power band called Symphony of Sorrow, Saga released no fewer than three Skrewdriver tribute albums in 2000 and 2002, along with several live albums, a collaboration with house musicians from the Swedish label Midgård Records in 2003, a 2007 solo album called *On My Own*, and a 2014 solo album called *Weapons of Choice*.[118] She has been known in particular for adopting a normalized appearance, shedding the skingirl couture of her 1990s Symphony of Sorrow persona for mainstream attire in her later solo career as a way of appealing to a wider and more mainstream audience.

Among white-power music fans, Saga seems to receive almost universal admiration, not only because of her anomalous status as a female performer in a heavily male-dominated genre, but also due to her genuine facility as a vocalist; in fact, *Resistance* magazine staff writer John Murdoch, who interviewed her for the magazine's Fall 2000 cover story, told her during the interview, "I would have to say that you are one of the most talented vocalists that we have worldwide. I'm not saying that merely because you are a woman; I am saying that because what comes across to the listener is a talented artist who has a lot of range in what she can do with her voice. We have very few true singers in the scene, and even fewer quality ones at that. Most of our people just shout into the microphone until they go hoarse."[119] In the interview, Saga replied to Murdoch's comment by saying, "I think that the ones who are not that familiar with the microphone and signing techniques in general can also have a lot of charm in what they produce. [. . .] And the shouting suits this kind of music in a way."[120] Yet, despite Saga's polite demurral, Murdoch is by no means the only white-power music fan to express this sentiment. In a 2010 review of her album *On My Own*, the Stormfront CD reviewer Ju-87 echoed Murdoch's sentiment by saying, "Lots of people on Stormfront complain that there's no

WN [white-nationalist] music for them outside the metal/HC [hardcore]/ RAC genre. Well. Here's your chance to score radio-friendly music. If it wasn't for the lyrics, you'd be seeing Saga music clips on MTV or your nation's equivalent. [. . .] It's difficult to rate this album. And I certainly can't compare or judge it with all the guitar 'noise' and brutal stuff I have in my collection."[121]

Like Murdoch—and many other white-power music fans who have discussed Saga's music—this user also makes gender-related comments about Saga in the review, explicitly constructing her as a white-power sex symbol through the unusual method of comparing her appearance with the final victim of Jack the Ripper, the prostitute Mary Kelly, writing, "I still find her prettiest as a blonde, even though I'm more into the brunette/dark haired 'Mary Kelly' look."[122] Uncomfortable references to nineteenth-century sex-workers-turned-murder-victims aside, this reviewer's focus on Saga's feminine attractiveness characterizes many discussions of her persona and her music in white-power circles. Saga, for her part, has summed up her feelings about being one of the few women performing white-power music by saying, "Why should we be less productive then men? White girl power—yeah!"[123]

Regarding her political beliefs, Saga spoke to the same British film crew that interviewed Shawn Sugg in 2006, saying, "It's a bad thing to be labeled a racist these days, and it's such a bad thing that people [would] rather shut up than express what they feel. I'm just trying to say that I don't want people who are not like me around me."[124] At least a handful of other Scandinavians clearly share this sentiment and have been willing to support it with real-world violence. Saga's most famous fan, the Norwegian terrorist Anders Behring Breivik, publicized an extended manifesto that praised Saga's music, doing so only hours before committing two politically motivated attacks that killed seventy-seven people in the Oslo area in July 2011.[125] Saga has denounced Breivik's massacres in an official statement on her website, but her music clearly praises other violent heroes of the white-power movement, including the late David Lane, who died in a US prison in 2007 and is the subject of one of the songs on Saga's *On My Own* album, a reworking of Elton John's song "Candle in the Wind" entitled "Goodbye David Lane."[126] Clearly, then, Swedish white-power musicians have had an influence not only on white-power *musicians* in other countries, but also on foreign *terrorists* such as Breivik.

Norway

Norwegian artists, like their Swedish counterparts, have produced music that has affected the international web of white-power music in profound ways. Several Norwegian white-power musicians have even become internationally famous for their own extreme acts of violence. Norway's white-power musicians have been relatively few in number, particularly compared with the large scenes in Britain, Germany, and Sweden. Still, these musicians' impact on the history and the sound of white-power music in recent decades is difficult to overstate. The Norwegian National Socialist black metal (NSBM) scene of the 1990s has, more than almost any other subgenre of white-power music since the original British white-power oi! punk of the late 1970s and early 1980s, inspired its own generation of copycat artists—and criminals.

As in the preceding histories of white-power music in other countries, it is important to begin this history of white-power music in Norway by explaining why white-power and neo-Nazi music appeared in Norway, as well as what specific socio-historical conditions have influenced Norwegian white-power musicians. It might seem surprising that Norwegians have contributed to recent neo-Nazi movements at all, because Norway spent the majority of World War II as an unwilling territory of the Third Reich, and many of its citizens resented the presence of German occupying forces in Norwegian territory. In fact, by the time the war ended in the spring of 1945, the covert Norwegian resistance organization Milorg—short for militær organisasjon or military organization—had actually morphed into a full-blown anti-Nazi military force of 40,000 trained soldiers.[127] Still, at least 45,000 other Norwegian citizens willingly voted for the Nazis and joined the collaborationist Nasjonal Samling (national unification) political party in support of Norway's Nazi puppet regime, which took control of the country in June 1940 under Vidkun Quisling and deported about 760 Jews to concentration camps, only twenty-four of whom survived the war.[128] After World War II, the Norwegian government executed Quisling for treason and distanced itself politically from the ideologies of its former Nazi occupiers, although a few of Quisling's former supporters continued to harbor pro-Nazi sentiments even decades later.

As is true in most other western European countries and particularly in those the German army took by force during World War II, only a small minority of postwar Norwegians has ever espoused hard-line neo-Nazism. Nonetheless, this marginalized demographic has been a relatively constant feature of the Norwegian political landscape since the World War II era. Ultra-right-wing racism has become an especially central topic of Norwegian public discourse since the Breivik attacks in 2011.[129] Iranian-Swedish politician Ali Esbati, who witnessed the deadlier of Breivik's two attacks at a left-wing summer camp on the Norwegian island of Utøya, argued in 2013 that racism in Norway had declined little since the Breivik attacks two years earlier, because "people reason that everyday racism is miles apart from Breivik's mass murder."[130] In fact, xenophobic right-wing political parties in Norway experienced *increased* electoral success after the Breivik attacks.[131] While their voter turnout is tiny compared to those of more moderate Norwegian parties, any measure of increased success for ultra-right-wing politics suggests that the Breivik attacks have not deterred Norway's far-right voter base from continuing to embrace racist parties and politicians.

It was members of Norway's ultra-right-wing demographic who, in the early 1990s, drew on pre-existing neo-pagan and black metal movements to create NSBM, a form of white-power music that had a uniquely violent effect on Norwegian society. Members of the small Norwegian NSBM scene engaged in a flurry of transgressive one-upmanship in the early 1990s that included murder, suicide, reported cannibalism, and dozens of successful and/or attempted church arsons.[132] The scene was known for the arsons in particular, because members destroyed several prominent Norwegian national historic landmarks, such as the twelfth-century Fantoft wooden stave church in Bergen.[133]

Black metal, normally a non-racist form of "extreme" heavy metal closely related to speed, thrash, gothic, and death metal, first developed in Northern Europe in the 1980s. Early, non-racist black metal groups included the Danish band Mercyful Fate, the British band Venom—which coined the term "black metal" as the title of a 1982 album—and the Swedish band Bathory, named after the seventeenth-century Hungarian Countess Erzsébet Báthory de Ecsed, who allegedly killed dozens or even hundreds of virgin girls and bathed in their blood to maintain her youth. These bands differentiated themselves from other heavy metal musicians by focusing almost exclusively on lyrical themes of nihilism, Satanism, and especially anti-Christianity.[134] Later musicians, particularly in the black metal subgenre of Viking black metal, also drew on the imagery and philosophy of neo-pagan Scandinavian mythology. In the 1980s, black metal bands adopted the indecipherable, growled vocals and hyper-speed drums of "extreme" metal cousins, but as the influence of Viking metal grew during the late 1980s and early 1990s, musicians began to experiment with their sound by blending in elements of neo-folk, electronica, military fife-and-drum, and western art music.[135] The resulting sound mixed typical aspects of heavy metal, such as wailing guitars and snarling vocals, with Hollywood-esque orchestral soundscapes aimed to invoke the martial, heroic, and bardic qualities of medieval Viking culture, at least as it appeared in the movies.

Many black metal "bands" were actually one-man studio projects, but those that did have full lineups developed increasingly flashy stage personae as the 1980s wore on. Performers wearing Viking-style armor, spiked leather, fake blood makeup, and elaborate "corpse" face paint often wielded props such as pigs' heads and inverted Christian crosses during live shows. Black metal's early performers intended for their genre to remain elitist, a conscious backlash to the increasing popularity of other forms of extreme metal in the mainstream. As Stormfront users often note, the practitioners of black metal tended to be white, and, in the early years, most often hailed from Northern Europe; one Stormfront CD reviewer, in fact, remarked in 2005 that "Black metal has nothing to do with black people. I actually don't think a single black person has ever played black metal. [. . .] Black people hate listening to [the Norwegian NSBM band] Burzum."[136] Another user responded to this first comment in order to point out that the actual lyrics to songs by Burzum and many other NSBM bands actually often express remarkably little of the racist elitism that NSBM musicians have expressed outside of their music, writing, "That's actually a bit folly to say, since Varg's [Burzum musician Varg Víkernes's] politics are always kept outside of his music. Same with most Norwegian Black Metal artists."[137] Nonetheless, as the first commenter suggests, even non-racist musicians in the black metal genre have been almost exclusively white.

Although black metal songs often feature *violent* texts, the genre did not take on an overtly *racist* tone until a small group of black metal bands known as the Black Circle congregated in an Oslo record shop called Helvete, Norwegian for hell, in the early 1990s. The owner of Helvete was Øystein Aarseth, guitarist of the black metal band Mayhem and owner of the black metal record label Deathlike Silence Productions, who nicknamed himself "Euronymous" after a demon in Greek mythology, Eurynomos (Εὐρύνομος). Fans of racist heavy metal music often express admiration for Aarseth's work in Mayhem; for example, the same Stormfront user quoted above as saying, "Black people hate listening to Burzum," a few weeks later reviewed the Mayhem album *Deathcrush*, stating,

I like Mayhem. They are legendary, and they also are the band that got me to start liking Norway so much. This album, or demo if you will, is very raw and primitive. I like that. It's barbaric, and barbarians are good people. The album's cover makes me feel that they may have been incredibly racist when this was released. Two black hands hanging from some rope.... hands with no body attached to them. The music itself is great (for raw black metal). [. . .] It is a classic, and it inspired more bands than that one could imagine. Mayhem was incredibly Satanic. 10/10 all time classic.[138]

Aarseth and Mayhem have clearly influenced a generation of NSBM musicians and fans with their seminal sound, as this album review suggests. The impact of Mayhem's music is not, however, the only reason why Aarseth has become one of the most famous musicians to have emerged from the international white-power music web to date. When Per Yngve "Dead" Ohlin, one of Aarseth's fellow Mayhem band members, committed suicide by shooting himself in the head in 1991, Aarseth photographed Ohlin's corpse—a picture that surfaced in 1995 on the cover of a South American Mayhem bootleg album called *Dawn of the Black Hearts*—and allegedly even ate parts of Ohlin's brain in a stew.[139] In 2012, Swedish guitarist Morgan Steinmeyer Håkansson of the black metal band Marduk (named for the patron deity of ancient Babylon in Babylonian mythology) admitted to the press that he still owned pieces of Ohlin's skull and brain, mementos that Aarseth had also sent to several other fellow black metal musicians as an apparent sign of respect.[140]

After the debacle surrounding Ohlin's suicide, Aarseth and other members of the Black Circle began to break other social taboos as well, consciously distancing themselves from mainstream society. In particular, they flouted the mores of polite society by espousing an esoteric brand of neo-Nazi ideology that mixed the Nietzschean and Satanist motifs of earlier black metal bands like Venom and Bathory with Vidkun Quisling's National Socialist philosophy and Third Reich–era racist occult imagery.[141] Their new appreciation for Nazi occultism, which in itself had venerated the mythos of Scandinavian paganism as a purportedly "Aryan" alternative to the Jewish-derived religion of Christianity, led the Black Circle to denounce not only Christianity, but also its parent religion, Judaism. Rather than attempting to offend outsiders simply by expressing Satanist occultism—a key feature of even non-racist black metal—the Black Circle blended elements of neo-Nazism into their occult ideology. They espoused anti-Semitism and Jewish world conspiracy theory, as well as homophobia, xenophobia, and the practice of Scandinavian neo-pagan religious rituals which they filtered through the lens of Nazi neo-pagan occultism. Mounting racism and homophobia within the Black Circle even contributed to a murder in 1992, when Bård "Faust" Eithun, drummer of the neo-Nazi black metal band Emperor, stabbed to death a homosexual man who had made advances toward him in a Lillehammer park.[142]

In the Black Circle's philosophy, Judaism and Christianity became two facets of the same problem: an oppressive foreign religion that had unjustly supplanted Norway's native paganism in order to subjugate Scandinavia's "pure," freethinking Viking warriors by polluting their culture with unwanted foreign traditions and people. This perspective, of course, ignored the fact that the pre-Christian Vikings' massive slave trade had brought medieval Scandinavians into cultural and genetic contact with populations from as far away as the Byzantine Empire at least partially by their own choice and not simply as a result of violent incursions from foreign invaders. By revising Viking history into a factually inaccurate story of violent heroic struggle against attackers from outside Scandinavia rather than portraying it as the story of deliberate outward expansion that it really was, early 1990s black metal musicians constructed Viking warriors as archetypal Nazis, voicing contemporary concerns about immigration and race-mixing via tropes of medieval Scandinavians and Viking warfare. This new philosophical branch of black metal earned itself the moniker National Socialist black metal (NSBM), and it quickly made head-lines in Norway for the extreme acts that its practitioners were willing to com-mit in order to express their hatred for all things "Judeo-Christian."

At the vanguard of 1990s NSBM was Kristian Víkernes, who entered the Norwegian black metal scene under the pseudonym Count Grishnackh—a name he borrowed from an evil orc character in J.R.R. Tolkien's *Lord of the Rings* saga—but quickly changed his given name from Kristian (meaning Christian, impolitic in black metal circles) to Varg (Norwegian for wolf).[143] Víkernes eventually became famous for his one-man NSBM band Burzum, meaning darkness in the fictional Black Speech language used in J.R.R. Tolk-ien's *Lord of the Rings* trilogy, but in 1992, he was a member of Aarseth's band, Mayhem. After Bergen's twelfth-century Fantoft stave church burned at a sym-bolic 6:00 AM on June 6, 1992, a juncture that, according to Víkernes, recalled not only the Satanist "666" but also the first Viking raid on English soil at the Lindisfarne monastery on June 6, 793 CE, Víkernes staged an elaborate press conference at his home to claim that he "knew about" the fire.[144] Víkernes was even brazen enough to use a photograph of the charred Fantoft church as the cover art for his Burzum album *Aske*—a title that means ashes in Norwegian. Subsequently, a jury which Víkernes claims was rigged with "pensioners" and "the one single Christian faith healer in Norway" found him guilty of three other church arsons, although not enough evidence emerged to convict him of the Fantoft fire itself.[145]

Although the Norwegian court found few physical links between Víkernes and the Fantoft arson, it had more reason to convict him of another charge: the murder of Øystein Aarseth. Víkernes and Aarseth had fallen out in 1992 over the financing of Víkernes's first Burzum album, *Burzum*, which Aars-eth had released on his Deathlike Silence label. Aarseth had borrowed from Víkernes the money he needed to press copies of the album, but had then used the loan for other purposes and failed to print the promised copies of *Burzum*. In response, Víkernes set up his own label, Cymophane Records. According to Víkernes, he chose the name "Cymophane Records" because it was Greek for "'Wave to appear,' the name of a gem that is shaped like an eye."[146] An incensed Aarseth began plotting to kill Víkernes, but early on the morning of August 10, 1993, in the presence of another Norwegian NSBM musician, Víkernes stabbed Aarseth to death in the stairwell of Aarseth's apartment building instead. Víkernes himself has described the murder in gruesome detail on his personal website, leaving little doubt of his guilt.[147]

The Norwegian court sentenced Víkernes to twenty-one years in prison for Aarseth's murder, as well as three arsons and the stockpiling of illegal explo-sives, but despite an ill-fated 2003 prison escape that added thirteen months to his sentence, he served only fifteen years before being released in May 2009.[148] While in prison, he produced and released two new Burzum albums using only a synthesizer, and since his release, he has continued to create new albums. European authorities have followed him closely since he left prison; as a result, he and his French wife were arrested in July 2013 for purchasing four rifles in France, where they now live. His wife carried a legal firearms permit, so the couple was soon released.[149] However, French authorities remain worried that he might carry out another Breivik-style attack, particularly because Anders Behring Breivik personally mailed Víkernes a copy of his manifesto, to which Víkernes has responded in both positive and negative detail on his website.[150] Víkernes has distanced himself from explicit Nazism since his release from prison, but the philosophies that he expresses on his website still include overt racism and eugenics.[151] In fact, at the time of his arrest for the firearms purchase in July 2013, he was scheduled to appear in court on separate charges that his website had violated French anti-racism laws.[152] He lost the hate speech trial in July 2014 and was sentenced to a six-month suspended jail term and a fine of €8000.[153]

Víkernes's influence on white-power music has spread beyond Scandinavia. While Víkernes was in prison, the managers of his Cymophane Records label even forged links with the burgeoning US white-power music scene. These links arose through a particularly close relationship between late Resistance Records owner William Pierce and a fugitive Cymophane Records branch manager named Hendrik Möbus, a German NSBM musician from the Thuringian band Absurd who operated under several aliases, including Randall Flagg—the name of an evil character from Stephen King's 1978 post-apocalyptic novel *The Stand*—as well as Jarl Flagg Nidhögg or JFN, referring both to King's character and to the Níðhöggr dragon of Norse mythology. Fans of NSBM often praise Absurd's music, even though the lyrics to the band's songs, like those of many other NSBM bands, do not express racist sentiments as explicitly as the musicians do offstage and outside the studio. For example, one Stormfront member who professes to be an NSBM fan and a fellow NSBM musician writes in a 2008 review of Absurd's 1999 album *Asgardsrei* (named for the supernatural "wild hunt," an omen of change or catastrophe in Scandinavian paganism), "Absurd's Asgardsrei is WP [white-power] music, but what BM [black metal] should sound like. It sounds like it's recorded in a garage with a 4 track. That's what BM is."[154]

Möbus, however, is similar to Víkernes in that he is more famous for his violent acts and his conflicts with law enforcement officials than he is for his music. In 1999, Möbus fled to the United States to escape a parole violation in Germany. Möbus and his bandmates had killed a high-school classmate as minors in 1993, and shortly after Möbus left prison on parole in 1998, police observed him giving an illegal Hitler salute onstage at a concert. At the time, Möbus was manager of the Cymophane Records branch, and was also the owner of the NSBM label Darker than Black (DTB) Records, although, due to his deteriorating legal situation, Darker than Black was taken over by Mirko Hesse's Hate Records in July 1999.[155]

In his international flight from German law enforcement officials, Möbus eventually found his way to the Hillsboro, West Virginia complex that by 1999 housed not only the headquarters of one of the United States' best-known hate groups, the National Alliance, but also a newly relocated Resistance Records, the world's largest and best-known white-power music retailer. Working together with National Alliance founder William Pierce, Möbus set up Resistance Records as the US distributor for Cymophane Records, bringing NSBM to the US white-power music market on a large scale for the first time. Pierce bought Cymophane outright in 2000.[156] Although US authorities finally captured Möbus in August 2000, Möbus's partnership with Pierce and Resistance allowed NSBM to reach an expanding audience of white-power music fans and helped to cement heavy metal as a key element of white-power music's sonic palette worldwide.[157]

The early 1990s Norwegian NSBM scene influenced not only the musical style of later white-power bands, but also their extra-musical activities. Whether or not Varg Víkernes committed the Fantoft church arson or any of the church burnings for which he was actually convicted, the Norwegian arsons provided the model for a number of copycat arsons. In addition to more than fifty NSBM-related church arsons which took place in Norway between 1992 and 1996 alone, an expanding NSBM scene has been responsible for dozens of other arsons and at least ten murders worldwide. In fact, three of the four members of a Polish NSBM band called Thunderbolt were convicted of arson and murder in their home country.[158] Although the Norwegian NSBM scene has remained small, the sensational press coverage of Víkernes and the church arsons launched NSBM into the Scandinavian mainstream consciousness and beyond, into the center of the white-power music world. By the late 1990s, prominent foreign white-power musicians had begun to experiment with NSBM, including George Burdi, a Canadian white-power activist who co-founded Resistance Records and fronted the band RaHoWa (short for racial holy war), as well as Ed Wolbank, front man of the United States' most famous white-power band, Bound for Glory, and its NSBM side project, Before God.

Since the early 1990s, however, Norway has produced only a few white-power bands—including Norhat (northern hatred), Norske Legion (Norwegian legion), Vidkuns Venner (Vidkun's friends, referring to Vidkun Quisling), and Rinnan Band (referring to the Norwegian Gestapo agent and infamous torturer Henry Rinnan)—but none who have interacted with or influenced the international white-power music scene to the same extent as the early 1990s NSBM musicians. This fact is particularly striking when one compares the small but influential Norwegian NSBM scene with the giant white-power music scene that flourished during the 1990s in neighboring Sweden. In all likelihood, the deluge of negative media coverage that followed the Black Circle's crime spree, along with the Black Circle's elitist penchant for excluding even white Norwegian-descended individuals they deemed unworthy, made white-power music an unpopular choice for many young Norwegians even as it was experiencing its golden years elsewhere. Norway's history as first an opponent and then a conquered territory of Hitler's forces during World War II may also make many Norwegians hesitant to support neo-Nazi ideologies. Nevertheless, the Black Circle has had an enormous influence on the international white-power music web.

By tracing this history of the Black Circle and its legacy, this section provides context for histories of NSBM scenes in other countries which will appear later in this book. In fact, without exploring the history of the Black Circle, it would be difficult to explain the trajectories of NSBM scenes in some countries outside Norway, especially the United States and Canada. Clearly, as the wave of violence surrounding the Black Circle and the Anders Behring Breivik attacks both demonstrate, Norway has experienced more than its share of terrorism from white-power musicians and fans in the past thirty years. While Norway's white-power music scene is smaller than most of the others explored in this book, its influence on both white-power musicians and white-power terrorists abroad has been just as important as the influence of numerically bigger scenes like the one in Sweden. Due to the Black Circle's influence, NSBM and other forms of heavy metal are now common in white-power music. The "native" Scandinavian neo-pagan religion of Northern Europe seems to have become the most prevalent religious choice among white-power musicians worldwide. White-power music may not have grown into a major force in Norway itself after the media circus descended on the Black Circle in the mid-1990s, but its impact has affected Norwegian society and international white-power music nonetheless.

The Western Mediterranean (France, Spain, Italy)

One might assume from reading the preceding histories in this chapter that the most influential white-power music scenes in the world all come from Northwestern Europe, and in particular from cultures that celebrate at least partial descent from ancient Germanic traditions. While the influence of neo-Nazism on contemporary white-power ideology means that Germanic and Scandinavian countries have played key roles in the history of white-power music overall, it would be a mistake to overlook white-power music from other parts of Europe. White-power musicians in many Western Mediterranean countries also participate in the international white-power music web, sometimes by espousing the same kinds of racism that circulate in Northwestern

Europe, and in other cases by adapting white-power racism to their own local histories and politics.

An important contemporary Mediterranean white-power music scene has developed in France, a country that is home to one of the most successful ultra-right-wing populist political parties in Europe. One might expect neo-Nazism to have received a hesitant welcome in France, a country which, like Norway, fell to the Nazis by force in World War II. French resistance fighters earned particularly fierce reputations for harassing and sabotaging the Nazi occupation forces during the war, often hiding and saving Jews from Nazi persecution in the process. Nonetheless, strands of anti-Semitic thought—which have influenced French society for at least a millennium, as becomes clear when one examines events such as the violently anti-Semitic Pogroms of 1096—also appealed to a significant percentage of the World War II–era French population.[159] In fact, anti-Semitism ran so high among the heavily influential Catholic Church in France during World War II that the church officials who finally issued a formal apology to the Jewish people in 1997 for having failed to stage organized intervention during the Holocaust cited a culture of "age-old anti-Judaism" and "constantly repeated anti-Jewish stereotypes" as key reasons why the church stayed silent during the deportation and murder of tens of thousands of French Jews.[160] Relations between the French Catholic Church and France's surviving Jewish community have improved in recent decades, but ultra-right-wing French politicians like Jean-Marie Le Pen still ridiculed the church's 1997 apology to the Jews, calling it "absolutely scandalous" and saying that it demonstrated "disdain for historical truth."[161]

In contemporary France, Jews are not the only national minority group that occasionally experiences prejudice and discrimination from government officials like Le Pen and his supporters. The contemporary French government now maintains an uneasy relationship with its Roma population and with citizens who have migrated to mainland France in recent decades from the empire's former colonies; as recently as 1961, in fact, French police actually *killed* between 32 and 200 peaceful Algerian-French protesters in what has become known as the Paris Massacre.[162] In 2009, the French government began a new campaign to expel illegal immigrants from France, deporting 8,300 Roma migrants back to Romania and Bulgaria by late August 2010.[163] The French government insisted publicly that it was not targeting the Roma in particular—in fact, France's immigration minister, Eric Besson, told the press that "[t]he concept of ethnic minorities is a concept that does not exist among the government"—but a memo leaked in August 2010 revealed that then-President Nicolas Sarkozy had indeed made Roma deportations a government priority.[164]

Then, in 2011, France implemented a controversial new law known collo-quially as the "burqa ban," which barred all garments denoting religious affili-ation from public places. Lawmakers expressly designed the statute to target the approximately 2,000 Muslim women living in France who wore full face coverings in public, although, after serious debate, they removed any spe-cific references to Islam from the final wording of the law.[165] French officials insisted that they instituted the law to ensure gender equity; Sarkozy himself publicly criticized the burqa as "a sign of subservience."[166] However, critics of the law point out that women who choose to wear full-face coverings for reli-gious reasons have lost considerable quality of life and freedom of movement since the statute went into effect.[167] In 2015, Muslim extremists associated with the ISIS terrorist organization began to target France with increasingly violent attacks, criticizing the French government's resolute support of secularism. An attack on the Paris offices of a satirical magazine killed twelve people in January 2015, and then a large-scale series of coordinated attacks in several places in Paris killed 129 people in November of that year. Public anger over the attacks sparked President Hollande to ask Parliament for constitutional changes to deal more effectively with terrorist threats in the future, and politi-cal analysts suggested that right-wing anti-immigrant politicians and parties would likely gain in the polls as a result of the increased threat.[168]

One of the parties that stands to gain the most from angry reactions to the 2015 terrorist attacks in France is the powerful, radical-right, populist Front National party, founded in 1972 by Jean-Marie Le Pen and now led by his daughter, Marine. The Front National has become a major force in French pol-itics since the mid-1980s.[169] Jean-Marie Le Pen's initial goal for the party was to unify a number of divergent branches in French extreme-right politics. This ultimately became possible because various French extreme-right groups like the neo-pagan *nouvelle droite* (new right) and the ultra-Catholic Chrétienté-Soliderité (Christian solidarity) factions might differ over issues like religion, but, according to political theorist Cas Mudde, "all share a populist radical right core ideology."[170] The Front National's platform includes support for restricted immigration, Islamophobia, and "Euroskepticism," a term that denotes desire for a country's withdrawal from the European Union.[171] Jean-Marie Le Pen—who was the first runner-up in the 2002 French presidential election—has even made repeated comments to the press and the European Parliament questioning the numbers of Jews killed in Nazi gas chambers and calling the gas chambers a "detail of Second World War history."[172]

In recent decades, French white-power musicians have traded on the popularity of radical-right politicians like the Le Pens. The earliest French racist skinhead bands, like Skinkorps, Snix, Tolbiac's Toads (referring to the French town of Tolbiac and the green color of the band's skinhead military surplus jackets), Légion 88, and Evil Skins/Zyklon B (German for cyclone B, the name of the de-lousing agent used to poison victims in the gas chambers at Auschwitz-Birkenau), appeared between 1982 and 1985, exactly as the Front National was gaining recognition as a political party of national consequence.[173] France, with different hate speech laws than Germany and other Western European countries, allows freedom of expression in art. This loophole allows many French white-power bands to slip under the radar of a French government that otherwise tracks political groups it considers to be subversive.[174]

One of the biggest names on the French white-power music scene to date has been Fabrice Robert, who has gone on to hold several elected positions in France, as well as to found the ultra-right-wing political party Bloc Identitaire (identity bloc), after ending his white-power music career. Bloc Identitaire now runs in official elections on a platform of Islamophobia and French nationalism.[175] Before he became a politician, Robert was a member of several white-power and neo-fascist bands, including Troisième Voie (third way, referring to the white-power call for a political philosophy outside both democracy and communism), Septembre Noir (black september), Freikorps (free corps, referring to volunteer German military and paramilitary units, particularly of the Weimar Republic era, a term adopted by some contemporary racist groups as well), and, in particular, the notorious oi!/hatecore punk band Fraction Hexagone (fraction hexagon), a band name later shortened to just Fraction, a group that forged links with white-power bands in other countries.[176] Musically, white-power music fans have praised Fraction Hexagone albums. For example, in a 2006 review of the 1996 Fraction Hexagone album *Rejoins nos Rangs* (join our ranks), the Stormfront reviewer Ju-87 writes, "The songs are relatively simple, but the band knows how to create entertaining riffs and vocal lines. It all sounds very militaristic. [. . .] Any sound White Nationalist will shout along with the lines, 'Europe, jeunesse, revolution [Europe, youth, revolution]!'"[177]

Robert and Fraction Hexagone developed a relationship with George Burdi's Canadian white-power band RaHoWa; in 1993, Burdi helped to found the white-power and neo-Nazi record label Resistance Records in Detroit. Under the influence of RaHoWa and Resistance Records, Fraction Hexagone and other French white-power bands began to adopt the radical anti-Semitism, neo-Nazism, and Jewish world conspiracy theory of the North American white-power movement. However, Fraction Hexagone's reliance on Nazi ideology and symbolism caused tension within the French radical right. The ultra-Catholic factions in the French extreme right wing have yet to forgive the Nazis for taking over France during World War II and tend to see fascist Italy rather than Nazi Germany as a role model. It is for this reason that Robert's new political party, the Bloc Identitaire, focuses more on radical

Islamophobia—popular in France, with its high numbers of recent Muslim immigrants—than on the anti-Semitism that characterized his earlier neo-Nazi activism.[178]

In its early days, the neo-Nazi-influenced Fraction Hexagone took for its logo the crossed hammer and sword of Otto Strasser's Third Reich–era pro-Nazi organization the Schwarze Front (black front). This crossed hammer and sword was already the logo of France's most prominent white-power record label, Rebelles Européens, run in the port city of Brest by the fascist Front National activist Gael Bodilis.[179] Rebelles Européens was Rock-O-Rama's only serious international competitor before Resistance Records began selling in the United States in 1994.[180] At its peak, Rebelles Européens offered a catalogue of almost 200 different albums, along with recordings of Third Reich–era military music and other white-power paraphernalia like T-shirts and books.[181] Bodilis explained his label's motivation to a skinzine by saying, "Music is an excellent way of expressing those [racist] ideas and it was becoming more and more necessary to have these skinhead bands known. Obviously there is one factor that I am not interested in— PROFITABILITY. The Jews could probably talk about it better than I do."[182] Despite the label's early significance to the white-power music movement, however, Rebelles Européens folded in 1994, with only a brief revival through an Australian label in 1995.

As Bodilis's comment demonstrates, Fabrice Robert and Fraction Hexagone were not the only French white-power activists to subscribe to anti-Semitic ideology in the 1990s. Nor were they the last. France and Belgium have their own division of Blood & Honour, called Blood & Honour Midgard, with its headquarters in Bruges, Belgium.[183] In 1994, the French band Vae Victis (woe to the vanquished) founded another racist music network as well, called Rock Identitaire Français, or RIF (French identity rock) after an ideologically driven genre of popular music called identity rock, which expressed pro-white racism through a range of different musical styles, including oi! punk, acoustic ballads, and even rap.[184] France has also spawned a number of other white-power and neo-Nazi musical groups over the past thirty years, including prominent bands like Jewicide, Legion A, Bunker 84, Choc Frontal (frontal shock), Panzerjäger (armored hunter), 9ème Panzer Symphonie (9th Panzer symphony), L'Infanterie Sauvage (the savage infantry), Elsass Korps (Alsace corps, referring to the Alsace region on the French-German Border), and Bagadou Stourm (combat troops, the name of a Breton nationalist organization).

While the French white-power music scene has reached neither the size nor the international significance of the larger and/or more influential networks in Britain, Germany, and Scandinavia, it has still carved an important niche in the worldwide white-power music web. Its focus on Italian Fascism and Mediterranean chauvinism as well as Germanic neo-Nazism demonstrates that the white-power music web is flexible enough to accommodate many different varieties of white-power ideology, incorporating white-power supporters and philosophies from ethnic groups that Hitler and his original Nazis likely would not have privileged.

Spanish white-power musicians are similar to those from France in that they idolize not only Nazi Germany, but also other authoritarian regimes of mid-twentieth-century Europe. Like French white-power musicians, they venerate Mussolini and the Italian Fascists alongside Hitler and the National Socialists, in addition to their own twentieth-century domestic dictatorship. In fact, Spanish and French white-power musicians demonstrate the same process of localizing the definition of "whiteness" to include Western Mediterranean groups alongside Germanic peoples at the top of the white-centered racial hierarchy. This web of white-power music scenes in Western Mediterranean countries is significant in that it poses subtle challenges to the Nordic-dominated racism of the original Nazis, and, indeed, of some neo-Nazi groups today.

Despite the presence of neo-Nazi and neo-fascist groups in contemporary Spain, Spain did not join World War II in *any* formal capacity. It remained non-belligerent for the duration of the war, although its government officially expressed ideological sympathy for the Axis cause. Spain ultimately remained neutral because in the years directly before the war, it had fought its own devastating civil war, in which Francisco Franco's right-wing fascist Nationalists had defeated the left-wing supporters of the democratic Spanish Republic. Both Hitler's Germany and Mussolini's Italy provided economic and material support for the Nationalist cause during the Spanish Civil War, sending combat units like an Italian fleet and the German Condor Legion to win control of Spanish Morocco for the Nationalists.[185] Under the influence of this support, the Nationalist government considered joining World War II on the side of the Axis powers, declining to participate in the end for financial rather than ideological reasons.

At home in Spain, more than 350,000 Spanish citizens died during the 1936–1939 Spanish Civil War, mostly as a result of Francoist government repression rather than battlefield fighting; 200,000 more perished in the brutal early years of the dictatorship between 1940 and 1942. Hundreds of thousands of Spanish refugees also flooded into foreign countries, although Spain's neighbors deported many of these refugees back to face persecution in Spain.[186] Ironically, at the same time, Jewish refugees were pouring *into* Spain from Nazi-controlled territory, despite Spain's 400-year ban on Jews living openly as Jews.[187] The violently anti-communist Franco regime—hostile to expressions of Judaism, which it equated with Bolshevism—did not allow these Jews to stay in Spain. Crucially, however, it allowed them to pass through Spanish territory on the way to neutral Portugal, and tens of thousands of Jews were able to escape Axis territory via this route.[188] Nonetheless, Spain refused to provide sanctuary for Jews during World War II, a harbinger of the cultural repressions that were to come under the postwar Franco government.

After the end of World War II, the Franco regime became increasingly nationalistic, banning cultural traditions from outside Spain, as well as a number of regional customs from within its own borders. Franco opposed in particular the cultural and linguistic autonomy of regions like Catalonia, Galicia, and the Basque country, enforcing policies of assimilation to the mainstream Castilian Spanish language.[189] The government relaxed some of these policies in the later years of Franco's rule, and much of this nationalism has subsided since Franco's death and the end of the dictatorship in 1975. Scholars even note that radical-right parties seem to be particularly weak in contemporary Spanish politics, remaining more isolated, technologically unsophisticated, and marginal than the influential radical-right populist parties in other Western European countries such as France and Austria.[190]

However, while tensions among most regions within Spain have relaxed since the 1970s, the Franco regime's historical xenophobia and opposition to minority or foreign cultural traditions does continue to carry over into contemporary Spanish white-power discourse. For example, in a 2014 reply to a thread entitled "European Mediterranean Folk Music [Greek, Dalmatian (South Croatian) & Italian etc . . .]" on Stormfront's Culture and History of Europe subforum, one user reprimanded fellow respondents for failing to check the racial pedigree of the Spanish-language music and videos to which they were linking in their posts, writing,

> We need to be careful with these "Spanish" compilations that have very little of Spanish and too much of Gypsy and Caribbean music. You just have to read the titles: *Exotico, Quetzal, Wandering Gypsy* . . . Even the musicians, what can you expect from [. . .] a dummy called Ottmar Liebert who makes a song called "Barcelona Nights" using Gypsy Flamenco patterns that have nothing to do with Catalan music? (italics in the original)[191]

This user clearly takes no issue with traditional Catalan folk culture, which the Franco regime *did* see as a threat, but admonishes other users to avoid conflating Spanish folk music with styles and influences from outside Europe. This insistence on differentiating European from non-European Spanish-language music is particularly interesting given the fact that many members of white-power music scenes in Latin America view white-power activists and musicians in Spain as their ethnic and linguistic kindred, a phenomenon I will discuss in greater detail in chapter 5. However welcoming or reticent individual white-power believers in Spain might feel toward their Latin American counterparts, though—and however small the contemporary Spanish white-power scene might be in comparison with the giant webs in countries like Germany, Russia, and the United States—the fact remains that a number of significant white-power bands *have* emerged from Spain over the past few decades.

Spaniards have indeed been active in white-power music at least since the early 1990s. Spanish white-power skinheads gave at least one large international white-power music concert in Valencia in 1992, the one to which the Welsh band Violent Storm was en route when its car slammed into a highway embankment, killing all of its members except Billy Bartlett. Upon hearing news of Violent Storm's accident, concert organizers quickly decided to go ahead with the event, turning it into an impromptu Violent Storm memorial that featured British bands No Remorse and Battlezone alongside the Spanish band División 250, a group named for the División Española de Voluntarios, or 250th Infantry Division, a unit of Spanish volunteers who fought on Hitler's eastern front during World War II.[192] Although the band División 250 broke up in 1993–1994 due to government pressure, its vocalist, Manuel Canduela, went on to become the leader of Spain's extreme-right-wing party Democracia Nacional (national democracy).[193]

Other prominent Spanish white-power bands have included Céltica, Estirpe Imperial (imperial bloodline), Tormenta (storm), Toletum (Toledo), Centuria Hispánica (Hispanic century), Sangre Joven (young blood), Odal (referencing the odal rune from the proto-Germanic Elder Futhark alphabet), Patria (homeland), Klan (a reference to the US-based Ku Klux Klan hate group), Legion Negra (black legion, meaning the World War II–era Crna Legija paramilitary arm of the Nazi-supported Croatian Ustaše regime), 14 Palabras (14 words, referring to the '14 Word' slogan by US neo-Nazi terrorist David Lane), Torquemada 1488 (also referencing Lane's 14 Words slogan, as well as the neo-Nazi numerical code 88 and the name of the first Grand Inquisitor of the Spanish Inquisition, Tomás de Torquemada), Batallón de Castigo (punishment battalion, an allusion to the punishment units sent into dangerous combat situations by the German military during World War II), Reconquista (recapture, meaning the ninth- to fifteenth-century-CE Christian displacement of Muslims from the Iberian peninsula), and Iberos Saiti (Saiti Iberians, supposedly referencing an ancient Celtic name for the band's hometown of Valencia).[194] Some of these bands, including Torquemada 1488, División 250, Batallón de Castigo, and Patria, have recorded on the homegrown Madrid label Rata-Ta Ta Tá Records.[195]

The Spanish scene boasts a Blood & Honour division, Asociación Cultural Sangre y Honor (cultural association blood and honor), which was founded in 1999.[196] A pre-existing division of Combat 18 had been founded in Barcelona in 1996, which may have been one of the reasons why the non-C18-aligned faction of Blood & Honour was anxious to establish itself in Spain in the late 1990s.[197] Blood & Honour Spain now oversees sections in several

Spanish cities, including Seville, Madrid, Toledo, and Barcelona.[198] The Spanish Blood & Honour division has been involved not only in organizing white-power concerts, but also in helping to produce and distribute albums for white-power musicians who have had difficulty finding mainstream companies willing to distribute albums with explicitly racist content.[199] It also began producing a Spanish *Blood & Honour* magazine free of charge to readers in 2001.[200] In addition to C18 and Blood & Honour, Spain is also home to Hammerskin chapters in Madrid and Gijon, as well as smaller, localized skinhead groups that help to organize concerts and promote regional bands.[201]

Members of the Spanish Blood & Honour division have run afoul of Spanish law on several occasions since the group's founding. In particular, on July 5, 2010, nineteen members—including two founders—were sentenced by a Spanish court for promoting anti-Semitic doctrine, Holocaust revision, neo-Nazi ideology, and discrimination, as well as for possessing and selling illegal weapons. Their trial focused on a concert the group had held at the Taj Mahal disco in the Talamanca del Jarama area of Madrid on February 12, 2005, after which police found a box containing the illegal weapons. The Regional Court of Madrid absolved only three of the nineteen defendants, sentencing fourteen of them to €2160 fines and thirteen of them to prison terms ranging from one to three years.[202]

Despite such legal problems, Spanish white-power bands have established strong connections with bands in other countries. In particular, they have worked closely with bands from the smaller white-power scene in neighboring Portugal. This connection has allowed them to market themselves through Portuguese fanzines to white-power believers and white-power music fans in South America.[203] As chapter 5 of this book demonstrates, although the Spanish white-power music scene has had a limited impact on the white-power music market in Europe itself, its link with predominantly Spanish- and Portuguese-speaking markets in South America has helped to bolster the South American white-power music scene, turning Spanish bands like División 250 into "classics" whose songs get covered at nearly every major white-power concert in countries like Argentina and Chile.

White-power musicians in Spain occupy an interesting position in the hierarchy of the international white-power music web due to Spain's long and tormented history of interaction with its Islamic North African neighbors. Despite the violence that has at some points accompanied Spanish-Muslim relations, long periods of peaceful Islamic rule have also characterized some eras in Spanish history. Millennia of intermarriage have left much of the Spanish population—including followers of white-power ideologies who might wish to deny this fact—with visible traces of both North African and European ancestry in outward appearance. Members of white-power music scenes from areas with statistically blonder populations, such as Germany and

Scandinavia, hold varying beliefs about the racial purity of white-power activists from Spain and other Mediterranean countries like Italy and Portugal. A 2007 Ju-87 Stormfront review of the Brigada Totenkopf album *Avanzando* (advance) also suggests that white-power music fans from the United States seem to be skeptical of Spaniards in white-power circles due to the influx of non-white, Spanish-speaking immigrants coming to the United States from Latin America: "A lot of Americans might get the chills when they hear this Spanish CD because of the beaner invasion over there. ☺ Just keep in mind that Spanish is a white language from origin" [*sic*].[204]

As Spain and Italy's inclusion in the Blood & Honour network demonstrates, white-power musicians from outside the Mediterranean world clearly are willing to work with Spanish and Italian musicians. However, whether they view them as true racial equals often depends on many different factors, including contextual expediency and the physical appearance of the individual musician. In other words, the white-power music world includes individuals who hold many different views about what "white" actually means, and while nearly everyone in the white-power music web seems to include ethnic Germans, Britons, and Scandinavians in this category, the status of some Mediterranean musicians—like that of some Eastern European musicians, who would have fallen into "inferior" racial categories under the Third Reich's taxonomy—remains more dubious.

Italian white-power musicians, like those from France and especially Spain, often fall into an in-between racial status in international white-power circles. However, Italians have their own historical racial hierarchy to draw on, one that stems most directly from the World War II–era racial theories of Benito Mussolini's Fascists, but also, in proto-racial form, from the uneasy and often violent relationships that the government of the classical Roman Empire had with non-Italian ethnic groups in the territory it conquered. For this reason, the Italian white-power music scene provides one of the clearest challenges to the dominance of Nordic-centered neo-Nazi ideologies in the international white-power music web.

In the case of Italian white-power music, it is difficult to overstate the importance of the World War II–era Italian Fascists as ideological heroes. Benito Mussolini's Partito Nazionale Fascista (national fascist party), which came to power in 1922 and ruled until Mussolini's ousting and execution in 1943, was indeed the world's original and archetypal fascist movement. Although anti-Semitism was not one of the Italian Fascists' core tenets, the fascist platform emphasized a radical form of nationalism that involved irredentist plans to rebuild the classical Roman Empire by re-conquering areas lost when the empire had broken up more than 1,500 years prior.[205] Mussolini therefore argued that Italy rightfully owned areas like Croatia, Albania, Corsica, Malta, Libya, Ethiopia, parts of Slovenia, and a few ethnic-Italian-dominated cantons in Switzerland.[206] He emphasized the superiority of Mediterranean peoples—occasionally even coming into conflict with Hitler over the Third Reich's Nordic-centered racial hierarchies—and he used his pro-Italian outlook to justify destructive colonial wars in Africa and Europe.[207]

After fascist Italy's defeat in World War II, the new postwar Italian constitution banned the Partito Nazionale Fascista and any future fascist successor parties.[208] However, the nationalist and racist elements of the Partito Nazionale Fascista platform did not disappear from Italian society, nor did support for archetypal Fascism among some sectors of the Italian population. In fact, during the 2008 mayoral election in Rome, crowds greeted the new mayor-elect Gianni Alemanno with fascist salutes and chants of "Duce!"— Mussolini's nickname.[209] Italian radical-right-wing parties are currently active in politics both at the Italian national level and in the European Parliament. Italy's nationalist, right-wing Euroskeptic party Lega Nord (northern league) was powerful enough to participate as a coalition partner in Silvio Berlusconi's government from 2008 to 2011.[210] Support for the Lega Nord has strengthened in northern Italy recently as economic crisis has struck that region with particular force.[211]

As the strength of Lega Nord and other far-right political groups in contemporary Italy suggests, support for extreme-right political ideologies has been high in recent decades, particularly in northern Alpine regions where some sectors of the population claim Germanic ancestry. White-power music has thrived in this environment. A homegrown Italian ultra-nationalist music scene actually pre-dated the racist skinhead bands of the 1970s, and was comprised mainly of singer/songwriters like Renato Colello and Amici del Vento, as well as neo-folk bands such as Compagnia dell'Anello (fellowship of the ring, referring to the title of the first book in J.R.R. Tolkien's *Lord of the Rings* trilogy).[212] While these early ultra-nationalist musicians generally avoided direct references to Fascism, Nazism, and even overt racism, they helped to establish a climate of national chauvinism in which a few skinhead bands could begin playing racist rock music in Italy in the early 1980s. The first racist skinhead bands in Italy included Plastic Surgery, which formed in Vicenza in 1981 as a non-political band and first began playing white-power music in 1983.[213] Later neo-fascist bands like Skin Army, Rommel Skins (alluding to Third Reich field marshal Erwin Rommel), and Peggior Amico (worst friend) began to advocate open neo-Nazism in the mid-1980s, followed in the late 1980s and early 1990s by bands like Block 11 (the name of the punishment block in the Auschwitz I concentration camp) and Corona Ferrea (iron crown, alluding to the medieval Iron Crown of Lombardy, allegedly forged in part from the nails used in Christ's crucifixion).[214] More groups arose over the course of the 1990s, such as the bands Final Solution and Bulldog Skin from the city of Messina, Razzia (raid) from Catania, Legio Viking (Viking Legion) from Livorno, Londinium SPQR (short for a Latin phrase meaning London senate and people of Rome) from Rome, and probably the best-known Italian white-power band to date, Gesta Bellica (acts of war) from Verona, formed in 1990.[215]

By 2000, Veneto Front Skinheads—since 1987, the operators of Blood & Honour Italy—had fifteen sections nationwide, and reported to *Blood & Honour* that they had "positive feedback" from mainstream political parties like Lega Nord.[216] The Veneto Front Skinheads, the center of a particularly active Northern Italian white-power music scene, operate their own record label, Tuono (thunder) Records, which was founded in Vicenza in 1993 under the direction of Massimo Bellini and is still in operation at the time of writing in 2015.[217] The group has also organized "activities linked to the history and knowledge of the Fascist era," including visits to Mussolini's crypt and meetings with Italian World War II veterans.[218]

Although the Veneto area tends to be the most active center of white-power music in Italy, other regions have developed their own white-power music scenes as well. The area in and around Rome has spawned important white-power bands such as the 1980s group Intolleranza (intolerance), and has been home to the racist record label Rupe Tarpea Produzioni (Tarpeian Rock productions, referencing both rock music and the name of the cliff on Rome's Capitoline Hill that functioned as an execution site in ancient times), which published a quarterly newsletter called *Non-Conforme* (non-conforming).[219] The skinhead scene in Milan has produced bands like ADL 122 (short for Anti-Decreto Legge 122 or Anti-Decree Law 122, referring to Italy's Decree No. 122 of April 26, 1993—often referred to as the Mancino Law—which allowed the Italian government to prosecute individuals for inciting violence), and has established not only its own record label, Assalto Sonoro (sonic assault) Records, but also a Milanese section of the Hammerskins.[220]

World War II–era Italian Fascism tends to be a major inspiration for these Italian white-power bands. One member of the band Gesta Bellica expressed the band's support for Mussolini in an interview with *Blood & Honour*, saying, "Mafia exists because our f*****g government doesn't exist. Benito Mussolini defeated the Mafia, and their bosses ran away to the U.S.A., but they came back in Sicily in 1943 on board the 'allied' tanks" [*sic*; profanity censored in the original].[221] Francesca Ortolani, an Italian white-power acoustic singer/ songwriter who performs under the stage names Viking and Aufidena (referring to the ancient Roman name of the Italian city Castel di Sangro, the ancestral home of the last members of the House of Caesar), echoes this veneration for World War II–era Italian Fascism. She told a British film crew in 2006, "I always say I am not a Nazi, I am a Fascist, because I think that I must defend my Italian history."[222] While some Italian white-power bands like Block 11 clearly also express support for neo-Nazism, this focus on homegrown nationalism and racism lends a particularly Italian character to Italian white-power music, one that influences white-power music in other Mediterranean countries like France and Spain. This Mediterranean rather than Nordic chauvinism represents an important challenge to the dominance of neo-Nazi ideology elsewhere in the white-power music world, although the Mediterranean and Northern European white-power music scenes obviously work together with one another. By providing a prominent example of how white-power musicians can adapt the ideologies of the international white-power movement to their own local purposes, the Italian white-power music scene functions as a role model for other white-power music scenes that privilege non-Germanic European heritage.

White-power music scenes in continental Western Europe have in many ways become the focus of worldwide white-power music in recent decades. This is partially due to the British scene's declining significance, but also to the strength, size, and spiritual appeal of the perennially robust German scene, which has been supported in no small measure by active scenes in nearby Germanic and Scandinavian countries. Western Mediterranean countries like France, Spain, and Italy have also developed white-power music that mixes sonic and ideological elements of the white-power music from Northern Europe with aspects of homegrown nationalism and philosophy, particularly Italian Fascism. As the next chapter will demonstrate, this ideological flexibility is also a key characteristic of contemporary white-power music in Eastern Europe. The fact that musicians from many different countries and sociocultural backgrounds have been able to adapt white-power music to their own goals and priorities explains why the genre has been able to grow and establish real staying power over the past thirty years. Although it might seem obvious that neo-Nazi music would entrench itself in territories that once belonged to the European Axis powers, white-power music clearly also appeals to some individuals from formerly neutral and Allied countries. This ability to work across historical, national, and ethnic boundaries has helped white-power musicians from continental Western Europe to cement themselves as major players in the international white-power music web in recent decades, and suggests that these may remain important centers for the genre in coming years as well.

4

The History of
White-Power Music
in Eastern Europe

Although the continental Western European white-power music subculture was and still is one of the most important parts of the worldwide white-power music web, right-wing Western Europeans were certainly not the only ones to learn of and take inspiration from the racist music emanating from England in the 1980s. In fact, racist skinhead subculture spread across Eastern Europe in the mid- to late 1980s as well, leaving grainy, hand-copied cassettes of early white-power albums in its wake. The fall of the Iron Curtain in the late 1980s and early 1990s, combined with the subsequent explosion of Internet technology, fostered a 1990s boom in Eastern European white-power music production and distribution.[1] While white-power music took slightly longer to spread to some Eastern European countries than it did to North America and continental Western Europe, once it arrived in the former Eastern bloc, it spurred the development of some of the world's largest and most dynamic white-power music scenes. Across Eastern Europe, disaffected youth dealt with collapsing economies, rising inter-ethnic tensions, and political instability by listening to white-power bands.

This chapter surveys the history of white-power music in Eastern Europe, much as the last chapter dealt with the history of white-power music in Western Europe. As in Western Europe, many different Eastern European countries have contributed musicians and fans to the international white-power music web, but not all of these scenes have reached equal size or significance. This chapter restricts itself to scenes from those countries that have had the most significant impact on white-power music internationally. White-power music scenes from countries like Serbia, the Czech Republic, Bulgaria, Romania, Estonia, and Slovakia, therefore, fall outside the scope of this project. This chapter focuses instead on white-power music from countries that have produced large numbers of internationally recognized white-power bands. It first examines Russia, along with closely related but smaller scenes in Belarus and Ukraine. It then explores the development of white-power music in Poland and Greece.

Unlike the histories of most of the Western European countries discussed in the preceding chapters, the post–World War II histories of almost all of these Eastern European countries share a history of communist governance. In all of the focus countries in this chapter except Greece, the communist era extended, with varying degrees of success, from the end of World War II until the critical period between 1989 and 1991 when the Soviet Union collapsed and European communist states reorganized themselves—sometimes violently—into variably functional democracies and market economies. In places like the former Yugoslavia, centuries-old violent conflicts re-emerged in the 1990s after the end of communism, while countries like Poland have transitioned more peacefully to capitalist democracy.

Yet even in the countries where this transition has been the smoothest, the process of converting entire economic and political structures from state socialism to capitalist democracy has been difficult and costly, not just in terms of capital investment, but also in terms of human suffering. People in many formerly communist European countries lost their life savings and financial stability when currencies collapsed and bloated industries slashed jobs to cut costs. The previous chapter discussed how this transition process affected the former East Germany, which could rely on a wealthy West German sibling to bear the costs of reunification. For citizens in other former Eastern bloc nations who could not turn to western counterparts for this kind of support, the switch from communism to market democracy has been even more challenging.

Frustration with limited opportunities and uneven economic growth has made many individuals in post-communist Eastern Europe amenable to extremist ideologies such as neo-Nazism. While some of this extremism takes localized forms, much of it responds to and corresponds with the racist ideologies from Western Europe discussed previously. Because these Western European variants of white-power ideologies typically focus on either Nordic or Mediterranean supremacy, white-power activists in Eastern Europe have developed their own pro-Slavic forms of neo-Nazism to appeal to racist groups and individuals closer to home. Of course, Hitler's original racist philosophies, linked as they were with the Third Reich's desire to expand German territory into areas controlled by Slavic groups, placed peoples of Slavic descent near the bottom of the World War II–era Nazi racial hierarchy.[2] While the Third Reich did not target ethnic groups such as Russians, Ukrainians, Poles, and Czechs for wholesale extermination to the extent that it did the Jews, Roma, and Sinti, it did exploit large segments of these populations as forced and slave laborers in its military-industrial complex, killing many of them in the process.[3] To this end, Nazi rule in the Third Reich's Eastern European colonies took on a far more brutal character than it did in most of Western Europe, with policies aimed at destroying native-born intelligentsia and forcing many individuals into hard labor for the German war effort.[4] Contemporary Slavic neo-Nazis, conscious of this history, construct variants of neo-Nazi ideology that include Slavs within the privileged "Aryan" category while still (at least sometimes) acknowledging the damage caused by the original Nazis during World War II. The country-by-country survey in this chapter discusses how this reformulation of neo-Nazi racism has taken shape in specific places. This pro-Slavic re-conception of neo-Nazi philosophy attests to the dominance of neo-Nazism among worldwide white-power groups, but it also demonstrates how dynamic and flexible contemporary racism can be. By adapting neo-Nazism to appeal to a wide range of European-descended ethnic groups, Slavic neo-Nazis have not only increased the size of the base population from which international neo-Nazi movements can draw supporters, but have also crafted a powerful argument for pan-white unity in the face of supposed threats from Jews and their purported Third World minions.

Some neo-Nazis from Western Europe still harbor deep Nordic and anti-Slavic chauvinist biases; one neo-Nazi musician from the premier Russian band Kolovrat (spinning wheel or swastika), for instance, has complained that "nationalists from Finland are still living in the '40s of the last century," and that "some Germans just can't see the obvious difference between 'Russian' and 'communist'"; he also insists that "all these pseudo racial 'theories' about 'Mongoloid subhuman' Russians (and Slavs in general) are nothing more than just pure bullshit."[5] As later chapters of this book argue in more detail, the pan-European "white nationalist" theory of racial superiority espoused by these Eastern European white-power groups seems slowly to be winning out over the older intra-European squabbling.

Russia, Belarus, and Ukraine

Russia, as the center of the former Soviet empire, seems the logical place to begin a study of white-power music in Eastern Europe. If the development of neo-Nazi music in former Allied countries like Britain and France initially seems puzzling, this must be doubly so for Russia, which bore the brunt of Hitler's massively destructive eastern campaign and suffered 20–25 million deaths, nearly half the overall death toll of World War II.[6] Even today, many young Russian couples choose to take their wedding photos at the Tomb of the Unknown Soldier in Moscow rather than in religious institutions or parks, and Hitler's book *Mein Kampf* is banned in Russia as "extremist." World War II—referred to in Russia as the Great Patriotic War—is one of the defining events in the Russian collective memory, and anti-Nazi sentiment remains high among the general population.[7]

Yet the Soviet system shared important features with the Third Reich that may have helped to make neo-Nazi ideologies seem logical to at least some Russians in the years immediately after the collapse of the USSR. Like the Third Reich, the Soviet state—despite the fact that many white-power groups mistakenly conflate Bolshevism with Zionism and a Jewish world conspiracy—harbored deep anti-Semitism stemming from centuries of anti-Semitic prejudice under the preceding Tsarist system. In fact, it was Tsarist Russian officials who forged the notoriously anti-Semitic *Protocols of the Elders of Zion* pamphlet in 1905.[8] This document first popularized the idea of a Jewish one-world conspiracy, a concept that forms the center of contemporary neo-Nazi ideology. Despite the fact that the *Protocols'* illegitimate provenance came to light more than a decade before Hitler took power, this pamphlet helped to shape Hitler's own anti-Semitic worldview and the racist policies of the Third Reich.[9]

The Soviet state maintained official atheism, but the government anti-Semitism of the Tsarist period nonetheless continued into the Soviet era.[10] It was only Stalin's death in 1953 that prevented the USSR's Jews from sharing the fate of the many "repressed" peoples who suffered mass exile, imprisonment, hard labor, and genocide in the USSR's far east.[11] Stalin's Russian anti-Semitism overlapped with major elements of Nazi ideology, and not entirely by accident; many Germans and Austrians reacted with alarm to the stream of Russian-Jewish immigrants who escaped the Russian pogroms of the late nineteenth century by moving to Central and Western Europe, meaning that Hitler and his comrades came of age in an environment of increased anti-Jewish sentiment that had been at least partially precipitated by nineteenth-century Russian anti-Semitism.[12] In some cases, Russians who supported the *USSR*'s Russian-centric ethnic policies discovered that with only minor modifications, *Hitler*'s anti-Semitic ideologies could appeal to their sense of national chauvinism as well. Even in the decades directly after Hitler's armies had laid waste to vast tracts of Soviet territory, neo-Nazi groups began to appear in the Soviet Union. Vsevolod, the singer for the Russian neo-Nazi band Vandal—who, like many white-power musicians, avoids publicizing his last name in order to shield his identity from government agents and anti-racist activists—explained to *Blood & Honour* magazine in 2001 that the Russian Nazi and neo-Nazi movements that existed before the fall of communism included Russian volunteers who had fought for the Third Reich during World War II, along with an underground Russian National Socialist Party which established itself in 1954, the year after Stalin's death, in response to the brutal treatment of ethnic Russians in the Stalinist-era Gulag system.[13]

Another of the key similarities between the two regimes was that, like the Third Reich, the USSR—especially in the Stalin years—was profoundly xenophobic. In some cases, simply having spent time under foreign influence as a prisoner of war in a German concentration camp was reason enough for the Soviet government to brand an individual an enemy of the state and to sentence him or her to a long term of hard labor in the Gulag system.[14] This xenophobic paranoia extended not only to actual foreigners, but also to many of the USSR's internal minority groups; even as Russia was helping first to defeat Hitler and then to try leaders of the Third Reich for their roles in the Holocaust, Stalin's regime was committing its own acts of genocide against groups like ethnic Ukrainians, Crimean Tatars, Kalmyks, and Chechens.[15] Russian-centric policies of ethnic and linguistic assimilation coerced millions of non-ethnic Russian Soviet citizens into russifying their names, abandoning traditional religions and customs, and speaking Russian instead of their native languages.[16] Although these policies relaxed slightly under Stalin's successors, they created an atmosphere of race-based suspicion and Russian national chauvinism that did not disappear when the USSR collapsed.

In fact, the end of the Soviet state was only a new beginning for Russia's internal turmoil. Economically, the chaos of leader Mikhail Gorbachev's *perestroika* (перестройка, meaning restructuring or rebuilding) era in the 1980s, which immediately preceded and precipitated the fall of the Soviet system, allowed a handful of wealthy Russian businessmen to buy up the majority of Russia's formerly state-owned infrastructure, turning themselves into oligarchs and leaving the majority of Russians with little to show for decades of labor in the socialist system.[17] Politically, the Russian government granted some of its former member states their independence, but it clung firmly to other territories, leading in particular to a series of bloody wars in Chechnya.[18] The costly Chechen conflicts, combined with factors like a late-1990s financial crisis among Russia's Southeast Asian trading partners, weakened Russia's fledgling market economy in the first decade after the breakup of the USSR and triggered a six-month period of financial collapse and hyperinflation in 1998.[19] Many ordinary Russians lost their life savings in the crash, leading to widespread poverty and dissatisfaction.

To make matters worse from the Russian perspective, Chechen terrorists, radicalized after decades of genocidal Soviet policies and heavy-handed post-Soviet wars, began attacking Russian civilian targets during this period. Apartment buildings, theaters, commuter trains, subway stations, airports, and even a crowded elementary school in a small southern Russian town became bombing targets starting in the late 1990s and 2000s, with a body count that still continues to climb.[20] Prominent researchers, including John Dunlop, a fellow at Stanford University's Hoover Center, have researched these attacks and argued that a string of 1999 apartment complex bombings that killed hundreds of people, which the Russian government blamed on Chechen militants, may actually have been staged by government officials to increase support for both a war on Chechnya and the initial election of Vladimir Putin as president of Russia; however, other attacks, such as the one on the elementary school, were more clearly the work of real Chechen terrorists.[21] Due to the public furor over the bombings, regardless of who the actual perpetrators were, racism has been particularly pervasive against "immigrants" from the Caucasus— immigrants who were actually Soviet citizens until the breakup of the USSR. Vsevolod of Vandal put this view succinctly when he told *Blood & Honour* in 2001 that "The reason for being a NS [National Socialist] Skinhead is the reaction to the bad economy and influx of coloured immigrants in our lands."[22]

For years, Russian white-power groups have been among the most violent in the world. Human rights groups have seen a spike in racist attacks over the last decade, although numbers are difficult to verify because the Russian government does not keep public statistics on racist violence.[23] At least two Russian extreme-right paramilitary organizations even hold training camps to teach young racist activists how to use weapons.[24] Moscow's anti-racist SOVA Center, which tracks racist attacks, has collected evidence of about 450 racist killings and more than 2,500 injuries from racist attacks that occurred between January 2004 and May 2010; the center's director, Alexander Verkhovskii, cautions that due to under-reporting, the real tallies are probably double these figures.[25] Some of these killings, such as the August 2007 double murder of a Dagestani and a Tajik man literally beneath the banner of a swastika flag, have been broadcast to the world via Internet videos.[26] Moreover, neo-Nazi groups have been known to attack and kill anti-racist activists, such as Nikolai Girenko, a researcher who was set to testify as an expert witness in the trial of several neo-Nazi skinheads before he was shot to death through the door of his Moscow apartment in 2004.[27]

The racism of Russian neo-Nazi groups finds support from mainstream organizations like the administration of Moscow State University, which in 2005 forced students to attend a virulently anti-American, anti-Semitic, and anti-Chechen lecture by the dean of the Sociology Department, as well as from leaders in the Russian Orthodox Church, some of whom have expressed public Holocaust denial.[28] In this climate, growing numbers of immigrant groups and national minorities have become the targets of racist violence. This includes not only Chechens and other peoples from the Caucasus region, such as Azeris, Georgians, and Dagestanis, but also Jews and individuals from Central and South Asia. Some of these groups, like Tajiks, are former Soviet citizens, while others are recent immigrants from places like Vietnam and China.[29] Surveys by Russia's anti-racist Levada Center have revealed that for every year between 2001 and 2006, more than half of Russians agreed with the slogan "Russia for Russians," a level of xenophobia fueled by the threat of Chechen terrorism and the increase in migration of individuals from the Caucasus and Central Asia to European Russia.[30] Motivated by economic insecurity, increasing numbers of middle-class Russians have begun to support extreme-right ideologies and to perpetrate racist attacks; in the early 1990s, perpetrators of violent racist crimes came mainly from poor neighborhoods in large cities, but the proportion of university students and children of business owners among perpetrators has grown since then.[31]

The Russian government has often proven reluctant to oppose the racism and violence of white-power groups, although in recent years, courts have begun to crack down on some of the most violent offenders, citing the Russian constitution's ban on incitement of national, racial, or religious enmity.[32] Especially in Moscow, the government has made strides to combat racist violence by appointing a new public prosecutor in 2008 to deal with racist attacks, as well as by creating an anti-extremism unit staffed with former organized crime investigators within the Ministry for Internal Affairs.[33] One group of nine neo-Nazis calling themselves the White Wolves was convicted in 2010 of killing at least eleven foreigners and posting videos of the attacks on the Internet; their case suggested that the Russian government was starting to take racist attacks more seriously.[34]

Still, the Russian courts' increasing attention to *racist* violence does not necessarily mean that neo-Nazi groups have discontinued their attacks on purported "enemies" altogether. Rather, they seem to have shifted the violence onto the *homosexual* population in Russia, which has become newly vulnerable since Russia passed a law against "homosexual propaganda" in June 2013.[35] Groups with names like Occupy Pedophilia have begun posting false gay dating profiles on the Internet, and then attacking and humiliating anyone who agrees to an in-person date. In many cases, the groups have filmed these attacks and distributed the videos publicly, outing homosexuals in order to isolate them from their social support networks. Suicide rates have been high among these victims—especially teenagers—and in one particularly gruesome case in June 2013, a Volgograd man was even tortured to death by anti-gay activists, succumbing to a vicious beating after suffering sodomy with a beer bottle and injuries to his genitalia.[36] The Russian government, for its part, has contributed to this climate of fear by scrubbing evidence of gay rights demonstrations from Russian Internet servers and jailing gay rights activists such as the members of the feminist punk collective Pussy Riot, which had staged and filmed a major anti-Putin protest performance in Moscow's landmark Church of Christ the Savior in February 2012.[37]

Given the relatively public profile and high levels of violence among contemporary Russian white-power activists, as well as Russia's long history of xenophobia, homophobia, and anti-Semitism, the fact that white-power and neo-Nazi music took root in Russia becomes less surprising than it might seem at first glance. In fact, homegrown white-power musicians began to play racist rock music in Moscow only shortly after the collapse of the Soviet Union. According to Denis Gerasimov, lead singer and driving force behind the big-name Moscow white-power band Kolovrat, white-power and neo-Nazi bands like Crack, which came from Moscow, as well as the St. Petersburg group Totenkopf—a band name that is German for death's head, referencing the skull-and-crossbones insignia of the SS—began to develop in Russia in the first years of the post-Soviet era.[38] (NB this Russian white-power band called Totenkopf is distinct from German, Italian, and Singaporean white-power bands that have all used the same band name.) However, these early Russian neo-Nazi bands used neo-Nazi iconography for its shock value rather than out of deep conviction, performing a proto-neo-Nazi transitional role akin to that of the Böhse Onkelz in Germany. Later Russian white-power bands have ridiculed these early groups for their shallow use of neo-Nazi symbols; Gerasimov, for instance, suggests that "their 'NS' [National Socialism] was the kind of 'NS' that Sid Vicious of 'Sex Pistols' showed in a Jewish district of Paris while demonstrating a swastika T-shirt, just cheap poseurism and epatage, nothing more."[39] To a hardcore neo-Nazi like Gerasimov, this kind of flirtation with neo-Nazism—long a favorite shock tactic even for supposedly nonracist mainstream punk musicians like the Sex Pistols and Siouxie Sioux—may represent an annoying misconception of real neo-Nazism. Still, these early Russian white-power bands set the stage for serious Russian neo-Nazi bands, demonstrating to future fans and performers that violent racism had an audience in post-Soviet Russia.

Gerasimov founded his band Kolovrat in 1994–1995 under the name Russkoye Getto (Русское Гетто or Russian Ghetto), referencing the musicians' working-class neighborhood in Moscow, as well as their sympathy for Russian politician Alexander Petrovich Barkashov's party Russkoye Natsional'noye Edinstvo (Русское Национальное Единство or Russian National Unity), which argued that Russia should turn itself into a ghetto-style fortress isolated from foreigners. Gerasimov and Kolovrat were among the first Russian musicians who, as Gerasimov puts it, "started to play RAC music on the territory of the ex-USSR with the serious ideological attitude."[40] Kolovrat's song lyrics in the past twenty years have focused on a laundry list of racist topics, including "politics first and foremost (I mean the criticism of today's so called 'democratic' and 'liberal' capitalist system); great European heritage, its glorious history and rich traditions; the tragedies of WW2, which we call 'Brother War' [a white-power term for a war among European nations]; Slavonic unity and our pride to be Slavs; the support of our Serbian brothers in their unequal fight for their holy land Kosovo; our struggle for the survival of our kin, etc."[41] Kolovrat's songs include "Арийский Реванш" ("ariiskii revansh" or "Aryan revenge") and "Наш Символ—Свастика" ("nash simbol—svastika" or "our symbol—swastika"), along with cover songs like the popular "88 RAC'n'Roll Band," a version of Landser's "88 Rock'n'Roll Band." Such pieces make heavy use of neo-Nazi and other racist symbolism, arguing for both Russian and pan-European white supremacy.

In Kolovrat's early years, neo-Nazi lyrical themes caused relatively few problems for Russian white-power musicians. However, starting in about 2000, Russian police began raiding neo-Nazi concerts. Kolovrat—as one of the scene's leading bands—became a key target of these raids. One Kolovrat gig in 2000 descended into a fight against police officers, after which 100 attendees were arrested, and a November 2002 Ian Stuart Donaldson memorial concert in the Moscow area resulted in the arrest of more than 300 concertgoers.[42] Kolovrat reports that many more of their concerts have been raided in the intervening years, and that "we're still under constant oppression and active monitoring in Russia so it's almost impossible for us to play even a small private concert for 100 comrades in our native city in the last couple of years."[43] Still, by 2010, the group had played more than 250 concerts all over Russia and many more abroad, making them by far the most famous Russian white-power band on the international stage.[44]

In addition to attracting increasing attention from the Russian police for their large concerts and neo-Nazi propaganda, some members of Kolovrat have incurred legal difficulties elsewhere in Europe. In February 2004, Gerasimov himself was arrested in the Prague airport for promoting Nazism and neo-Nazism after Czech customs officials discovered neo-Nazi symbols like "88" and "Ian Stuart" on his clothes, as well as neo-Nazi CDs in his suitcase. Czech courts acquitted him of the charges in October 2004 and allowed him to return to Russia, but only because—at least in the judge's eyes—he could not have been promoting Nazism or neo-Nazism with his CDs when all the objects were "shut in a suitcase."[45] In December 2004, a higher court overturned this acquittal, although Gerasimov was safely back in Russia by this time.[46] The band has complained openly about this incident, which members view as political persecution.[47]

Despite government crackdowns, the Russian white-power music scene has grown rapidly from its humble beginnings in the mid-1990s. As early as 1995, Russian skinheads opened a Blood & Honour chapter in Moscow after meeting with members of the Blood & Honour Berlin chapter at an international white-power music concert in Budapest.[48] As a result of such activism, 1996 and 1997 saw more Russian neo-Nazi bands with serious racist convictions appear on the scene, including Shturm (Штурм, or storm) and

Radegast (Радегаст, the god of hospitality in Slavic mythology). A mainstream heavy metal band from Yaroslavl called TKNF, which had expressed racist sentiments occasionally in the past, began to explore open neo-Nazism in 1996–1997. After Shturm and TKNF held a gig in Moscow that drew an unexpectedly large crowd of 350, more neo-Nazi bands formed, such as the Moscow-based group Vandal (Вандал, later Банда Москвы—Banda Moskvy, or Moscow Band) and the band Ultra—originally known as S.T.S. or Shit-Town Streetbulls—which came from the city of Ivanovo and took its band name from the die-hard "ultra" fans of European soccer culture. This growing white-power music scene began to hold concerts in Moscow to regular turnouts of 450 to 600 fans.[49]

In addition to the punk- and metal-oriented bands of the early Russian white-power music scene, a number of Russian white-power bands have chosen to play pagan-oriented, acoustic, and neo-folk music, responding to acoustic releases by Western European musicians like Frank Rennicke and Ian Stuart & Stigger. Some of these have found a warm reception among fans even outside Russia. For example, the white-power neo-folk band Volkolak (Волколак, or werewolf), which comes from the Amur region in the Russian Far East, employs flutes, tamborines, and other instruments that are uncommon in white-power music. In a 2008 review of the 2004 Volkolak album *Слава Яриле* (slava Yarile or glory to Yarilo, referring to the Slavic pagan god of vegetation, fertility, and springtime), a Croatian fan on Stormfront writes,

> One can feel power and white pride in their songs and can have the feeling that such beautiful songs can't be made by someone who is not white. This is not racism but pure fact. In the clear voice of the singer can be felt a great amount of hate and pride blending into one. Pride in being Russian, and hate for all those who are living in Russia and aren't Russian. I heard this album many times. It is sort of magical for me, although I'm not Russian. I think that everyone can feel pride while listening to this, even if he doesn't speak Russian. [. . .] If you want to hear something to relax, or to feed your ears with something that is NS [National Socialist], but not black metal or rock, and you think that Prussian Blue is too childish and funny, this is right thing for you.[50]

Although this particular fan's other CD reviews on Stormfront are almost exclusively for NSBM albums, Volkolak's technical proficiency, unapologetic racism, and neo-folk sound have clearly left a deep impression. As this review suggests, like other non-rock-based white-power musicians, Volkolak appeals in particular to white-power music fans who dislike heavy forms of rock music.

The majority of Russia's key white-power bands, however, still play punk- and metal-derived music. One of the most famous and longest-running Russian white-power rock bands has been the group Korroziya Metalla

(Коррозия Металла, or metal corrosion, referring to heavy metal music). Like TKNF, Korroziya Metalla is a heavy metal group that pre-dated the fall of the USSR, but Korroziya Metalla only began to focus on racist and neo-Nazi lyrical themes after 1989. The band's leading figure is bassist Sergei "Pauk" (spider) Troitsky, who has served as singer and guitarist for the band at various points as well.[51] Troitsky—who has run unsuccessfully for mayor of several major Russian cities, including Moscow in 1993 and 2013, as well as Khimki in 2012—has been open not only about his fascism ("What might bother [my parents] about that?" he asks journalist Jacek Hugo-Bader), but also about his blatant misogyny: "In Moscow a good prostitute costs 10,000 [rubles], but in the provinces you can get a top model for the whole night for 800 rubles (£16). Three of them came with us to concerts for the next bit of the tour [after a concert in Novokuznetsk] and danced naked on the stage at concerts. They were stars, but we threw them out along the way because we like to have new ones in each city."[52] This kind of misogyny is different from the patriarchal and militaristic ethos of most white-power bands from Western Europe, particularly as regards Troitsky's unapologetic attitude toward having sex with Russian prostitutes, a practice that many white-power musicians from outside Russia would likely regard as degrading to otherwise "pure" white women.

Troitsy's band is generally known for playing thrash metal, but they have experimented with NSBM as well. In order to release music with lyrics too extreme for most mainstream Russian recording studios, Troitsky founded his own record label, KTR, short for Korporatsiya Tyazhyologo Roka (Корпорация Тяжёлого Рока, or corporation of heavy rock). The cover of the band's 1995 album *1.966* showed a swastika overlaid with two triskelions, or three-armed swastikas; the lyrical content of the album corresponded with the political sentiment of the cover art, including a song called "White Power" that warned of a white genocide and explicitly advocated violence against black and Chinese immigrants. Several former members of Korroziya Metalla, including Maxim Layko and Vasiliy Kazurov, have gone on to play in the prominent Russian white-power band D.I.V., which sings songs such as "Mein Kampf" and "Rap Monkey."[53]

In May 2013, the Russian government went so far as to place one of Korroziya Metalla's songs—"Bey Chertey" ("Бей Чертей" or "beat the devils")—on a list of extremist materials.[54] This is because the band uses the Russian word for devil—chyort (чёрт), based on the Russian word for black—chyornyy (чёрный). Therefore, when Troitsky's 1999 lyrics urge listeners to save Moscow and even Russia itself by beating "devils," the song refers not only to religious sentiment, but also to direct racist violence. When Hugo-Bader confronted Troitsky about the fact that fans have used the racism in Korroziya Metalla songs such as "Bey Chertey" as inspiration for actual violence against minorities in Russia, Troitsky responded by complaining that "Music is pure abstraction—you can't take it so literally. [...] It's not my fault if someone understands me wrong."[55] A Moscow court disagreed, however, and banned the song.[56] This is just one example of a growing trend toward government repression of white-power music and neo-Nazi groups in Russia, the pattern to which Kolovrat's Denis Gerasimov refers when he asserts that "there are brutal repressions during the last several years in Russia, about 1500 comrades are doing the time behind the bars, and more than 10 comrades were condemned to life sentences."[57]

Although police surveillance and censorship have made life increasingly difficult for many white-power musicians in Russia, the Russian white-power music scene has from its outset maintained an international profile with especially close links to white-power music scenes in neighboring Ukraine and Belarus. Although Ukraine and Belarus suffered under *both* Soviet *and* Nazi occupation during the twentieth century—the carnage in mid-twentieth-century Ukraine, Belarus, and Poland was, in fact, so severe that historian Timothy Snyder has gone so far as to label this battleground area, which lay geographically between the German and the Russian empires, "the bloodlands"—some individuals in these countries nevertheless find neo-Nazi ideologies attractive today. Like white-power musicians in Russia, white-power musicians from Ukraine and Belarus tend to emphasize pan-European and pan-Slavic unity rather than national chauvinism, re-defining Nazism to include Eastern Europeans. As one member of the Ukrainian white-power band Sokyra Peruna told an interviewer in 2010, "This is an old Slavic proverb: let bygones be bygones."[58]

Of course, the existence of such proverbs does not preclude lingering resentment over Nazi injustices in Ukraine, but because the Soviet regime committed its own atrocities against ethnic Ukrainians both before and after World War II—knowingly starving millions of ethnic Ukrainians via ruthless farm collectivization policies in an early 1930s genocide now referred to as the Holodomor (Голодомор, or extermination by hunger), then sending many more to die of starvation, overwork, and inhumane conditions in the Gulag system—the USSR and its Russian successor state, rather than the Nazis, often tend to bear the brunt of ethnic Ukrainians' hostility over historical injustices.[59]

In fact, mistrust of Russia among ethnic Ukrainians has been so extreme in recent years that when the Ukrainian President Viktor Yanukovych chose to sign a treaty with Russia instead of a trade agreement with the European Union in late 2013 and early 2014, violent protests in the capital city of Kyiv devolved into full-blown revolution, forcing Yanukovych to resign and flee the country.[60] Russian President Vladimir Putin exacerbated the tension by sending troops into Ukraine's majority-ethnic-Russian Crimean Peninsula, encouraging a contested March 2014 referendum in which Crimean residents voted to join Russia.[61] Both NATO and the UN have declared this move illegitimate, and the UN resolved in late March 2014 to continue recognizing Crimea as part of Ukraine, not Russia.[62] Ethnic Ukrainians now worry that Putin might try to re-incorporate other areas of eastern Ukraine into Russia as well.[63] This crisis is still unfolding, and the final results for Ukraine, Russia, and the international community are far from clear. What *is* obvious is that tensions remaining from the Soviet era continue to affect relations among ethnic groups in post-communist Eastern Europe, particularly in the contemporary tinderbox that is eastern Ukraine.

Nonetheless, in white-power circles, white nationalism and calls for pan-European unity have begun increasingly—though by no means always—to trump expressions of national chauvinism among racists from various national and ethnic backgrounds. This process is evident, for example, in discussion threads about the conflict in eastern Ukraine on the Stormfront Russia subforum. Pro-white racists from around the world share differing opinions on the showdown between Russia and Ukraine, some of them expressing support for old-style Soviet imperialism and some conveying frustration with what they see as a Jewish-controlled Russian power structure abusing the people of Ukraine. In one exchange, a forum moderator discourages support for any infighting at all among European-descended groups, saying, "Crap government in Ukraine, even more crap government in Russia. More immigrants, more crap laws in Russia currently than in Ukraine. Soon, possibly, the Eurasian Union [a neologism expressing disapproval for non-white immigration into the European Union] and integration with 80 million 'compatriots.' Advocate to start a war, maybe even WW3, waste many lives, to take territory from one crap government to another?"[64] Another member responds to this rhetorical question by stating,

> EU and NATO government will be even more crap in my opinion. They take a stronger hold of their countries. Putin's propaganda is weak and it is easier to dispel. The RF [Russian Federation] will be easier to overthrow. With the EU and NATO you will get just as many Turks and other muds [a reference to dark-skinned and purportedly pre-human "mud people" in the mythology of the racist Christian Identity creed] as Germany has now.[65]

The moderator replies,

> Simply objectively compare Eastern Europe with Russia, and verdict is obvious: Putinistan [a neologism conflating Vladimiar Putin and Russia with immigrants from Central Asian republics] is worse from WN [white nationalist] point of view. 10 years ago people, at least, could say "but at least in Russia we don't have

these Holocaust denial laws, laws that punish politically incorrect opinions" as in Europe and so on. But now all that is gone and there is a police state as bad as the worst European examples like Germany.[66]

Here—as in many exchanges among white-power believers online—one can see individuals with different opinions coming together to discuss how best to approach the Russia/Ukraine conflict. Hardline pro-Russian and pro-Ukrainian sentiments do appear on the Stormfront boards, but far more often, members engage in discussions like this one, debating how best to counter what they see as an overarching problem with Jewish domination of both countries in the context of a political powder keg. While this conversation illustrates the fact that pro-white racists certainly do not always agree with one another on matters of intra-European conflict, it also demonstrates that the general consensus among white-power believers internationally seems to be that white people should concentrate on fighting Jews and non-white immigrants no matter what their specific national heritages or political persuasions. In this way, pro-white racists from Ukraine, Russia, and surrounding countries ironically seem to be modeling the idea of "let[ting] bygones be bygones" and engaging in mutually beneficial relationships across national and ethnic lines more readily than most people in the societies around them.

As in Russia, white-power music scenes developed in Ukraine and Belarus in the early to mid-1990s. The scenes in these two countries have been smaller than the Russian scene, partially because Ukraine and Belarus are far smaller than Russia in both geographical size and population. In Ukraine, one of the earliest and best-known white-power bands was Nokturnal Mortum (Latin for nocturnal dead), a death metal and NSBM band that started in 1991 under the name Suppuration, and has spawned side projects such as the band Aryan Terrorism.[67] Another key Ukrainian white-power band has been Sokyra Peruna (Сокира Перуна, or Perun's axe, referring to the Slavic pagan god Perun), originally known as Bulldog, which formed in 1998 out of two early 1990s hatecore bands.[68] Later Ukrainian white-power bands that have also played key roles in the scene include the Kharkiv-based group Dub Buk (oak and beech), a band formed in 1997 by an erstwhile Nokturnal Mortum guitarist, which released its songs in the Russian language rather than its native Ukrainian language. Other key groups have included Munruthel, Whites Load, Drudkh, Nachtigall (German for nightingale), and Khors (named for the god of the sun in Slavic mythology).

Among these groups, Nokturnal Mortum draws particular praise from its listeners due to the musicians' prowess as multi-instrumentalists; in contrast to most NSBM bands, which use computer programs to imitate the sounds of instruments that band members do not know how to play, the members of Nokturnal Mortum, in the words of one fan who writes a Stormfront review of the 2003 demo album *Weltanschauung* (German for worldview), "use real wind instruments including bagpipes, flutes, fiddle, even real cow's horn."[69] Likewise, another fan writes, "I'd have a hard time putting in words how highly I think of NM's [Nokturnal Mortum's] 'Weltanschauung.' I've always thought that traditional folk music and black metal fit together like bread and butter and this album is definitely great proof of that."[70]

Dub Buk and several of the other bands that have involved musicians from Nokturnal Mortum have also elicited positive fan response both from within and outside Ukraine. Dub Buk fans report, in particular, enjoying the heavy use of Slavic pagan themes in Dub Buk's music, as in this 2008 Stormfront review of the 1999 album Місяць Помсти (misyats' pomsti, meaning moon vengeance or month of vengeance) by the same user quoted above in a comment on Nokturnal Mortum's facility as multi-instrumentalists:

> Dub Buk is more melodic [than Nokturnal Mortum] but heavy and hateful with very fast paced Pagan songs amazing drumming that although fast remain melodic, along with strong keyboards giving folk sounding riffs, sounds very Pagan and the amazing work you expect from a Ukraninan band. The production quality is quite low not something you wouldnt expect from a BM [black metal] band it just adds to the atmosphere. This album does have a lot of repatative riffing for long spans of time one songs lasting 11 min. With these Ukranian Melodic BM bands you have to have patience to listen to them and appreciate the music. The lryical themes are all sung in russian, deal with Nationalistic feelings, Paganism and anti christianity. [*sic*][71]

Slavic paganism and anti-Christianity are not the only important lyrical themes that appear in Ukrainian white-power music, though. Like their Russian counterparts, many Ukrainian white-power bands also express clear affinity for neo-Nazi ideologies. In the same post that contains the review of Dub Buk's Місяць Помсти, this Stormfront user also comments on the 2002 Dub Buk album Иду На Вы! (idu na vy!, or I go to you!), writing, "The last song ['Героям Слава!,' 'geroyam slava!,' or 'glory to the heroes!'] is a type of orchestraic Nationlistic song, similar to those of the Third Reich. Great way to end the album." Significantly, this listener is responding not only to Dub Buk's use of neo-Nazi-themed lyrics, but also to the way the band references the *sound* of Third Reich–era German military marches in their music, making it clear that many white-power music fans consume white-power music not only for its lyrical content, but also for important aspects of the non-verbal racist symbolism that white-power musicians employ.

By drawing on neo-Nazi symbolism and ideology in both their song lyrics and their sonic style, Ukrainian white-power bands make the argument that they, like Russians and other Slavic groups, should be considered part of the neo-Nazi Aryan racial elite. This is, in fact, a common theme in white-power music across Eastern Europe. While the Ukrainian white-power music scene is smaller than the Russian scene, its members still play an important role in shaping how neo-Nazis from around the world conceive of what it means to be both white and neo-Nazi. The small size of the Ukrainian white-power music scene in comparison to that in Russia, which is home to one of the biggest scenes in the world, belies the strength of Ukrainian neo-Nazism. Like in Russia, Ukrainian authorities may oppose overt neo-Nazi propaganda, but racism toward national minorities still runs high; Amnesty International, for example, has charged that Ukrainian police consistently fail to respond to racist attacks on Jews, Roma, and foreigners.[72]

The Belarusian scene, which has remained smaller than the Ukrainian scene, has been dominated by a band which from 1995 to 2003 called itself Apraxia—the name of a motor planning disorder in which the affected individual cannot execute planned movements, regardless of his or her desire and physical ability to move—but which since 2003 has continued to play under the name Molot (Молот, Ukrainian for hammer).[73] Other notable Belarusian bands include Blackmoon Warrior 88, Panzerterror SS, and Kamaedzitca (Камаедзіца, named, at least according to the band, for an annual March 24 bear-awakening celebration in the Slavic pagan religion).[74] The fact that the Belarusian white-power music scene is smaller than those in Russia and Ukraine does not necessarily mean that bigoted ideals are less popular in Belarus than in Russia or Ukraine. Actually, as one Belarusian Stormfront user phrased his overview of the Belarusian socio-political climate in a 2014 forum post, "In Belarus a large portion of the media is owned by the state. That really is a good thing these days. It prevents western Jewry from buying up the media. [. . .] Overall Belarus is a great white nation that utterly rejects western poisons like LGBT rights and what not."[75] Of course, this statement represents the views of one individual and not of an entire country; many white-power believers in former Eastern Bloc countries do criticize the extent of the states' control as remnants of what some see as Jewish communism. Still, this account suggests that white-power believers in contemporary Belarus do not seem to feel as threatened by left-wing and purportedly Jewish-driven ideals and interests as their Western European counterparts. The lack of a large white-power music scene in Belarus, then, may stem not just from a simple political disagreement with white white-power ideologies among the populace, but rather from other factors, such as a potential lack of interest in the punk- and metal-driven sounds that characterized the majority of white-power music in the first three decades of the genre's existence.

The presence of a large white-power music scene in Russia, along with that of its smaller cousins in Ukraine and Belarus, reveals the flexibility of white-power and neo-Nazi ideologies. Seventy years ago, it would have been ridiculous to think that German Nazis might agree to work with Russians, Belarusians, or Ukrainians on anything approaching equal terms. Today, the strength of the white-power subcultures in Eastern Europe has changed this dynamic. In fact, a 2007 statement from the Russian section of the International Society of Human Rights indicated that Russia alone is home to more than 50,000 skinheads, more than in the entirety of Western Europe; in Russia, unlike in Western Europe, this skinhead movement is primarily racist-oriented, and some estimates suggest that 2,000–3,000 racist skinheads just in the city of Moscow are prepared to attack and even kill immigrants.[76] By demonstrating that they are willing to commit extreme acts of violence against racial and sexual others—and, all too often, by demonstrating that their national governments will allow them to get away with such violence—these skinheads and neo-Nazis have made themselves impossible for Nordic-centered Western European neo-Nazis to ignore or laugh away.

According to one member of Nokturnal Mortum, bands from Eastern Europe now not only communicate with those from Western Europe, but also cooperate in violent crimes: "Europe has shown a lot of interest in Ukrainian bands. [. . .] We're together in terrorist acts. [. . .] In the past we burned down churches. Nowadays we're more into political movements against sub-people."[77] If white-power groups can reconcile historical animosities such as that between Russia and Germany—or, for that matter, between Russia and Ukraine—this means that many of them are serious about their belief in pan-European white supremacy, and that they are willing to re-envision old racial hierarchies in order to respond to new demographic pressures from outside Europe. This kind of adaptability is what helps to keep racist ideologies alive even through major socio-historical changes such as the fall of the Iron Curtain, and suggests that without concerted efforts to counter discriminatory attitudes, violent racism may continue to be a part of Eastern European culture for a long time to come.

Poland

Poland, like Russia, is home to one of the largest white-power and neo-Nazi music scenes in Eastern Europe. Like Belarus and Ukraine, Poland suffered terribly at the hands of both the Nazis and the Soviets in the mid-twentieth century. A fledgling Polish state had received its independence when the Austro-Hungarian Empire crumbled in 1918—its first period of independence in more than a century—but in 1939, Nazi and Soviet delegates signed the secret Molotov-Ribbentrop Pact to divide Poland between them.[78] After only a few short weeks of fighting in September 1939, the western half of Poland fell to the Nazis and the eastern half to the Soviets.[79]

Neither occupying force held a particularly high opinion of the native Poles, never mind the millions of Jews whose ancestors had come to Poland centuries earlier to take advantage of the medieval Polish government's religious tolerance. Even before Hitler and Stalin began fighting each other in June 1941, both regimes attacked the Polish intelligentsia and forced large numbers of Polish civilians into slave labor.[80] The Nazi regime set up all of its six major extermination camps—Chełmno, Bełżec, Treblinka, Sobibór, Majdanek, and Auschwitz-Birkenau—on Polish soil. Many ethnic Poles, along with nearly all of their Jewish neighbors, perished in these camps. The Soviet secret police, for their part, sent thousands of ethnic Poles to die in Stalin's Gulag system, massacring almost 22,000 members of the Polish intelligentsia in the Katyn Forest near Smolensk in 1940 alone and then trying to blame the atrocity on the Germans.[81] By the time the dust of World War II had settled, approximately 2,770,000 ethnic Poles and somewhere between 2,700,000 and 2,900,000 Polish Jews had been killed, and the victorious Soviets had set up a Polish communist government as a Soviet satellite state.[82]

Terror and violence continued in Poland until Stalin's death. Even after 1953, the Soviet-supported Polish government continued to persecute some sectors of Polish society, especially the powerful Catholic Church, to which 96 percent of contemporary Poles belong.[83] Because of these repressions, unlike in Russia, the communist regime never enjoyed widespread support in Poland; by the 1970s and 1980s, mass labor protests had erupted under leaders like future Polish president and Nobel Peace Prize recipient Lech Wałęsa of the Solidarność (solidarity) movement.[84] The Polish government declared martial law between 1981 and 1983 to try to end the unrest. Nonetheless, severe economic instability, combined with the collapse of the Soviet Union, led to the fall of Polish communism in 1989.[85] Due in part to the Poles' suffering under Soviet-controlled communism, even before the fall of the Iron Curtain, at least a small sector of the Polish population viewed the violent Nazi period as having been preferable to Soviet occupation; after all, as Polish historian Jan Gross writes in his history of post–World War II Polish anti-Semitism, not all Poles even during the war years had viewed everything about the Nazi regime as hostile or negative: "Broad strata of Polish society took advantage of Nazi policies and joined in the spoliation of their Jewish neighbors. [...] That Polish society proved vulnerable to totalitarian temptation and that numerous Poles joined in Nazi-organized victimization of their Jewish fellow citizens was facilitated by indigenous anti-Semitism."[86] As in Russia, disgruntled Poles began to re-define Nazism in the later years of the communist era by re-envisioning the Nazi regime's brutal policies toward Slavic ethnic groups, positioning themselves as Aryans and arguing for pan-European unity on the basis of shared anti-Semitism and xenophobia.

Some prominent German white-power musicians in recent years have expressed public disagreement with this idea that Poles are, in fact, Aryans. Landser's song "Polacken Tango" (Polack tango), for instance, explicitly mocks the Polish claim to Aryanness, reveling in the fact that Germany defeated Poland in eighteen days at the beginning of World War II and took many Poles as prisoners of war.[87] Likewise, other German bands like Radikahl and Gestapo have spoken against the idea of including Hungarian, Greek, and Russian bands within the purview of the white-power music web.[88] Even Ian Stuart Donaldson appears in at least one film clip disparaging Poles from the stage, provoking outrage from many Polish white-power music fans, such as a Stormfront user who expressed shock and disbelief after first seeing Donaldson's anti-Polish comments in 2007:

> O **** . . . he actually did say ****ing Poles, the scum of the earth . . . I never heard
> it before:| He wrote a good song about Poland and years later he actually says
> we're the scum of the earth plus Skrewdriver is probably my favorite band . . .
> I bet he didn't actually mean it, he just said it so the Germans will like
> him . . . but probably not . . . I bet he would be writing songs now how ****
> we are and all that. He talks about European brothers and unity all the time,
> but he insults Poles, like they're just Jews. (Ellipses, asterisks, and emoticon
> in the original)[89]

Yet increasing numbers of Western European bands have called for unity with Eastern Europeans, proclaiming, for example, in songs such as Kraftschlag's "Festung Europa"—German for fortress Europe, a Third Reich–era term that refers to the Nazis' plans to fortify all of Europe against Allied invasion—that *"wir sind Europäer"* ("we are Europeans").[90] One Stormfront user, in fact, condemned Landser's anti-Polish chauvinism in 2011 by writing, "Chauvinists are our WORST enemies. Worse than Jews, Communists, Liberals or anything else" (capitalization in the original).[91]

Despite some opposition to Poles and other Slavs in organized white-power movements, white-power skinheads and white-power music have existed for decades in Poland. The first white-power bands actually appeared in communist Poland in the mid-1980s, well before the fall of the Iron Curtain.[92] This early racist music scene experienced significant difficulties with the communist authorities. Western white-power music was hard to obtain, and Polish rock bands could not record albums or play regular concerts due to government repression.[93] Most of these bands expressed transitional white-power ideologies, drawing on peripheral elements of organized white-power beliefs from Western European white-power groups, but avoiding the most overt symbols of neo-Nazism, such as swastikas and references to World War II. Communist-era Polish skinhead bands like Ramzes & the Hooligans therefore seem not to have been ideologically committed neo-Nazis. They did, however, draw on the pervasive racism, Polish national chauvinism, and xenophobia that permeated some demographics in Polish society, just as bands like the Böhse Onkelz, and Totenkopf were doing at the same time in Germany and Russia.[94]

The irony of this xenophobia is that Poland had historically been one of the most racially tolerant and diverse countries in Europe, drawing its large prewar Jewish population from elsewhere in Europe through its welcoming legislation.[95] However, the Third Reich killed 90–95 percent of Poland's Jews, along with many of the country's other racial minorities.[96] Those who did survive the Holocaust came home to a postwar atmosphere of violent anti-Semitism and other racism among the Polish populace which drove most survivors to leave for the United States and Israel.[97] By the 1950s, Catholic-dominated Poland had become one of the most ethnically homogenous countries in the world, with a population comprised of more than 95 percent ethnic Poles.[98] The Polish youths who grew up during the communist era therefore had little experience living with people outside their own ethnic group, making them particularly susceptible to xenophobic rhetoric when their horizons began to expand in the late 1980s and early 1990s.

One band comprised of such youths was Legion, an early and influential Polish white-power band which aligned itself with one of the first Polish extreme-right-wing political parties of the post–World War II era, a group called the Narodowe Odrodzenie Polski (national revival of Poland or national rebirth of Poland). The Narodowe Odrodzenie Polski, although a far-right group, was not a neo-Nazi organization; in fact, the Polish skinhead scene divided itself between the typical neo-Nazi skinheads who appeared in other countries and a homegrown Polish Catholic ultra-nationalist faction. Legion was one of the few Polish white-power bands to emerge before the fall of communism, along with Honor—one of the preeminent bands in white-power music internationally—and lesser-known bands like BTM, Baranki Boże (lambs of god), Zadruga (a band name taken from a form of South Slavic clan-based village), and Szczerbiec (the name of the Polish coronation sword that constitutes the only extant piece of the medieval Polish crown jewels).[99] One of Legion's cassettes reportedly sold more than 30,000 copies even before the fall of the Iron Curtain.[100]

After 1989, the Polish white-power music scene exploded with a massive influx of new Polish white-power skinheads and dozens of white-power bands.[101] These bands included the notorious neo-Nazi group Konkwista 88 (conquest 88) from Wrocław, which was the first Polish white-power band to release its own vinyl single in 1993; before this time, Polish white-power bands had only released their music on cassette tape.[102] The members of Konkwista 88 collaborated with Honor and other neo-Nazi bands to found a Blood & Honour-style organization called Aryjski Front Przetrwania (Aryan survival front) and an associated Polish-language magazine, *Szturmowiec* (storm-trooper). This organization collapsed, however, when a key member defected from the white-power movement and provided important details of the group's organization to the left-wing press.[103]

Other groups stepped into the space that the Aryjski Front Przetrwania had left behind, including a professional white-power record label named Fan Records, which recorded racist bands from both the neo-Nazi and Catholic ultra-nationalist wings of the Polish skinhead movement, including Legion, Surowa Generacja (raw generation), Odrodzenie 88 (revival, rebirth, or renaissance 88), and Szczerbiec.[104] Fan Records folded in 1997 after a police raid, but in the early 1990s, many of its white-power albums actually appeared in mainstream Polish record shops.[105] Other successors to Aryjski Front Prztrwania included a fleeting Polish division of Blood & Honour in the city of Olsztyn in 1996, which was forced to close after a government raid and was not re-established until 2002, along with a similar promotion organization, Narodowa Scena Rockowa (national rock scene), which handled only ultra-nationalist Catholic bands and not neo-Nazi musicians through its Hard Records label.[106] The mid-1990s also saw more new Polish bands enter the white-power music scene, such as Ofensywa (offensive or attack), Nowy Lad (new order), Sztorm 68 (storm 68)—which included the singer of the band Szczerbiec—Feniks (phoenix), Odwet 88 (retaliation or revenge 88), Ekspansja (expansion), and Salut (salute), although only a few of these bands survived through the late 1990s. Big-name foreign white-power bands like the United States' Bound for Glory and Extreme Hatred, Britain's No Remorse and Brutal Attack, Italy's ADL 122, and the Czech Republic's Excalibur began playing concerts in Poland in the mid-1990s as well.[107] In the 2000s—despite the fact that Honor was forced to disband after the 2005 death of its singer, Mariusz Szczerski—a number of new Polish white-power bands appeared on the scene. These included Antisemitex, Hammer of Hate, White Devils, Tormentia, White Master, The Invasion, Głos Prawdy (voice of truth), Agressiva 88 (Portuguese for aggressive 88), and Gammadion (an alternate word for swastika).[108]

In the late 1990s, further trends from outside Poland began influencing the Polish neo-Nazi music scene. The Norwegian NSBM scene, in particular, inspired a number of Polish white-power musicians to begin producing NSBM on their own. Chief among these musicians was Robert "Rob Darken" Fudali, the musician behind the one-man NSBM studio projects Graveland and Lord Wind.[109] Other Polish NSBM acts have included Dark Fury, Abusiveness, Selbstmord (German for suicide), and Gontyna Kry (Old Slavonic for temple of blood).[110] The acoustic white-power music of German artists like Frank Rennicke and Annett Moeck has also influenced the Polish scene, which produced the anti-Semitic singer/songwriter Leszek Czajkowski.[111]

Polish police have been more lenient with white-power musicians than have authorities in some other European countries over the last twenty years, although the Polish penal code technically lists relatively strict laws against hate speech. Anti-fascist activist groups like the Nigdy Wiecej (never again) organization and its Music Against Racism campaign, however, have worked with prominent anti-racist Polish and foreign bands to promote anti-racist attitudes among the Polish populace.[112] During the 1990s, Polish white-power bands were able to hold gigs in large concert halls, but have found these large-scale concerts difficult to stage openly since Poland joined the European Union in 2004, complaining that they have come under increasing police surveillance in the last decade.[113]

As in Russia, Ukraine, and Belarus, the presence of neo-Nazi musicians and other activists in Poland within living memory of World War II demonstrates that at least some Poles have been able to reformulate the history of the Third Reich and the philosophies of National Socialism both in their own minds and in the Polish collective memory. Many Polish white-power musicians follow neo-Nazi and white-power activists elsewhere in arguing that threats from Jews and other foreign minorities will soon cause a demographic collapse in Poland. What this perspective fails to consider, of course, is the fact that Poland has *already* undergone a profound demographic collapse in the form of the Holocaust, which in less than six years took Poland from a multiethnic country with a centuries-old history of racial tolerance to one of the most ethnically uniform nations in the world. This process of collective forgetting has allowed some Polish white-power musicians to argue that the Third Reich was actually *good* for ethnic Poles, a sentiment that conveniently excises the history of Nazi-inflicted massacres and forced labor that affected ethnic Poles as well, albeit to a lesser extent than they impacted Polish Jews and Roma/Sinti.

By romanticizing the Nazi regime in order to demonize the Soviet occupation and the later Polish communist satellite government, neo-Nazi Poles are arguing that Poles and other Slavic-descended peoples can re-envision Nazi philosophy in such a way as to include themselves within its most privileged racial categories. Poles saw more of the Holocaust unfold in their backyards than perhaps any other nationality in Europe, and they know as well as anyone that Hitler never intended Slavic peoples to enter his racial elite. Still, Eastern Europe in the post-1989 era is a different place than it was in 1945, and one should not discount Polish neo-Nazis' ability to change the world of white-power activism. Given the high rates of non-white immigration into Europe in recent decades, Nordic-centered neo-Nazis from Northern and Western Europe have begun to concede that their Eastern European neighbors may have more in common with them than Hitler would have believed. Increasing cooperation with German white-power activists—particularly in the wake of the 2000 Blood & Honour Deutschland ban, which has hampered German distributors' ability to market white-power music through homegrown companies—has further bolstered Polish neo-Nazis' claims to Aryanness.[114] Rather than signifying simply a hypocritical misunderstanding of twentieth-century history, then, Polish and other Slavic neo-Nazism actually represents a significant step in the evolution of white-power ideology, one that responds to the increasing ease of global migration and communication by reducing its focus on nineteenth-century-style national chauvinism in order to emphasize racial unity across state borders. This ability to develop new racist philosophies that resonate with contemporary generations means that neo-Nazism and other forms of white-power activism are far more dynamic and less obsolete than many people might like to believe.

Greece

Contemporary Greece, like Poland, is home to a vibrant white-power music scene comprised of bands that express both old-style national chauvinism and newer pan-European and neo-Nazi ideologies. In the early years of white-power music, the Greek white-power music scene seemed insignificant compared with larger scenes in places like Britain and Germany. As a result of the recent financial crisis, which has devastated the Greek economy and caused some of the worst recent socioeconomic problems anywhere in the European Union, Greek white-power music circles and neo-Nazi organizations have increased exponentially.

Greece is unique among the countries surveyed in this chapter in that, unlike Russia, Ukraine, Belarus, or Poland, post–World War II Greece never fell under the control of the Soviet Union or a Soviet-supported communist satellite government. Originally a neutral state in the war, Greece rebuffed an Italian invasion in 1940, only to fall to Hitler and the Nazis in 1941; the brutal German occupation ended only in October 1944, when Greek partisans and British troops finally seized Athens.[115] Greek communists did struggle for leadership of the country in a civil war between 1944 and 1949, but eventually lost to democratic forces supported by both Britain and the United States. With the help of Marshall Plan aid, the Greek economy recovered quickly after the end of the Civil War, making Greece seem to be one of the democratic success stories of post–World War II Europe.[116]

However, deep divisions between the political left and right remained salient in Greece long after the end of the Nazi occupation and the conclusion of the civil war. In the mid-1960s, while left-wing and right-wing politicians squabbled among themselves, a group of military officers saw a chance to seize power. On April 21, 1967, these right-wing officers staged their own coup d'état by using the element of surprise to snatch important political and military installations and arrest key opponents.[117] They installed an ultra-nationalist military junta in place of the ousted democratic government, stripping Greek citizens of most political freedoms and civil liberties by playing on fears of a communist takeover.[118] During the seven years that the junta remained in power, its authorities arrested, detained, and tortured thousands of political opponents in prisons on coastal islands.[119] In 1974, under mounting public opposition, the junta descended into political infighting that led to its collapse.[120] Greece at this point restored its democratic government and began, once again, to expand its economy. Yet as in other European countries which experienced right-wing dictatorships during the mid- to late twentieth century, the demise of the junta did not mean that supporters of ultra-nationalist ideologies simply disappeared. With economic growth came increasing numbers of migrant workers and refugees from the Third World, who constituted as much as 10 percent of the Greek labor force by the mid-1990s.[121] Compounding this influx of foreign workers into Greece has been the recent civil war in Syria, which has spurred a massive wave of refugees and asylum-seekers to flee to the European Union; Greece, as one of the primary ports of entry for these migrants, saw 124,000 immigrant arrivals in the first seven months of 2015, an increase of 750 percent over the first seven months of 2014.[122] This influx has caused outrage not only among old-style Greek ultra-nationalists, but also among an increasing number of young neo-Nazis, including skinheads.[123]

In fact, the racist skinhead movement had arrived in Greece around 1979. Early Greek skinheads in the years directly after the junta were instrumental in blending neo-Nazi and pan-European racist ideologies with Greek national chauvinist philosophies. In the beginning, they organized themselves mainly as small local gangs or crews, as they did in Britain and Germany during the late 1970s and early 1980s. Around 1987, however—exactly as Ian Stuart Donaldson was creating connections between racist skinheads and right-wing political organizations in Britain—Greek skinheads started to work with Greece's ultra-right-wing political organizations, such as Εθνική Πολιτική Ένωσις (ethniki politiki enosis, or national political union) and Λαϊκός Σύνδεσμος—Χρυσή Αυγή (laïkós sýndesmos—chrysí avgí, or popular association—golden dawn, usually referred to simply as Chrysí Avgí or Golden Dawn).[124] In the late 1980s and early 1990s, this new breed of politicized Greek skinheads produced its first crop of homegrown Greek white-power rock bands—most of whom played oi! punk—such as Last Patriots, Cause of Honour, Apolitistoi (uncivils), Aryan Resistance, No Surrender, Rock'n'Roll Rebels, Southrise, United Boots, and Warrior's Pride.[125]

The 1990s saw a blossoming of white-power music in Greece that mirrored the growth of white-power music among European-descended populations elsewhere. Greek white-power bands began to experiment with the new musical genres that were influencing white-power music scenes in Western Europe and North America, including heavy metal and hatecore. Under the influence of Norwegian NSBM, by the mid-1990s, Greek bands like Naer Mataron—a band name which, according to band members, comes from the ancient Sumerian name for Hades, the Greek god of the underworld—had also begun to produce NSBM on their own.[126] The Greek white-power music scene had grown so much by the end of the 1990s that Blood & Honour founded a Greek division in February 1999, called Blood & Honour Hellas (referring to the ancient Greek name for Greece, Ελλάς, or Hellas), which began producing its own English-language *Blood & Honour Hellas* magazine in May of that year.[127] Alongside Blood & Honour, homegrown white-power music zines and organizers have also continued to produce their own concerts and publications.

Since 2002, newer Greek bands like Boiling Blood, the hatecore group Iron Youth, and der Stürmer (German for the stormer, the title of one of the Third Reich's main propaganda newspapers) have been representing the Greek white-power music scene on international white-power compilation albums and at international white-power concerts.[128] Many of these bands have received praise from white-power music fans outside Greece, in venues such as a glowing 2005 Stormfront review by the Dutch user Ju-87, who wrote about the Iron Youth album *Durch das Volk, mit dem Volk, für das Volk* (German for "through the nation, with the nation, for the nation," a slogan of East Germany's ruling post–WWII communist party), saying, "Every WN [white-nationalist] metal/hardcore fan should buy this. They are definitely one of the most professional bands in the scene."[129] In recent years, Iron Youth and other white-power groups of the early 2000s have influenced an even newer generation of Greek bands such as Pogrom and Legion Hellas.

The Greek white-power music scene for a time even had its own concert venue, Skinhouse Hellas, which opened in 2005 in the city of Trikala, a main center of the Greek white-power music scene.[130] This hall hosted many of the international white-power music web's biggest bands from abroad, including Brutal Attack, Mistreat, Vinland Warriors, Sleipnir, Bully Boys, and Whitelaw.[131] While some white-power bands and music organizations have had friendly relations with particular venue owners in the past, this type of publicly advertised white-power-only venue represented an unprecedented step in white-power music, and demonstrated that white-power musicians in some regions of Greece enjoyed deep connections not only with venue owners, but also with police and the mainstream public, who allowed such a business to continue operating for a decade. However, by late 2015, Skinhouse Hellas's official website had disappeared, suggesting that the venue had closed, likely due to government crackdowns against Chrysí Avgí and its supporters.

Spurring the friendly relations between the Greek mainstream public and white-power groups has been the recent financial crisis. In an atmosphere of economic uncertainty and unrest, the Chrysí Avgí party gained unexpected electoral success, especially in 2012, and many "ordinary" Greek citizens began to express racist and xenophobic political ideologies that once flourished only on the fringes.[132] Many Greek white-power musical groups, such as the bands Iron Youth and Stosstrupp (shock troop, referring to the early Nazi Party organization *Stosstrupp Adolf Hitler*), played on their mainstream appeal, allying themselves with Chrysí Avgí and participating both in political activism and street-level violence.[133]

Some individual musicians, such as Giorgos "Kaiadas" Germenis—who was not only the bassist for the Greek NSBM band Naer Mataron, but also one of Chrysí Avgí's representatives in the Greek parliament—used Chrysí Avgí's electoral success to secure political office, continuing all the while to engage in street-style violence. In May 2013, Germenis used his parliamentary identification to circumvent a security cordon surrounding Athens mayor Giorgos Kaminis, attempting to attack the mayor and actually trying to pull a gun before the mayor's security team subdued him.[134] In the struggle, Germenis accidentally hit a twelve-year-old girl in the face instead of harming the mayor.[135] While white-power musicians like Russia's Sergei Troitsky have run for office elsewhere in Eastern Europe, the fact that known white-power musicians and publicly active Greek neo-Nazis like Germenis actually found national-level electoral *success* demonstrates both the depth of Greece's current political instability and the strength of white-power ideologies in contemporary Greece.

Following the murder of a left-wing musician in September 2013 by a Chrysí Avgí member, however, the Greek government ruled Chrysí Avgí a "neo-Nazi criminal gang" and imprisoned Giorgos Germenis, along with several other key party leaders, for allegedly running a criminal organization.[136] Greece's state-run Athens News Agency alleged that Germenis "had the role of an 'army major' in the recruitment and training of new members as well as in migrant attacks."[137] Upon being brought from prison to address the criminal charges before the Greek Parliament in May 2014, Germenis stated that "This will go down in history as the day an elected lawmaker appeared in Parliament led in handcuffs from prison. [. . .] We are political prisoners."[138] His former colleagues in Parliament ignored him, lifting the diplomatic immunity of all eighteen Chrysí Avgí politicians elected to national office in 2012. The imprisoned Chrysí Avgí leaders went on trial starting in May 2015.[139]

Stormfront users, predictably, reacted to the news of the crackdown with anger; one Greek user, upon hearing that Chrysí Avgí leader Nikolaos Mihaloliakos had been arrested in September 2013, even went so far as to express desire to take violent revenge: "This is unacceptable. This is the pseudo-democratic that sell us all these years. I feel so much anger that I want to get the shotgun and go there to get their heads. All politicians are scumbags and rascals."[140] Other Stormfront members were more guarded in their disapproval, but one user from summed up the general tenor of the response on Stormfront by writing, "The marxist jews are afraid of Golden Dawn. It interferes with their multi-cultural cesspool plans and to make us all slaves, while they live like kings" [sic].[141]

Despite the fact that Chrysí Avgí's fortunes have fallen, the political success of such a white-power-music-friendly Chrysí Avgí party helped Greek white-power music rise to international prominence rapidly in recent years. Unlike scenes in countries such as Germany and Sweden, the Greek white-power music scene experienced something akin to a golden age in the early 2010s. Whether Greek white-power musicians can continue their public violence and overt neo-Nazi activism into the future will depend not only on the outcome of the Chrysí Avgí trial, but also on how the Greek government chooses to address Chrysí Avgí's former rank-and-file supporters and on how the international community responds to the catastrophic recession in Greece. Whatever the future holds for Greek white-power music, the links between Greek white-power musicians and the Greek national government made the Greek white-power music scene, at least for a short time, one of the world's most politically influential. It is for this reason that the Greek scene deserves mention here, despite the fact that Greece—as a small country—cannot produce the large numbers of white-power bands that operate in countries like Russia and the United States. Nordic-centered neo-Nazi groups may have been skeptical about white-power bands from some Mediterranean countries in the past, but the vehemence of the Greek scene seems to have changed their minds. Like white-power musicians from Northeastern Europe and the Western Mediterranean, Greek white-power musicians are working to help redefine what it means to be a neo-Nazi and a white-power activist. If their contemporary strength is any indication, Greek white-power musicians may have a particularly influential voice in this process.

Greek and other Eastern European white-power musicians hold similar racist ideals to their Western European counterparts. Nonetheless, their very existence embodies the flexibility of contemporary white-power and neo-Nazi ideology; under Hitler, most of these musicians would never have been considered Aryan, never mind have been allowed to campaign for Nazi political objectives alongside Germans and Norwegians. The white-power music scenes in Eastern Europe are important to the international white-power music web for the same reason that the Western Mediterranean white-power music scenes are important. They show that white-power and neo-Nazi ideologies are not simple reiterations of archaic political debates, but rather fluid and homologous philosophies that attract contemporary adherents due to their resonance with current events.

White-power music scenes in Eastern Europe are also important to the international white-power music web because they represent the last decade's most significant growth area for the genre. In contrast to their Western European brethren, many of whom have spent the past fifteen years struggling at the hands of attentive and well-equipped law enforcement agencies, white-power musicians in countries like Russia and Greece had often enjoyed the toleration—and sometimes even the direct support and participation—of local authorities. This has allowed white-power music to grow in Eastern Europe in ways that have been impossible in Western Europe. While some white-power musicians from Germanic countries remain opposed to the presence of Slavic and Mediterranean white-power activists in neo-Nazi groups, many seem to have watched the rapid development of Eastern European white-power and neo-Nazi groups with admiration. Eastern European white-power musicians are clearly changing the dynamics of the white-power music web away from the traditional Nazi ideology of Nordic superiority and toward a pan-European white nationalism that can include groups which Hitler would have preferred to exclude. This means that they likely have a place not only in the history of white-power music, but also in its future. As the next decades unfold, national governments and international organizations will determine whether or not white-power musicians from various Eastern European countries can continue to play racist music virtually unchecked. If left to their own devices, these musicians have demonstrated that they will be happy to continue building white-power music scenes that propagate hatred and violence.

5

The History of
White-Power Music
outside Europe

The previous three chapters have all dealt with white-power music scenes in Europe itself—first in Britain, then in continental Western Europe, and finally in Eastern Europe. This emphasis on the European continent makes sense for a book on white-power music, because the focus of white-power ideology is on maintaining the supposed biological purity, cultural superiority, and international dominance of European-descended peoples. However, over the past 500 years, Europeans have left the European continent in large numbers to conquer and colonize other parts of the world. The expansionist, exploitative, and chauvinistic ideologies that characterized religious and political conflict in Renaissance- and Enlightenment-era Europe have followed these conquerors and settlers across the globe, helping to justify violence and oppression against the populations who already lived in areas that Europeans wanted to colonize. Genocide, slavery, environmental destruction, and entrenched pro-white racial hierarchies followed in the Europeans' wake, continuing in many cases even after the settler colonies had gained nominal political independence from their former colonizers. Given this history of both structural and interpersonal racism across Europe's former settler colonies, it is unsurprising that white-power music has appealed to some European-descended individuals living outside Europe. In fact, some of these current and former European colonies have produced important leaders in the international white-power music web. For that reason, this

104

history of white-power music must trace the histories of white-power music scenes not only in Europe itself, but also among the descendants of European settlers in places outside Europe.

This chapter will explore white-power music as it has developed in three key non-European regions: first, the United States and Canada; second, Latin America; and, third, Australia. I have chosen to group the histories in this chapter together by region and not by country—with the exception of Australia—because the national white-power music scenes in these three areas interact heavily within their regions. Moreover, white-power musicians in these areas respond to socio-historical pressures that affect these entire regions in ways that separate the regions from one another and from Europe. The reason that these three histories appear together in this chapter is that the shared history of European colonialism gives them similar core traits that are not necessarily common to white populations living within contemporary Europe itself.

It is important to note here that limited numbers of white-power and neo-Nazi bands do exist in parts of the world other than Europe, the Americas, and Australia. In particular, Southeast Asia has produced a few bands like the Singaporean group Totenkopf and the Japanese group Hakenkreuz (German for swastika), which tend to emphasize nostalgia for the World War II–era alliance between Nazi Germany and imperial Japan. I have chosen to exclude these groups from the purview of this study, because the vast majority of European-descended musicians and fans involved in the international white-power music web reject these Asian and Asian-descended groups as non-white. Their music, therefore, does not circulate through the same production, distribution, or reception channels as the rest of the music I discuss in this book. This does not mean that these groups do not draw on salient aspects of Nazi ideology in their song lyrics and ideologies, and it does not even mean that these groups' affinity for Nazi racial policy and claims to Aryan lineage do not correspond with ideas that some leading Third Reich officials also held. It simply means that these groups lie outside the scope of this book, and that this music deserves consideration elsewhere.

I will begin my discussion of white-power music outside Europe by exploring white-power music scenes in the United States and Canada. The white-power music market there has for decades been one of the largest in the world. Notably, this region has also been home to many of the genre's most important recording companies and music distributors. To begin, I must explain both how racism has developed historically in the United States and Canada and why white-power ideologies appeal to some individuals in these countries, because race relations have developed differently in these former European settler colonies than they have in the mainland European countries that I have surveyed in the previous three chapters.

The United States and Canada

Pro-white racism in the areas that are now the United States and Canada stems from many different historical processes, including struggles between Europeans and indigenous groups; culture conflict *among* the European immigrants of various nationalities who poured into North America after the Columbus voyages; the importation of millions of African slaves to the United States in the seventeenth, eighteenth, and early nineteenth centuries; resentment toward the non-European immigrants who began to arrive in North America in large numbers in the nineteenth century; and the United States' twentieth- and twenty-first-century involvement in violent conflicts overseas. Various ethnic groups have served as targets for pro-white racist sentiment in North America over the centuries, including non-Europeans, as well as European settler groups such as Irish and Italian Catholics.[1]

Undoubtedly the longest-suffering ethnic minority population in North America has been the group that once formed the *entirety* of the continent's population, its indigenous tribes. Over several centuries, Europeans opened up vast tracts of land in North America for white settlement, facilitating and often directly perpetrating an indigenous population collapse that by the early twentieth century had totaled a 90–98 percent decline from estimated pre-Columbian numbers.[2] Then, in both the United States and Canada—as in other former British settler colonies like Australia—once the worst of the killing had quieted in the late nineteenth and early twentieth centuries, government officials began programs of forced child removal that took indigenous children away from their parents and communities for re-education in brutal off-reservation boarding schools, a practice that the United Nations now classifies as genocide in itself.[3]

Statistically, indigenous groups and individuals in both countries continue to live in poverty at much higher rates than the populations in general. A 2008 study reported, for instance, that in the United States, indigenous individuals lived in poverty at more than twice the national rate, were far less likely to earn high school diplomas and bachelor's degrees than members of the general population, suffered much higher unemployment rates than other ethnic groups, were more likely than members of any other ethnic group to fall victim to violence and to commit suicide, suffered mental health disorders at higher-than-average rates, and were more likely to abuse alcohol and drugs than their counterparts in other groups.[4] A similar report by Canada's National Collaborating Centre for Aboriginal Health stated that Canadian indigenous populations, like those elsewhere in the world, suffered higher-than-average rates of health problems such as child and maternal mortality, infectious disease, malnutrition, substance abuse, violence including homicide and suicide, obesity and related conditions like diabetes and hypertension, and "diseases caused by environmental contamination."[5]

Statistics such as these indicate that indigenous Americans and Canadians suffer heavily now, as they have for more than five centuries. However, they have not been the only group to experience structural violence, discrimination, and exploitation at the hands of Europeans and their descendants during this period. Particularly in the colonies that later became the United States, individuals of African descent have also been targets of racist oppression. European-descended landowners began importing African slaves to the North American colonies as early as 1619.[6] Through a gradually tightening network of legislation, slavery in the United States turned into a chattel system in which African slaves and their descendants became the legal property of their white owners in perpetuity.[7] By the time the US government emancipated the African-descended slaves in 1863, at least 8.5 million Africans had left their home continent on slave ships whose conditions were so brutal that an estimated 15 percent of the human cargo died before arrival.[8] The slave system had become so entrenched in the cultures of some Southern US states that a few, especially Mississippi and South Carolina, had slave populations that actually exceeded their European-American populations in numbers.[9]

Anti-slavery legislators intended for the 1863 Emancipation Proclamation, along with the 1865 Thirteenth Amendment to the US Constitution, which banned slavery in the United States forever, to improve the lives of its newly freed slaves. However, these lawmakers failed to anticipate the strength of the backlash against the new statutes from angry Southern whites, who founded the Ku Klux Klan as a terrorist organization in 1866, and, within a generation, had set up a system of racist laws that had reduced the African American communities in most Southern states to near-slavery conditions once again.[10] It was not until the post–World War II era that African Americans achieved any measure of legal equality with whites on a national level, and even this nominal legal equality has failed to bring the African American community any equality of wealth or status with European Americans in the United States today.[11] Race riots in both Baltimore, Maryland and the St. Louis suburb of Ferguson, Missouri in 2014 and 2015 have drawn national attention to ongoing issues such as police brutality toward African Americans and deep-rooted systems of structural inequality that leave this group living in poverty at rates far higher than the national average.[12] Nostalgia for the slavery era remains prevalent, particularly in former slave states. Clothing, bumper stickers, and other items bearing symbols of the country's slaveholding past, particularly the battle flag of the pro-slavery 1860s southern Confederate government, still appear for sale in shopping malls via Dixie Outfitters and other mainstream retail chains in many parts of the US South.[13] The government of South

Carolina, in fact, only stopped using the Confederate flag as its state flag after a 2015 mass shooting by a white teenager left nine black parishioners dead at an African American church, fomenting a national discussion about the racist implications of the state symbol.[14] Even in Canada, which never developed a complex chattel slavery system like that of the United States, anti-black animus also exists on a relatively large scale; York University researchers discovered in 2009, for instance, that the average experiment participant in Toronto was *more* likely to choose to work with a white over a black partner on a puzzle exercise after the potential white partner made a racist remark about the black participant.[15]

Discrimination toward non-white immigrants has also marred race relations in Anglophone North America during recent centuries. In the late nineteenth and early twentieth centuries, both Canada and the United States enacted racist immigration laws that strictly limited and in some cases even banned immigration from places like Southeast Asia and Africa; the explicitly stated goal of these policies was to maintain European-dominated population demographics.[16] Although both Canada and the United States have since repealed these laws, studies demonstrate that animosity toward Muslim populations in both countries has risen sharply since the September 11, 2001 terrorist attacks and the United States' subsequent wars in Afghanistan and Iraq. In fact, the percentage of people in the United States who said they held "unfavorable attitudes" toward Muslims leapt from 24 percent in early 2002 to 46 percent in early 2006.[17] In Canada, a 2013 opinion poll by the Angus Reid Public Opinion firm found that 54 percent of the country's population harbored an unfavorable view of Muslims, up from 46 percent in 2009.[18] The United States, which shares a border with Mexico, also has an uneasy relationship with immigrants from Latin America, who, along with their descendants, made up 17.4 percent of the country's population as of 2014; the state of Arizona, for instance, passed a 2010 law, widely criticized by watchdog groups for encouraging racial profiling by law enforcement officers, which required all immigrants to carry identification paperwork and compelled police officers to interrogate anyone they even *suspected* of being an illegal alien.[19]

Yet despite differing opinions among the general populace about structural inequality and immigration in both the United States and Canada, the expressions of violent, unapologetic interpersonal racism that appear in white-power and neo-Nazi groups have become increasingly taboo in North American public discourse since the end of World War II. Historian Mattias Gardell points out, in fact, that for many individuals who have joined pro-white hate groups in the postwar era, the radical, illicit, and stigmatized nature of white-power and neo-Nazi ideologies and practices is often part of their appeal; Max Resist singer Shawn Sugg's comments about his attraction to "outlaw" and "extreme" lifestyles, discussed in chapter 3, provide a clear example of Gardell's point.[20] Even the earliest post–World War II neo-Nazi groups, such as George Lincoln Rockwell's American Nazi Party, formed in the United States in 1959, and André Bellefeuille's associated Canadian Nazi Party, formed in 1960, appeared on the margins and not at the center of the North American political system, particularly because memory of having fought Nazi Germany during the war ran high in both countries less than two decades after the Third Reich's collapse.[21]

Because of lenient hate speech laws, though, white-power and other neo-Nazi groups like Rockwell's and Bellefeuille's have been able to operate legally in the United States and Canada in the intervening decades, making public white-power activism easier for individuals in these countries than for white-power believers in many European nations. In the United States in particular, white-power activists only incur legal difficulties if courts can prove that they have incited *specific* acts of violence against individual victims; the First Amendment to the US Constitution otherwise protects blanket bigoted and violent statements.[22] Taking advantage of their protected legal status, US and Canadian racist activists have participated in the international white-power music web on a large scale, founding some of the world's most famous white-power bands and operating several of its biggest white-power record labels. In fact, in a rare moment of support for a US government policy from a white-power believer, the Stormfront reviewer Ju-87 wrote in a 2006 review of the album *Purge* by the US band Code of Violence, "Very outspoken lyrics sometimes. Courtesy of the US First Amendment. That's something we desperately need in Europe."[23]

The United States was actually home to several of the very first white-racist popular musicians whose work still circulates widely among fans of white-power music today, predating the British white-power oi! music scene of the late 1970s and early 1980s by more than a decade. This so-called hate country music emanated from the racist Reb Rebel Records label, along with a few other less prominent companies like Nash-T Records, Reb-Time Records, and Conservative Records.[24] Reb Rebel Records operated between 1966 and 1969 in the town of Crowley, Louisiana under the leadership of owner Joseph Denton "Jay" Miller—the same J. D. Miller known as the father of the swamp blues, who recorded both black and white artists at his Master-Trax Studios in Crowley, helped to popularize African American music among whites in the Southern United States, and wrote the 1952 Kitty Wells country hit "It Wasn't God Who Made Honky Tonk Angels."[25] Via Reb Rebel Records, Miller distributed racist country songs that argued against racial desegregation and African American civil rights. Reb Rebel artists like Leroy "Happy Fats" Leblanc, Billy Joe "Son of Mississippi" Norris, and especially Clifford "Johnny Rebel" Trahan wrote and recorded songs that most famously include examples such as Trahan's "Kajun Klu Klux Klan" [*sic*], "Nigger Hatin' Me," and "Move Them

Niggers North." The Ku Klux Klan itself supported racist musicians like Leblanc, Norris, and Trahan, and seems to have helped to distribute their records
across the US South, with the 1971 Reb Rebel compilation LP *For Segregationists Only* selling heavily at an official Klan booth at the North Carolina State
Fair in the early 1970s.[26]

The 1960s hate country artist whose career has enjoyed the highest degree
of long-term success has undoubtedly been Johnny Rebel. Rebel—Clifford
"Pee Wee" Trahan—took his stage name from a nickname used for the soldiers
of the pro-slavery Confederate Army during the US Civil War in the 1860s.
He was born in 1938 to a Cajun family, and had begun playing guitar and singing at local clubs by the time he graduated high school. He recorded country,
rockabilly, and swamp blues songs under a number of stage names between
the late 1950s and early 1970s, including "Tag Along" as Tommy Todd, "Black
Magic" as Jericho Jones, "I'll Knock Three Times" and "Play That Song One
More Time" as Johnny Blaine, and a handful of others as Pee Wee Trahan and
Pee Wee Trayhan, even working in Nashville as a studio musician for a short
time in the 1960s.[27] Some of the songs he recorded under pseudonyms other
than Johnny Rebel have appeared on recent re-release collections by non-
racist record labels, such as the 2013 Ace Records compilation album *Boppin
by the Bayou Again*, which features his songs "Bop and Rock Tonight" and
"I'm Gonna Learn." He also wrote and co-wrote a number of non-racist songs
for other musicians like Jimmy C. Newman and Johnnie Allan.[28] As Johnny
Rebel, though, Trahan voiced the rage and anxiety that many whites in the
United States' Deep South felt over the 1960s movement for African American civil rights, which some sectors of the white population in his native Louisiana saw as a threat to their traditional way of life. He told an interviewer
in 2003 that his main motivation for recording the Johnny Rebel songs had
been financial, and that he had actually been friends with a number of the
African American artists who recorded for J. D. Miller: "I would do anything
to make a buck. Hell, I made a few bucks off of it. [. . .] I don't know if he
[Miller] had a statement to make then, but at that time he was recording a lot
of blacks. Most of his artists were blacks. I was big buddies with these guys.
Lightning Slim, I even used his car one time to go on a date! That's how much
blacks bothered me." Still, in the same interview, he also echoed some of the
same racist sentiments he had expressed as Johnny Rebel in the 1960s: "Blacks
develop an attitude towards whites, and they won't let it go. They won't let go of
what happened."[29]

In fact, although Trahan has attempted to downplay his personal bias
in recent interviews, the occasionally violent racism that he wrote into the lyrics of songs like "Kajun Klu Klux Klan" was off-putting to many local audiences even in Louisiana in the 1960s, and largely because of that violence, he
was not the most successful of Reb Rebel Records' artists while the label was

actually in operation. As Happy Fats, for instance, Leroy Leblanc reportedly sold 200,000 copies of Reb Rebel's first release in 1966, "Dear Mr. President," but even in 1960s Louisiana, radio stations refused to play Trahan's more explicit Johnny Rebel songs.[30] One Stormfront member nonetheless reports that Rebel's songs appeared frequently in jukeboxes in the South in the 1960s, writing, "Believe it or not, I can remember Johnny Rebel when I was a teenager in the 1960s. Most redneck bars had several of his 45's on the jukebox and the bartender usually had a stack of them under the counter for sale. Glad to hear the old boy is still around and kickin'!"[31] Clearly, then, some members of the original target demographic for Trahan's Johnny Rebel recordings, including the fan recounting this particular memory, still enjoy listening to 1960s hate country music.

Likewise, the catchy Johnny Rebel stage name and Trahan's unapologetic racism appealed to Ian Stuart Donaldson and the legions of white-power musicians and fans who formed the international white-power music web starting in the 1980s.[32] Trahan reports that he was unaware of his white-power following until 2001, when a fan named Brad Herman contacted him through J. D. Miller's sons and offered to help him re-package his old Johnny Rebel material and record new songs.[33] At Herman's suggestion, Trahan returned to hate country music after a hiatus of more than thirty years to release an Islamophobic song called "Fuck You, Osama Bin Laden!" in 2003 and then a new full-length album, *It's the Attitude, Stupid!*, in 2006, which featured songs like "Send 'em All Back to Africa" and "Quit Your Bitchin,' Nigger!" As a result of the new material, Trahan was even interviewed on the mainstream US radio program *The Howard Stern Show*, which had a reputation for discussing controversial topics, and which played some of Trahan's Johnny Rebel music on the air.[34] White-power music fans on Stormfront express widespread praise for Johnny Rebel songs, often lamenting the fact that so few white-power musicians have produced hate country music in comparison to white-power punk and metal music. One Stormfront user commented in 2014, "Johnny Rebel is a true patriot, his prophecy is uncanny; if only people would listen in sight of retrospective! Everything he said about Negroes back then is true today, Negroids spiritually stink and when enlightenment comes they'll be shunned!"[35] Another wrote more simply of having affection for Trahan's Johnny Rebel music in 2008: "Johnny Rebel, windows down driving through coon town, full volume, cig in my mouth, nothing better."[36]

Despite the fact that an audience for racist country music obviously outlasted the 1960s, the Louisiana-based hate country scene dissipated in the 1970s. Still, through Ian Stuart Donaldson, the influence of hate country music—along with racist oi! punk and second-wave skinhead culture—came back to North America in the early 1980s, where it circulated among newly politicized white-power skinheads in the United States and Canada. A few

homegrown racist skinhead bands appeared in the United States in the early
1980s, such as the Bully Boys, formed in Dallas, Texas in 1983.[37] As the 1980s
and 1990s wore on, the leaders of established white-power groups such as Willis Carto of the Institute for Historical Review and Tom Metzger of White
Aryan Resistance began to court members of the emerging North American
racist skinhead scene for their own organizations.[38]

Violence—including at least seven murders by the end of the 1980s—
followed the skinheads into the fold of recognized US white-power groups.[39]
Skinheads under Tom Metzger began generating national attention in the
United States by appearing on talk shows such as *Geraldo*, where Metzger's son
and friends made headlines by actually breaking host Geraldo Rivera's nose
with a chair.[40] In 1988, Portland, Oregon skinheads affiliated with Metzger's
White Aryan Resistance group murdered an Ethiopian immigrant, Mulageta Seraw. After police found White Aryan Resistance materials in the kill-
ers' vehicle, Metzger lost a civil trial for incitement to murder. He incurred a
US$12.5 million fine that resulted in the loss of his home and most of White
Aryan Resistance's profits.[41]

Before losing almost everything to the court settlement, Metzger had
spent considerable effort fostering a homegrown white-power music scene
in the United States. The new bands that he nurtured included the Tulsa
Boot Boys from Tulsa, Oklahoma and Bound for Glory, formed in 1989 in
St. Paul, Minnesota.[42] Bound for Glory, in particular, was to become one of
the most important groups the international white-power music scene has
ever produced, recording and touring abroad alongside Skrewdriver, Brutal Attack, and other big-name bands from the European scene.[43] Bound for
Glory's frontman, Ed Wolbank, has since been involved with other white-
power bands such as Before God, Plunder & Pillage, Kriegsgruppe 23 (German
for war group 23), Bully Boys, and Bound for Attack, and is a former director
of the Northern Hammerskins division of the neo-Nazi Hammerskin Nation
skinhead network.[44] Wolbank, who says he would like to play a concert "in the
White House! (When it's in better hands)," told *Blood & Honour* in 2000 that
he considered Nazi war criminal Rudolf Hess, the subject of Bound for Glory
song "46 Years in Hell," as "one of the greatest humanitarians of the twentieth century."[45] Stormfront users, who are often critical of white-power music
that they view as musically or lyrically inferior, resoundingly praise Bound for
Glory's music; the Stormfront reviewer Ju-87 writes of them, in fact, that they
are "The best band the USA has spawned. Was it not for their WN [white-
nationalist] lyrics they could've become big in the mainstream."[46]

Along with Bound for Glory, other North American white-power bands
forged connections with white-power bands overseas in the early 1990s.
George Burdi, aka George Eric Hawthorne, Canadian lead singer of the
Windsor, Ontario–based white-power band RaHoWa, started white-power

music's premier record label along with friends in the winter of 1993–1994.[47] While white-power musicians had been recording up until that point with the Rock-O-Rama and Rebelles Européens labels, Burdi's label, Resistance Records—originally headquartered across the river from Windsor in the US city of Detroit, Michigan in order to take advantage of the United States' milder hate speech legislation—offered prominent white-power musicians a newly professionalized and internationally minded outlet. Resistance Records' in-house magazine was one of the first white-power music publications to feature a glossy, full-color cover and professional printing.[48] Burdi told an interviewer in 1995 that the label had pressed 5,000 copies of the magazine's first issue, but had increased to 15,000 copies per issue by the time the fourth issue came out ten months later.[49] This level of publicity made Resistance Records an attractive label for international bands, including not only RaHoWa and Bound for Glory, but also prominent European groups such as Paul Burnley's star British band No Remorse; the distribution figure of 15,000 copies per issue has been disputed by the magazine's former printer, however, who suggests that at least for later issues of the magazine, she printed only 5,000 copies per issue rather than the 15,000 that both Burdi and other label officials had claimed.[50] In the first eighteen months of Resistance Records' operations, the label reported that it sold 50,000 CDs and turned a US$300,000 profit.[51] Because the United States' hate speech laws are among the most lenient in the world, Resistance Records was able to achieve a level of stability that white-power music labels in many other countries—fearful of government raids, inventory seizures, heavy fines, and even jail time—could not hope to match.[52]

This did not mean that US and Canadian officials did not try to target Resistance Records for other reasons. In 1997, authorities in the United States and Canada staged a simultaneous joint raid on Resistance's office in Detroit and on Burdi's home across the river in Windsor, Ontario, charging that the company had been failing to pay sales taxes.[53] Resistance settled the case quickly by paying a fine. The label avoided serious tax fraud charges because a significant proportion of its buyers came from outside the United States and Canada and were therefore exempt from local sales taxes.[54] Shortly after Resistance settled the tax case, however, Burdi went to prison in Ontario for kicking a female anti-racist activist in the face with a steel-toe boot at an abortive RaHoWa concert in Ottawa in 1993. Control of the label passed to a former editor of *Blood & Honour* magazine, Eric Davidson, who would later go on to co-found one of Resistance's biggest competitors, Panzerfaust Records.[55] Burdi was released a year later, but he shocked everyone by renouncing racism and forming a multiethnic band called Novacosm.[56]

The influence of Burdi's band and especially of his record label did not simply fade away after his defection from organized white-power activism, though. Some of Burdi's former bandmates went on to play in other

white-power bands; RaHoWa's lead guitarist and multi-instrumentalist Jon
Latvis, for example, played in the prominent Toronto-based band Aryan in
the late 1990s.[57] Also, RaHoWa's two full-length albums—1992's *Declaration
of War* and 1995's *Cult of the Holy War*—are now considered major classics of
the white-power music genre, irrespective of Burdi's widely publicized exit
from the industry. For example, Stormfront user Ju-87 writes in a 2005 review
of *Cult of the Holy War*,

> This album is a classic. [. . .] The lyrics are the best ever written in the WN
> movement. [. . .] I prefer these above all the simple 'kill all ni . . . ers' lyrics of
> many US bands. Those are nice to blow off some steam, but will not attract
> new members to the WN cause. RaHoWa is a much better tool for recruitment.
> Lots of variation let you keep playing this album over and over again. The
> vocals of Burdi sound like a man who stands 100% behind them. I still cannot
> believe he took a 180 degree turn. (racial slur censored in the original)[58]

This writer clearly understands the fact that Burdi now repudiates his former
white-power beliefs and therefore has no plans to produce further RaHoWa
albums, but still considers the RaHoWa albums that Burdi and his band
recorded while Burdi was still involved in white-power groups to be "classic,"
particularly the much-celebrated *Cult of the Holy War.*

Many other white-power music fans—or at least those who post on the
Stormfront forums—also seem to agree with this reviewer. Between March
and October 2005, a thread on the Stormfront Music and Entertainment
board called "What Was The First WN [white-nationalist] Band You Listened
To?" received almost one hundred replies; the respondents to this thread
listed RaHoWa as second only to the monolithic Skrewdriver in its influence
on their early forays into white-power music fandom.[59] Further, when users
posted between January 2012 and June 2015 to a long-running Stormfront
Music and Entertainment thread entitled "YOUR TOP 10 WHITE POWER
BANDS"—a thread that also received almost one hundred replies—RaHoWa
was *still*, nearly two decades after Burdi's defection from white-power activism,
receiving enough votes to place in the top fifteen out of nearly two hundred
bands that various users mentioned liking.[60]

Clearly, Burdi and RaHoWa left a lasting impact on the world of white-
power music, even if some fans did stop listening to their RaHoWa CDs after
Burdi left white-power activism. The heavy influence that Burdi had on the
growth of the white-power music industry and on the development of
the white-power music sound in the early- to mid-1990s helps to explain
why the North American white-power music web initially struggled to
regain its bearings when Burdi announced that he would no longer participate
in the industry he had worked so hard to build. In fact, for a while after Burdi's

defection, it appeared as if the white-power music industry in North America had collapsed.

Then, in 1998, prominent US white-power activists began to show interest in the dying Resistance Records. Willis Carto of a Holocaust denial powerhouse called the Institute for Historical Review, along with former Reagan White House staffer Todd Blodgett, purchased Resistance in 1998 and relocated the company's headquarters to Etiwanda, California, near San Bernardino.[61] Then, a court case forced Carto to declare bankruptcy, and Blodgett took the opportunity to sell Resistance for an alleged sum of $250,000 to Carto's nemesis, Dr. William Pierce, founder of the neo-Nazi group the National Alliance.[62] Pierce relocated Resistance to the National Alliance's headquarters in Hillsboro, West Virginia, and set about expanding the label's catalogue. His next power play came in the autumn of 1999, when he subsumed Resistance's Swedish ally, Nordland Records. Pierce wrote of the buyout in the Winter 2000 issue of *Resistance* magazine, saying, "We [. . .] bought the entire inventory of Nordland, one of the best and biggest distributors of resistance music in Europe, when the folks at Nordland were facing bankruptcy as the result of harassment by the Swedish government. The buyout doubled the size of our inventory and also doubled the number of titles we are able to offer."[63] After buying Nordland's inventory, Pierce also created links with Varg Víkernes's NSBM label Cymophane Records. By working with the fugitive German murderer and white-power musician Hendrik Möbus of the band Absurd, who was a Cymophane branch manager, Pierce added a large NSBM inventory to Resistance's catalogue.[64] George Burdi's band RaHoWa had actually experimented with an NSBM sound on *Cult of the Holy War* before Burdi's defection from the white-power movement, and this background, along with Möbus's support, had convinced Pierce to start distributing NSBM albums from Cymophane under the new name Unholy Records. Pierce even chose to record several NSBM artists alongside more traditional white-power punk groups on the Resistance label.

The elderly Pierce died in 2002, leaving Resistance to his embattled protégé, Erich Gliebe. Upbeat about white-power music's potential to foment a racial revolution, Gliebe had written in a 2000 *Resistance* magazine editorial, "Through resistance music, we have the ability to transcend national boundaries and reach out to our racial brothers and sisters around the globe. With the rising tide of nationalism and racial awareness in eastern Europe and Russia, and with the huge advances in technology and travel that we have today (created by our race, of course), now is the time to promote and market our music in every White enclave in the world to bring our folk together."[65] Despite this early optimism, the ineffectual Gliebe lost control of the label briefly in 2005–2006, regaining it in 2007 only because Resistance's new CEO, Shaun Walker, went to prison.[66] Around the same time, Gliebe was forced to stop printing new issues of *Resistance* magazine after his printer—the Cleveland, Ohio-based Graphic Litho Inc.—refused to continue pressing copies on ideological grounds.[67] Fans like the Stormfront CD reviewer Ju-87, an avid buyer and collector of white-power albums, were also beginning to note by early 2006 that the label had "stagnated concerning new [album] releases."[68] Resistance Records finally folded entirely in 2012 under Gliebe's mismanagement. National Alliance membership had fallen from 1,400 members when Pierce died in 2002 to about 75 in 2012.[69] Even white-power music fans on the Stormfront online message board greeted the news of Resistance's closing with statements such as "Resistance has sucked for years now," although a Stormfront user calling himself "Ian Moone" stated cryptically in February 2014 that "Resistance Records is actually coming back under new ownership. I know the guy who bought the remaining stock from Erich Gliebe."[70] By early 2016, a web shop operating under the Resistance Records name and logo was in business again, albeit selling only to customers with US mailing addresses.[71]

Regardless of whether the newly re-launched Resistance Records actually regains the power and influence that the label wielded in the 1990s and early 2000s, Resistance Records' impact on white-power music in recent decades has already been enormous. In fact, in response to Resistance's success, other white-power record labels also began to spring up in the United States as early as the mid-1990s. A white-power musician calling himself simply "Ryan," who was a member of the prominent US white-power bands Nordic Thunder, Chaos 88, and Blue Eyed Devils, followed Resistance Records' lead and started a white-power music label called Tri-State Terror Records in 1994.[72] Tri-State Terror began by producing music only from the founder's own bands, debuting with Nordic Thunder's album *Final Stand* in 1994. By the time the label closed its doors in 2001, it had produced at least twenty-five albums by other US bands such as Angry Aryans, Aggravated Assault, The Voice, Attack, Infantry, No Alibi, Pure Rampage, Dying Breed, Stronghold, Sedition, Vaginal Jesus, Steelcap, and Mudoven (a band name that references the mud people of Christian Identity doctrine, as well as the crematoria or ovens of the Nazi concentration camps).[73] These albums included several staples of the white-power music canon, like Blue Eyed Devils's *Holocaust 2000*, Angry Aryans' *Racially Motivated Violence*, and Vaginal Jesus's *Affirmative Apartheid*. Blue Eyed Devils, in particular, have become one of the international white-power music web's most famous hatecore bands.[74] In fact, most of Tri-State Terror's releases featured bands that played in musical styles like hatecore and heavy metal.[75] This followed a trend in the worldwide white-power music web away from exclusively skinhead-based oi! punk music and toward a widening range of musical genres that especially include increasingly heavy rock and heavy metal music.

Another important record label in the US white-power music industry, Panzerfaust Records—named for the German phrase "armored fist," referring to a World War II–era German hand-held rocket launcher—was founded in St. Paul, Minnesota in September 1998 by racist skinheads Anthony Pierpont and the former Resistance staffer Eric Davidson.[76] Pierpont was a savvy businessman, and from the outset, Panzerfaust established itself as a major competitor to Resistance. Pierpont and Davidson soon found another partner in Resistance defector Bryant Calvert Cecchini, a.k.a. Byron Calvert.[77] Their label produced albums for prominent North American white-power bands like Youngland, H8machine, Involved Patriots, Griffin, and Stonehammer, and achieved brief mainstream notoriety by adapting the German *Projekt Schulhof* strategy for the US market. Panzerfaust's 2004 *Project Schoolyard* CD attracted the attention of hate group watchdogs like the Anti-Defamation League of B'nai B'rith and the Southern Poverty Law Center, in addition to that of local mainstream news outlets.[78] The album, which Panzerfaust planned to distribute free to 100,000 US students between the ages of thirteen and nineteen, featured an international array of white-power bands, including Bound for Glory and its members' NSBM side band Before God, as well as Max Resist, Brutal Attack, Youngland, H8machine, Final War, Midtown Bootboys, and Fortress.[79] In an interview with the mainstream nonprofit radio station Minnesota Public Radio, Cecchini downplayed the violent potential of the CD's message, saying,

When you hear people say, "My gosh, you guys are associated with violence," that's just nuts. I can tell you that I have never, once, in my life, attacked anybody because of their race. I've never done it. Obviously we don't suggest to kids that they listen to the CD and go out and do the stuff that's on the CD any more than the people that produced (the video game) *Grand Theft Auto III* are sued or held responsible for the rate of car thefts in the cities of America. My kid is four years old, he watches *The Three Stooges* and he hasn't yet poked out his brother's eye. You know what I mean?[80]

However, even at the time of Panzerfaust's greatest success with its 2004 *Project Schoolyard* album, the label was on the verge of imploding. At issue was Anthony Pierpont's ethnic background and criminal history. Pierpont's relatively dark skin had raised questions in white-power circles for years, but until 2005, he had managed to keep rumors under control. Then Cecchini found a copy of Pierpont's birth certificate, which listed Pierpont's mother as the Mexican-born Maria Marcola del Prado. To make matters worse for Pierpont, Cecchini also followed a tip from other white-power skinheads that led him to an Internet forum where Pierpont had posted lewd messages about having sex with Thai prostitutes during a sex tour he had taken in Thailand, something that the anti-race-mixing white-power movement regarded as a serious sin.[81] Finally, the anti-racist Southern Poverty Law Center posted an online picture of Pierpont with Hispanic friends in a California prison yard during his time behind bars for a drug infraction, and Pierpont's disgusted partners shut the doors on Panzerfaust Records. Davidson and Cecchini seized control of Panzerfaust Records' inventory and used it to found a new record label, Free Your Mind Productions, which—like the rest of the white-power community—vowed never to have anything to do with Pierpont again.[82]

Free Your Mind Productions, which was originally based in Valdosta, Georgia, now markets through the Arkansas-based white-power company Tightrope Records, advertising a reduced catalogue of white-power CDs alongside a wide range of white-power-themed clothing. In December 2008, Tightrope pressed 30,000 copies of a second volume of the *Project Schoolyard USA* album, which contained mostly older white-power songs by bands like the defunct RaHoWa and Skrewdriver, and even a few 1960s hate country songs by Johnny Rebel. Yet, despite the fact that Panzerfaust's successor labels have lived on in at least some form, neither Free Your Mind Productions nor Tightrope Records has ever approached the prolific levels of recording and distribution that characterized Panzerfaust Records in the Pierpont era. The Panzerfaust racial-purity debacle in fact seems to have sapped strength out of the US white-power music market in much the same way that the Browning-vs.-Burnley feud slowed the development of the British white-power music market during the previous decade.

For example, one Stormfront user wrote in July 2014, "What happened, when Panzerfaust went under, the American scene has never fully recovered. The Panzerfaust fiasco has and still is a big black eye."[83] Another user responding to the same thread also suggested, crucially, that the slowdown in the US white-power music market stemmed in large part from a general wave of US-based white-power record label closures over the past decade, and placed the blame not on squabbles between movement insiders, but rather on decreased revenues as a result of widespread Internet file-sharing since the turn of the new millennium: "I think the prevalence of online file sharing has diminished much of the revenue required to keep bands and labels economically viable. 10–15 years ago you had Resistance, Panzerfaust, Final Stand etc. One by one, it seems they all folded."[84] While the Panzerfaust scandal certainly shook the white-power music world, impacting white-power music fans and musicians in the United States in particular, as this second Stormfront user's statement illustrates, deep financial difficulties will likely present larger problems for the white-power music industry than scandals in the long term. If white-power musicians receive little financial compensation for plying their trade in a geographically diffuse niche market, and if they continued to be surrounded by communities that repudiate their belief systems, then the incentives to continue making new music—or even to found new bands in the first place—decrease markedly. If white-power music labels cannot turn profits because many fans of their music choose to download songs for free via online file-sharing services, then one of the main support networks for the musicians dies.

White-power music fans on the Stormfront forum are often vocal in their disapproval of users who admit to downloading illegal copies of white-power albums, arguing that fans of the music should support the industry by purchasing albums from white-power distributors. The Stormfront CD reviewer Ju-87 even tries to encourage other fans to purchase albums by discussing how much he enjoys interacting with the physical copies of albums, writing that it is worthwhile to "purchase the original release instead of soullessly downloading it from your PC. Music doesn't come alive in my ears if I can't look at the cover art, read the lyrics, and, the pervert I am, even sniff the new booklet sometimes."[85] Still, the frequency of white-power record label closures in the 2000s and 2010s indicates that labels have clearly felt the pressure of increasing music piracy in recent years.

Of course, several large white-power music labels in Europe, along with a number of their counterparts in the United States, still continue to operate, finding ways to stay afloat even in a difficult post-2008 economy where many fans seem unwilling to pay for new music. In addition to Tightrope Records and the new version of Resistance Records, other prominent labels that currently operate in the United States include Micetrap Records, out of Maple Shade, New Jersey; Label 56, located in Baltimore, Maryland; NSM88 Records, selling from Detroit, Michigan as part of the National Socialist Movement (NSM) organization; and the Milwaukee, Wisconsin–based Stahlhelm Records, which was named for the German phrase steel helmet, referring both to the steel helmets worn by front-line German soldiers during the World Wars and to the interwar German right-wing paramilitary organization Stahlhelm, Bund der Frontsoldaten, or "steel helmet, league of front-line soldiers." These recording companies complement major international white-power labels like the German companies PC Records in Chemnitz and OPOS Records in Dresden. Despite the fact that important recording companies like Panzerfaust and Tri-State Terror have collapsed, along with a few prominent European labels like the Belgian-based Pure Impact Records, which closed its doors in September 2014, the persistence of other record labels both in the United States and abroad, some of whom list albums from the older, now-defunct companies in their online catalogues, demonstrates that white-power music retail companies continue to find audiences who are willing to buy their music.

Partially due to the influence of the many and varied white-power recording labels that have operated in the United States over the past two decades,
US and Canadian white-power musicians play in a wide range of musical
styles. Alongside acoustic "hate folk" musicians from European white-power
music scenes, several US and Canadian white-power musicians have been
involved in hate folk and other types of white-power acoustic music. The
Toronto-based white-power singer and bassist Griffin, who played in the band
Aryan with former RaHoWa guitarist Jon Latvis and made the cover of *Resistance* magazine's issue 8 in 1996, has released a number of ballads, including a
full 2002 Panzerfaust Records ballad album called *Thunderclap*. Likewise, the
US musician Eric Owens released two acoustic hate folk albums in the 1990s,
1994's *Folk the System!* and 1998's *Res Gestae* (Latin for great achievement or
autobiography).[86]

By far the most famous hate folk band to emerge from North America has
been the now-defunct child group Prussian Blue, comprised of twins Lamb
and Lynx Gaede, born in 1992. The girls' mother, April Gaede, has long been
a prominent US neo-Nazi activist in groups like the National Alliance and
National Vanguard.[87] April Gaede homeschooled her twins and began encouraging them to play white-power music in public in 2001, when they were only
nine years old.[88] They mainly played covers of white-power songs by other
bands, but composed a few songs of their own, including a white-power bub-
blegum love song called "Skinhead Boy" and a piece entitled "Hate for Hate:
Lamb near the Lane," which Lamb Gaede co-wrote via telephone conversations with the imprisoned US neo-Nazi terrorist David Lane.[89] According to
a 2004 *Resistance* magazine cover story on Prussian Blue, the Gaede sisters
chose their band name because the phrase "Prussian blue" referenced not
only their Prussian ancestry and blue eyes, but also "the color of the Zyklon B
residue . . . ha! ha!," a reference to the nonexistent blue pigment that Holocaust deniers mistakenly believe would have coated the walls of the Auschwitz
gas chambers if the rooms had really been used to gas thousands of victims.[90]
The Gaede twins released their Prussian Blue albums *Fragment of the Future*
on Resistance Records in 2004 and *The Path We Chose* independently in 2005,
appeared in two television documentaries, featured in a relatively positive article in the mainstream *GQ* magazine, and nearly received a story in *Teen People*
magazine before rumors of a "sanitized" story without references to the words
"'hate,' 'supremacist,' or 'Nazi'" spurred major protests in front of *Teen People*'s
New York offices and caused the magazine's editors to withdraw the story.[91]

In their mid-teens, both Lamb and Lynx Gaede began expressing doubts
about the racist ideologies they had been conveying in their music. Upon
developing serious health issues in their late teens, the Gaede twins became
outspoken advocates for medical marijuana legalization in the United
States and made a complete break with the white-power movement.[92] Lamb

Gaede—who had said to *Resistance* magazine in 2004 that "I want to be an official spokeswoman for the National Alliance"—told a reporter in 2011, "I'm not a white nationalist anymore. [. . .] I was just spouting a lot of knowledge that I had no idea what I was saying."[93]

Reactions to Prussian Blue have been mixed in the white-power community. Even some of the most glowing reviewers on Stormfront acknowledge that the Gaede twins were relative musical novices when they produced their two Prussian Blue albums; one user, for example, wrote in a 2005 review of *Fragment of the Future* that "When you listen to the first tracks on the CD you can tell the girls are nervous. They make a few mistakes and there's a certain uncomfortable sound in their voices. [. . .] When listening to this it's important to remember that it's a debut CD produced by a pair of 11-year-olds. With that in mind the CD, as a whole, is quite impressive. They don't have the very polished, professional sound of the much more experienced, adult bands such as Saga or Annett, but in a few years they'll probably rival anyone."[94] At the same time, other Stormfront users are even less sanguine about the Prussian Blue legacy, pointing out that the popular-media firestorm surrounding the Gaedes portrayed the white-power movement as ruthless and corrupt: "I can't imagine how she [April Gaede] thought forming 'Prussian Blue' would actually benefit the WN [white-nationalist] Movement as a whole. As controversial as it is to say in WN circles—Prussian Blue did a whole lot more for our enemies than they did for us. Just think how many Jewish media moguls were literally salivating at the prospect of spinning the Gaede twins as being brainwashed into 'hate' and 'Nazism.'"[95] Still others adopt the view that any publicity for racist organizations is good publicity, and that Prussian Blue—along with white-power music in general—benefited white-power political organizations in considerable measure simply by attracting any mainstream attention at all to the cause. As one Stormfront user wrote in 2014,

> Remember at one point the twins were even featured in *GQ* magazine. That's some serious publicity and it wasn't so negative. Perhaps April thought the angelic looking twins could help nullify some of the preconceptions people had about "Nazis and racists." Another angle is that most Whites will not respond to an objective argument. They are ruled by emotion and so can only be reached through emotional appeals and entertainment. This is one reason why Dr. [William] Pierce went into the record business.[96]

Whatever the individual white-power believer's opinion of the band's impact, it is clear that despite the Gaede twins' short-lived white-power music career, Prussian Blue attracted more mainstream attention to the North American white-power music scene than almost any other act yet to emerge, including even Bound for Glory and other bands that have produced dozens of albums and generated significant, long-standing white-power fan bases. Prussian Blue also demonstrated to North American white-power music producers and distributors that acoustic hate folk music could sell. For fans, Lamb and Lynx Gaede provided an alternative to the more typical oi!, hardcore, and metal sounds of the average male-dominated, tattooed white-power rock band. The controversy surrounding them seems mostly to have abated now that they have retired from white-power activism, but they left an important mark on the North American white-power music scene nonetheless.

In addition to Prussian Blue, Griffin, and Eric Owens, several other North American white-power musicians have experimented with acoustic hate music, blending elements of European-derived folk music with electronica and orchestral soundscapes to create a nihilistic, Laveyan-Satanist form of white-power experimental noise music. Many Stormfront users have argued that white-power experimental noise music and NSBM have replaced the oi!-based punk sound of most 1980s and 1990s white-power music as the most popular sound of white-power music in the United States over the past decade.[97] This is a particularly interesting development, because as late as 2008, NSBM fans from Europe were almost universally panning the bands that emerged from what was then a tiny, fledgling US-based NSBM scene. A Stormfront user from Croatia, for example, in a 2008 review of the 2002 album *Vinlandic Stormtroopers* by the US-based NSBM band Gestapo SS, rates the album only 3 stars out of 10 and explains, "Gestapo SS is from the U.S.A. and the NSBM scene there is not worth[y] of attention. The real scene is in Poland, Norway, Ukraine, Russia, etc. [. . .] This album is awful. Guitars are good but vocals and guitars aren't tuned. Quality is also on the low level. [. . .] This album was released in 2002. It means that they haven't recorded a new material for six years and I hope it will stay that way."[98]

In recent years, however, US-based white-power metal and electronic musicians have begun to receive more attention from the international white-power community. White-power ambient "dark-wave" electronic songs by Michael Moynihan's band Blood Axis, for instance, mix fiddle tunes from the British Isles with electronica and spoken-word voiceovers to invoke both a martial and a purportedly traditional European folk ethos. Moynihan himself co-authored a 1998 book called *Lords of Chaos: The Bloody Rise of the Satanic Metal Underground*, which glorifies Varg Víkernes and other members of the violent 1990s Norwegian NSBM scene, de-emphasizing the racism although not the violence inherent in the genre's lyrics and ideologies. A friend of Moynihan's, the minimalist white-power dark-wave experimental musician Boyd Rice of the band NON, made public connections with both Tom Metzger's White Aryan Resistance hate group and Bob Heick's neo-Nazi American Front.[99] In fact, Heick himself has dabbled in white-power industrial and dark-wave music under the pseudonym Robert X. Patriot.[100] Moynihan has also helped to record other white-power dark-wave experimental and neo-folk bands, such as R. N. Taylor's "apocalyptic folk" band Changes, collaborating with the fascist experimental musician Thomas Thorn in bands like Slave State and Sleep Chamber.[101] While these groups have not confined themselves only to acoustic music, they have used elements of European-derived folk and acoustic music strategically as a way of claiming sonic links with supposedly primeval pre-modern European folk traditions. Some US white-power bands now even play actual white-power electronica, including the one-man studio project Genocide Lolita, responsible for songs such as "Holocaust Erotica," "Gulag Mentality," and "I Want to Kill the President."

Of course, the United States and Canada have also been home to many white-power bands who play in the genre's more traditional punk and heavy metal musical styles. The United States' Bound for Glory and Canada's RaHoWa have been among the most famous of these, complemented by other star acts like Blue Eyed Devils, Bully Boys, Empire Falls, Max Resist, Nordic Thunder, Intimidation One, Vinland Warriors, and Youngland.

At least one spectacular mass murderer has emerged to date from these musicians' ranks, the bassist Wade Michael Page. Page had been involved for many years with US white-power bands like End Apathy, Youngland, Max Resist, Definite Hate, Intimidation One, Aggressive Force, Blue Eyed Devils, and 13 Knots, a band that took its name from the fact that there are thirteen knots in a noose. He had even worked with a few European groups, such as Billy Bartlett's long-running Welsh band Celtic Warrior and the embattled German group Radikahl.[102] In early August 2012, Page shot to death six people at a Sikh temple in the US city of Milwaukee, Wisconsin, subsequently killing himself as well.[103] In the aftermath of the shooting, police discovered that he had belonged to and/or been involved with several white-power extremist organizations in the United States, including the National Alliance, the Ku Klux Klan, Volksfront, and the Northern Hammerskins, of which he had become a patched member about a year prior to his shooting rampage.[104] Page's shooting spree brought white-power music to the attention of many people in the United States for the first time, although watchdog groups and government organizations had been tracking white-power music and musicians for at least two decades before his attack.

Before Page, other US-based white-power musicians had also been involved in major, ideologically motivated criminal activities. Among the most notorious were Scott Stedeford and Kevin McCarthy of the band Day of the Sword, one of the few major bands in the international white-power music web to advocate the racist doctrine of Christian Identity rather than variants of indigenous Northern European paganism. Even though most fans of white-power music seem to identify themselves as racist pagans rather than as racist Christians, the fan response to Day of the Sword's music has been consistently positive in the two decades since the band released its albums; Stormfront's Ju-87, for example, wrote in 2005 that Day of the Sword was "one of my favorite WN bands. Scott is a great singer and the lyrics are absolutely fantastic. Although a lot of them are Christian based (a religion that I loathe), it is not disturbing. Strong, proud pro-white texts and great music."[105]

Both Stedeford and McCarthy were members of a terrorist cell called the Aryan Republican Army, which robbed dozens of banks in the United States' Midwest region during the mid-1990s as part of a plan to fund and foment an Aryan revolution in the United States. The ARA funneled hundreds of thousands of stolen dollars into white-power projects that included not only Day of the Sword recordings, but also—according to reputable researchers such as the American criminologist Mark S. Hamm and the British journalist Ambrose Evans-Pritchard—the Oklahoma City bombing plot of their known associate Timothy McVeigh, who may even himself have been involved in some of the ARA's bank robberies prior to his arrest.[106] McVeigh's bombing of the Murrah Federal Building in Oklahoma City killed 168 people, including nineteen children—the deadliest act of domestic terrorism in US history.[107] No members of the ARA were ever arrested or tried for complicity in the bombing, despite evidence of at least some collaboration with McVeigh in the months prior, but they certainly stood trial in the late 1990s for their bank robberies.[108] Kevin McCarthy, the youngest member of the cell, served as the prosecution's lead witness against Scott Stedeford and other members of the ARA, receiving only a five-year sentence and then disappearing into the US federal witness protection program.[109] Stedeford is still serving his thirty-year sentence, but has publicly renounced racism, continuing to play music in a prison band that avoids racial bias.[110]

Even if the links between these former Day of the Sword members and the Oklahoma City bombing prove to be inconsequential, as the US government asserted when it chose to prosecute only Timothy McVeigh and Terry Nichols for the attack, the white-power music scene in the United States and Canada clearly has a broad reach. In fact, this scene is one of the biggest in the world, and its importance lies not only in its numerical strength, but also in its ability to provide the international white-power music web with relatively stable locations from which to host recording labels and Internet sites like the Stormfront community. While mainstream society in the United States and Canada generally considers the overt display of neo-Nazi and white-power imagery to be taboo, and while governmental and non-governmental organizations often monitor hate groups' activities, white-power groups can generally operate without fear of direct government censorship in the United States and Canada unless they engage in actively violent behavior. US and Canadian white-power bands often write and perform songs with lyrics that are more overtly racist and violent than those by European bands, simply because they *can* do so without fear of imprisonment. These musicians might complain about government persecution in the lyrics to their songs, but these two countries—and the United States in particular—maintain some of the most lenient policies toward hate speech in the western world. The long-term existence of North American white-power recording and distribution labels like Resistance Records has provided the international white-power music web with a level of permanence that has proven elusive in many European countries.

Although some subgenres of white-power music are based in musical traditions that developed primarily in Europe, it is also important to note that the rock 'n' roll music which constitutes the basis of the white-power music soundscape is—like its country music cousin—fundamentally a North American innovation, born out of the confluence of European and African traditions in the US South among the descendants of freed slaves and their white neighbors in the immediate post–World War II era. In fact, for decades after rock 'n' roll began to appear on pop-music charts around the world, prominent white-supremacist activists were decrying rock 'n' roll music as one of the United States' *worst* international exports, echoing the sentiments of the 1950s pro-segregationist spokesman Asa Carter, president of the racist Alabama White Citizens' Council, who commented to news cameras in 1956 that "the obscenity and vulgarity of [. . .] rock 'n' roll music is obviously a means by which the white man and his children can be driven to the level with a 'nigra.'"[111]

Yet once punk and heavy-metal musicians had begun to play forms of rock 'n' roll music aimed almost exclusively at white audiences, using elements of Nazi iconography for shock value and stripping overt markers of African-derived musical traditions like complex polyrhythms and cyclical structures away from their music, white-power activists found it relatively easy to reformulate a genre of music with mixed-race roots into a vehicle for violently pro-white political ideologies. In fact, the loud volume and stage-centric nature of standard rock concerts—as well as the tradition of celebrity hero worship common among fans of mainstream rock musicians like the Rolling Stones and Nirvana—suit authoritarian political movements particularly well. These elements foster performance situations in which the sheer volume of the concert hinders audience participation in or real-time feedback on the sound or the message of the music, and charismatic musicians like George Burdi and Ian Stuart Donaldson can style themselves as figureheads of their political movements in the same vein as actual dictators like Hitler, Mussolini, and Franco. Moreover, the popularity of rock 'n' roll in late-twentieth- and early-twenty-first-century youth culture has made rock music a convenient tool for attracting new adherents to white-power politics and organizations. In other words, while white-power musicians are clearly conscious of the fact that rock 'n' roll music has an embarrassing mixed-race parentage, they draw on rock 'n' roll for sonic material because the genre bears enough contemporary advantages to outweigh its inconvenient history. While the music that has emerged from North American white-power music scenes does not tend to sound particularly different from European white-power music—at least with the exception of hate country music, which *has* emanated almost solely from US-based musicians—this is because North American–derived musical traditions have had a heavy impact on popular music styles in Europe and elsewhere over the past century, rather than because North American white-power musicians have contributed little to the sound of white-power music on an international level.

As the prominence of mixed-race artistic movements like rock 'n' roll and country music attest, the United States, Canada, and other former European settler colonies have long served as "melting pots" of white identities from across the European continent. For this reason, white-power musicians from the United States and Canada have helped to encourage the idea of pan-white unity among white-power believers in Europe itself, arguing that whites should abandon national-chauvinist ideologies in order to focus on the purported threat to their entire race from non-whites. The white-nationalist discourses of ZOG conspiracy theory and "no more brothers war" therefore owe much of their popularity to the activism of white-power musicians and believers from North America. It remains to be seen how the white-power music scene in the United States and Canada will develop now that its most prominent and long-lived record label, Resistance Records, is starting life anew. Given the prevalence of racism and the lenient hate-speech laws in these two countries, it seems the scene will likely continue to reinvent itself and to produce new bands and recordings into the future.

Latin America

The United States and Canada are home to the *biggest* white-power music scene in the Americas, but not the *only* one. In fact, Latin America has for decades produced its own white-power musicians. The presence of violent white-power racism and white-power music in Anglophone and Francophone North America, areas that are currently home to majority-white populations, makes at least some sense to most outside observers. The fact that white-power music also exists in Latin America, albeit on a smaller scale, seems more puzzling on initial examination. In fact, local white-power bands have been playing in some South American countries, such as Argentina and Brazil, since the early 1980s, initially developing there exactly at the same time as white-power music began to appear among European-descended communities elsewhere in the world. Some South American white-power bands maintain the hard-line, Nordic-centered racism of Northern European white-power music scenes, while others earn the ridicule of white-power believers elsewhere by featuring mestizo members in their lineups.

Both white-power music and pro-white racism in Latin America stem from many of the same historical processes that have influenced the development of racist music and racist movements in the United States and Canada. While populations in most of South and Central America are heavily dominated by the indigenous and mestizo descendants of South America's original inhabitants—and, in some areas like northern Brazil and the Caribbean, also by large numbers of African Americans whose ancestors labored as imported slaves on Spanish and Portuguese plantations—Latin America is home to white settler communities descended not only from the area's original Spanish and Portuguese colonizers, but also from later immigrants from countries like Germany, Russia, and Ukraine. As in the United States and Canada, the forbears of these Latin American white populations perpetrated the wholesale slaughter and mass enslavement of many Latin American indigenous groups, destroying native empires like the Inca and the Aztec in order to exploit local labor and resources.[112] For many indigenous and even mestizo groups, this oppression is ongoing; a right-wing Guatemalan government supported by US and Canadian anti-communist military forces, for instance, used mass murder, systemic rape, and torture to commit genocide against Guatemala's indigenous Maya in the 1980s, and continues to oppress this group violently today.[113]

As in many other parts of the world, widespread poverty and the economic exploitation of non-whites have accompanied this racist political oppression and naked violence in much of Latin America. Areas with majority-indigenous and/or majority-black populations like Brazil's northern Bahia province are typically the poorest places on the continent; to cite just one of many such examples, a 2007 United Nations report found that people of African descent made up 48 percent of Brazil's total population, but their incomes constituted only 20 percent of the country's GDP, and 78 percent of them lived below the poverty line.[114] This vast income inequality is representative of the rest of Latin America as well.[115] Indigenous, mestizo, and African-descended sweatshop workers across Latin America produce low-cost clothing and other consumer goods for western markets, often toiling in dangerous conditions for below-subsistence wages.[116] In short, European settlers may not dominate the population demographics in most Latin American countries the way they do in the United States and Canada, but the vestiges of European colonialism appear in the region's economic and political systems nonetheless.

Given the racism inherent in the European colonial and post-colonial systems in Latin America, it should come as little surprise that at least a few of the European-descended individuals in the region—including even some mestizos—have identified strongly with European racist and authoritarian movements. In fact, some of the post–World War II dictatorships in South America, such as the Perón regime in Argentina and the Vargas regime in Brazil, took influence from the philosophies of Hitler, Mussolini, and Franco, building right-wing governments that mixed homegrown South American populism with European fascism.[117] This fascism sometimes manifested different forms of pro-white racism than Hitler's Nazism or even Mussolini's archetypal Fascism, as when the genocidal WWII–era dictator of the Dominican Republic, Rafael Trujillo, agreed to accept thousands of Jewish refugees from Nazi-occupied Europe in a bid to "whiten" the population of his country, even while orchestrating the murders of tens of thousands of African-descended Haitians living along the Dominican Republic's border with Haiti.[118] Nonetheless, this affinity with the Nazis and other European totalitarian regimes in the World War II era led several Latin American countries to provide safe haven to many notorious Nazi war criminals after the war's end. In the years immediately following the war, South American governments accepted—sometimes knowingly—as many as 9,000 wanted Nazi war criminals, including top-level personnel like Adolf Eichmann and Josef Mengele (Argentina), Walter Rauff and Paul Schaeffer (Chile), Franz Stangl and his subordinate Gustav Wagner (Brazil), and Klaus Barbie (Bolivia).[119]

When these Nazi refugees from international prosecution arrived in South America, they found local South American Nazi supporters waiting for them. The most prominent of these was the Chilean diplomat Miguel Serrano. Serrano—despite his widely known World War II–era background as a member of the Movimiento Nacional Socialista de Chile (National Socialist movement of Chile) or Nacistas (Nazis), as well as his editorship of a wartime Chilean Nazi magazine—was appointed Chilean ambassador first to India, then to Yugoslavia, and finally to Austria between 1953 and 1970, serving also as a representative to both the United Nations Organisation for Industrial Development and the International Atomic Energy Commission.[120] Serrano wrote prolifically, publishing Nazi and neo-Nazi materials before, during, and after his international diplomatic career. He advanced an eclectic philosophy of esoteric Nazism that mixed the Jungian *völkisch* nationalism and anti-Semitism of the Third Reich with indigenous Aztec cosmology, Gnostic Christianity, and Indo-Aryan mysticism derived from the writings of both the Greek-French Nazi mystic Savitri Devi (nee Maximiani Portas) and the Italian neo-fascist Julius Evola.[121] Serrano, like Evola, argued that the white race was descended from extraterrestrial gods called Hyperboreans, and that Hitler was a Hyperborean avatar come to Earth to end a dark age of race-mixing. To establish the racial legitimacy of South American Nazism, Serrano drew on the work of early-twentieth-century pseudo-scholars who had posited the existence of a Viking empire in South America. He tried to demonstrate that

Aryan demigods had come to the Americas thousands of years before Columbus, but had been largely displaced by Jewish-influenced indigenous tribes.[122]

Although many of Serrano's theories sound bizarre, it is important to remember that some of the Third Reich's highest officials—particularly Heinrich Himmler—also explored the links between Hitler's pro-Aryan movement in Germany and ancient Indo-Aryans outside Europe.[123] Serrano's writings resonate with many individuals who are interested in the esoteric and occult Nazi theories propagated by Himmler's colleagues and subordinates. The success of fictional mainstream feature films portraying sensationalized versions of this Nazi mysticism, most notably *Indiana Jones and the Raiders of the Lost Ark*, suggests that this topic enjoys relatively widespread appeal among individuals who repudiate Nazi crimes as well as among those who seek to emulate them.

Given Serrano's international prominence and his long tenure in South American neo-Nazi movements—he was active in Chilean Nazism from before World War II well into the 1990s, and died only in 2009—it is unsurprising that some members of the South American neo-Nazi community today subscribe to elements of his Nazi occult belief system.[124] The Chilean white-power band Triskel, for instance—named for the triskelion, triskele, or rolling sevens symbol, significant in white-power music circles because it serves as the logo for Blood & Honour—performs a song called "Hyperborea," referencing Serrano's belief that the white race descends from divine extraterrestrials who settled on a now-submerged continent called Hyperborea, located at the North Pole. Some Latin American white-power and neo-Nazi bands, like the Mexican NSBM group Kukulcan (named for a Mayan snake deity), follow Serrano in celebrating indigenous Mayan and Aztec mythology as a homegrown aspect of their neo-Nazism. A supporter of racist skinhead groups, Serrano actually spoke to an interviewer about his interactions with neo-Nazi skinheads in the early 1990s, saying that their street-level attacks on homosexuals and drug addicts in Chile were "stupendous!" and adding that racist skinheads "represent the most profound and important values of the Chilean people."[125]

For Latin American white-power activists, Serrano represents an important bridge between the World War II era and the contemporary racist skinhead movement. His activism helped to introduce Nazi and neo-Nazi occult theories to a new generation of racist believers in the 1980s and 1990s, demonstrating how Latin Americans of European descent could incorporate indigenous Latin American mythology and cultural traditions into a racist movement that often viewed indigenous Americans as racially other. The origins of contemporary Latin American white-power musicians' pro-Latin-American brand of neo-Nazism in Serrano's Nazi mysticism suggest that, far from being a fluke or a misunderstanding of real Nazi philosophy, the eclectic and international mélange of occult racism that appears in some contemporary Latin American white-power music actually stems from traditions that date back to the Third Reich's own obsession with esoteric mysticism and historical revisionism. Not all Chilean white-power activists support Serrano's interpretation of Nazism; a musician who performs under the name Alejandro Rex, for example, blames Serrano for "confusing" indigenous Chileans into believing that they can be Nazis: "His ideas or bad interpretations had generated confusion in Chilean National-Socialists (making many Chilean native people from here enter to this worldview [National-Socialism])" (brackets in the original).[126]

Nostalgia for Third Reich ideology—both mystical and otherwise—has in fact been present in Latin American white-power music from the inception of the racist oi! punk scene there in the early 1980s. Latin American white-power music appeared first in Argentina in 1983 with the foundation of the racist oi! skinhead band Comando Suicida (a band name that is Spanish for suicide command, and which refers to the musicians' outrage at the British slaughter of Argentine troops in the 1982 Falklands War). From the outset, Comando Suicida expressed clear neo-Nazi sympathies, unlike early racist bands in countries like Germany and Russia, where radicalization occurred more gradually. For example, one member of Comando Suicida issued the following statement on post–World War II non-white immigration into Europe: "Since World War II ended there's been a plot to destroy Europe, a racial destruction. [. . .] They filled Germany with Turks, France with Algerians, England with Pakistanis. . . . That's a way of filling Europe with shit [. . .] to spoil the good that is left in European blood."[127] This musician, of course, communicates frustration with non-white immigration into previously white-controlled areas, which is a key tenet of white-power and neo-Nazi ideologies worldwide. Also, his statement of solidarity with white Europeans against non-white immigrants suggests that he wants European white-power and neo-Nazi sympathizers from outside South America to view him as a fellow member of their white racial elite. Moreover, Comando Suicida's song lyrics repeatedly express hostility toward Catholics, Jews, and homosexuals, further aligning the band with European neo-Nazi political platforms. These blatant neo-Nazi sentiments are important primarily because the group played a central role in the early Latin American white-power music scene. Comando Suicida continues to be the most famous group ever to have emerged from Latin American white-power music, filling for the microcosm of Latin American white-power music a role similar to that of Skrewdriver and Ian Stuart Donaldson in the international white-power music web overall. Despite breaking up and re-forming several times throughout the 1990s and eventually folding for good in the 2000s, Comando Suicida helped other musicians to ascertain what it meant to be in a Latin American white-power band.

By the late 1980s and early 1990s, other white-power skinhead bands had begun to appear in Argentina alongside Comando Suicida. These included most prominently Ultrasur (a band name that references Madrid's Ultras Sur organization, comprised of die-hard "ultra" fans of the Real Madrid soccer team), Razón y Fuerza (reason and force), Accion Radical (radical action), Reaccion Violenta (violent reaction), Legión Argentina (legion Argentina), Producto Nacional (domestic product), and Krisis Nerviosa (nervous break-down). Few of these groups achieved the longevity of Comando Suicida, but they did contribute to a sustained Argentinean white-power music scene that continues to exist today. Some of their songs, such as Ultrasur's "NS [National Socialism]," appear in cover versions by contemporary Argentinean white-power bands like Muerte y Calaveras (death and skulls).[128]

In recent years, a new generation of white-power and neo-Nazi bands has dominated the Argentinean scene, led not only by Muerte y Calaveras, but also other groups like Battaglione (Italian for battalion) and Borcegasso.[129] Interestingly, these groups take influence not only from Skrewdriver and the seminal 1980s British white-power oi! scene, as do white-power musicians elsewhere in the world, but also from Spain's "classic" 1980s and 1990s white-power bands. Latin American white-power bands today often use covers of older Spanish white-power songs to close their sets at gigs, because their audiences recognize and enjoy many of these songs; a few of these Spanish white-power songs, like Klan's "Skinheads por Siempre" (skinheads forever) and División 250's "Revuelta" (revolt) seem to function as "standards" that members of multiple bands know and can play together as encores.[130] This affinity for Spanish-language white-power music from Europe helps members of the Latin American white-power scene to situate themselves as members of the international white-power music web and to emphasize their cultural and biological links with the European continent.

White-power musicians from all over Latin America, not just from Argentina, use their music to express love for European-descended culture. In fact, although the first white-power band in Latin America formed in Argentina, the white-power skinhead movement as a whole began in neighboring Brazil. The very first Latin American ultra-nationalist and neo-Nazi skinhead gangs developed there in 1981 in São Paulo, a city that was once home to Franz Stangl, the fugitive former commandant of the Nazi death camps at Sobibór and Treblinka, and that has served as the center of Brazil's white-power skin-head activities in the decades since Stangl's arrest.[131] Early São Paulo white-power skinhead gangs like White Power Skinheads, Carecas do Suburbio (skinheads of the suburbs), and Carecas do ABC (skinheads of ABC, referring to the first letters of three different working-class São Paulo neighborhoods) tormented the city's homosexuals and *Nordestinos*—that is, northeasterners, economic migrants to the white-dominated cities of the Brazilian south from the country's impoverished and African-Brazilian-dominated northeastern states.[132] In at least one case in 1994, members of the Carecas do ABC gang even murdered a homeless black teenager.[133] In the late 1980s, skinhead gangs rapidly began appearing in other Brazilian cities as well, although the highest numbers remained in São Paulo; by the end of the decade, the country was home to approximately 1,000 racist skinheads, the most of any country in Latin America to date, partially due to its large total population in comparison to those of other Latin American countries.[134]

While the Brazilian white-power music scene started slightly later than the scene in Argentina, it has produced several well-known neo-Nazi and white-power bands. The first was Locomotiva (locomotive), which also sometimes referred to itself as Locomotiva 88, and which formed in the Mauá municipality of São Paulo in 1987.[135] Among the band's many racist tenets was the belief that Brazil's southern states should separate from its northern states in order to prevent a further influx of African-Brazilian economic migrants to the south from the northeast. Band members edited the white-power music skinzine *Raça & Pátria* (race & fatherland), styling it after the British magazine *Blood & Honour* and publishing in both Portuguese and English to appeal to an international market. They also organized a large concert called Rock Against Communism São Paulo in December 1989, the first of its kind in South America. Locomotiva broke up in the early 1990s after running afoul of Brazil's new 1988 constitution, which for the first time labeled racism a crime and allowed the city of São Paulo to pass a law banning the swastika. Two members of the band, however, did return for a short-lived reunion in 2007.[136] Locomotiva served as the premier band in a burgeoning Brazilian white-power music scene that soon grew to include bands like Evil, Frente Nacional (national front), Grupo Separatista Branco (white separatist group, again referencing the idea that southern Brazil should split from the northern parts of the country)—which later changed its name to Brigada NS (NS [National Socialist] brigade)—and Rêsistencia 1945 (resistance 1945). A few recent Brazilian musicians have even begun to play NSBM, including a one-man NSBM studio project that operates under the band name Command.

The new Brazilian constitution's statute against racism clearly had an overall adverse effect on the Brazilian white-power music scene, which peaked in the early 1990s. Like Locomotiva, members of the prominent Brazilian white-power band Defesa Armada (armed resistance) found themselves in legal trouble in the 1990s. Formed in the São Paulo suburb of Santo André in 1995 as one of the few white-power rock bands anywhere in the world to feature a female lead singer, Defesa Armada had to change its name to D.A. in 1997 to avoid being associated with two CDs featuring illegal racist sentiments that it had recorded in its first two years. While the group toned down its racist rhetoric after that point, it continued to denounce "the communist menace" and "the mistake of promoting homosexuality" in the lyrics to its songs, sentiments that are still legal under Brazilian law.[137] Other, later Brazilian white-power bands such as Grupo Separatista Branco/Brigada NS, Southern Warriors, and São Paulo Reich have chosen to continue expressing neo-Nazi sentiments despite the risk, even traveling to play concerts for white-power audiences in Argentina.[138]

Like Argentina and Brazil, Miguel Serrano's home country of Chile has produced several white-power bands of note. The most prominent band to emerge there was a group called Rockanoi!, whose members were direct followers of Serrano's esoteric and occult neo-Nazi philosophies.[139] Rockanoi! went so far as to write a song about Serrano, entitled "One in a Million," in addition to songs dedicated to prominent figures from the Third Reich, including Adolf Hitler ("Someone Like You Will Never Be Forgotten") and Rudolph Hess ("Camarada Rudolph Hess," Spanish for comrade Rudolph Hess). By the mid-1990s, a core of Chilean white-power skinheads numbered around 200, and had spawned an increasing number of bands, such as División Gamada (swastika division), Tropa SS (SS troop), Sieg'88 (German for victory '88), and Odal Sieg (a band name that is German for odal victory, referring to the Proto-Germanic Elder Futhark odal rune, whose name denoted nobility, lineage, and race, making this band name a combination of ancient and contemporary Germanic words meaning something akin to "racial victory" or "victory of the noble race").[140] Today, Santiago remains the center of white-power music in Chile, but the scene in Magallan—home to recent bands like Marcha Violenta (violent march)—has also risen in size and reputation.[141] While the Chilean white-power music scene is numerically smaller than those in Argentina and Brazil, several of its bands have toured elsewhere in Latin America, playing important roles in the white-power music scenes of the region in general.

Scattered white-power bands and local white-power music scenes also exist elsewhere in Latin America, although the scenes in Argentina, Brazil, and Chile are the most prominent in the region. A limited white-power skinhead scene in Uruguay fostered a 1990s neo-Nazi band called Escuadrón 88 (squadron 88), and while this band broke up after recording only one demo album, one member re-formed it in 2012 and began performing again. In 2009, another Uruguayan neo-Nazi band called Contra Ataque 88 (counterattack 88) joined Escuadrón 88, and is still playing gigs and recording albums.[142] Colombia—where racist skinhead groups have developed since 1993 in the cities of Bogotá, Medellin, Pereira and Cali—has also produced several white-power bands, including Orgullo Nacional (national pride) and Huetramannaland (a band name which, according to the band, is an ancient name for America meaning "land of the white gods," and which the band chose because it references Miguel Serrano's idea that Aryans arrived in the Americas thousands of years before Columbus).[143] Isolated white-power bands have emerged in other places, such as the Guatamalan band Nazgul SS (a band name that references both Hitler's SS and the evil ring-wraiths or *Nazgûl* from J.R.R. Tolkien's *Lord of the Rings* trilogy), Comando de Exterminio (extermination commando) and Kukulcan from Mexico, Auschwitz from Puerto Rico, and Khristienn Corpse and Schutzstaffel (German for protective force, the full name of Hitler's SS military organization) from Venezuela.

One interesting feature of some of these Latin American white-power bands is that they occasionally seem to feature members whom white-power believers from Europe regard as non-white. Because white-power activists typically consider individuals with any amount of non-European heritage to be an embarrassment to their cause, members of white-power and neo-Nazi bands nearly always claim exclusively European descent, making it difficult to ascertain whether specific musicians really *are* of non- or only part-European heritage. However, rumors circulate widely throughout the international white-power music web that members of particular Latin American white-power bands are actually mestizo, Jewish, part-African, or otherwise not fully white. As was true in the case of Panzerfaust Records founder Anthony Pierpont in the United States, these types of rumors certainly appear in white-power music scenes outside of Latin America too, but white-power musicians and fans from outside Latin America seem far more skeptical of Latin American white-power bands than those from anywhere else in the world.

The rumors that follow these bands often conflict with one another, demonstrating that even the accusers often have little idea whether or not their claims are correct. The neo-Nazi *Revolt NS* blog reported in 2012, for instance, that "Expulsos Do Bar [kicked out of the bar] is a OI band of Espirito Santo state [in Brazil]; [. . .] the band have a nigger on his formation, ridiculous" [sic], an accusation which stands in direct contrast to a Greek zine interview with the Brazilian white-power band Southern Warriors, who denounce a number of other "crossbred idiots" but are happy to report simply that "EXPULSOS DO BAR it is a nationalistic band."[144] Likewise, the Greek Stormfront user galazoaimatos-hellas—a heavy contributor to Stormfront threads about white-power music in Latin America—questions even the ethnic backgrounds of the founding Latin American white-power bands Comando Suicida and Locomotiva, writing,

> commando suicida has members mestizo, this band was anticommunist patriotic argentinian and football fans of san lorenzo [the soccer team San Lorenzo de Almagro] we cant say it is w.p. [white power]

some bands probably have also mestizo members like paliza88 [beating88],
huetramannaland, sociedad violenta [violent society], bandeira de combate
[combat flag], estirpe 86 [race 86], armada oi! [navy oi! or fleet oi!]

locomotica from brazil was the first latin rac band from 1988 but they had one
brazilian jewish member if i a m correct. [*sic*][145]

The same user follows this account—which mistakenly names Locomotiva and
not Comando Suicida as the earliest white-power band in Latin America—
with another post that asks, "can anyone exp[l]ain me why so many mestizo
people in latin america use these ns [National Socialist] symbols and tries to be
white i can t understand that!!!" [*sic*][146]

Actually, the willingness of some mestizo Latin Americans to tolerate and
even to embrace violently pro-European racist ideologies like Nazism stems
from a particular understanding of racial hierarchy and miscegenation that
developed in Latin America, a system markedly different from the Anglophone North American concept of hypodescent or "one drop of blood," which
automatically assigns individuals of mixed-race heritage to the racial categories of their lowest-ranking ancestors, meaning that someone in Anglophone
North America with only one non-white great-grandparent or great-great-
grandparent might in some cases still be considered just as black as someone
of completely African descent. In much of Latin America, in contrast, race-
mixing has historically represented a gradual means of "whitening" the population, and the greater an individual's proportion of European ancestors, the
higher he or she has usually ranked in the region's racial hierarchies.[147] Rather
than appearing as despised mongrels, the way mixed-race individuals often
have in Anglophone North America and in Nazi Germany, mestizos in places
like Brazil and the Dominican Republic have tended to comprise large segments of the upwardly mobile middle classes.[148]

In Latin America, portraying oneself as white even when one obviously
had some non-European ancestors could historically serve as a means of social
advancement. The World War II–era Dominican dictator Rafael Trujillo was
rumored to wear light-colored makeup to make his skin appear whiter than it
really was, using this as a way of legitimizing his claim to leadership.[149] Small
wonder, then, that some mestizos in Latin America today adopt the ideology
and symbolism of pro-white racism. Their posturing carries on a long-running
Latin American tradition of mestizos asserting white identity in order to
place themselves in a privileged racial caste—even when others in that privileged caste might view their claims as dubious or fraudulent—and thereby to
advance themselves socially. To European white-power activists such as those
who respond to Stormfront posts on Latin American white-power music,

Latin American bands who mingle indigenous Aztec, Incan, and Mayan mythology with Nazi ideology or who play in mestizo neo-Nazi bands simply represent a miscarriage of true Nazism. The reality is more complex. In Latin America, the use of Nazi symbolism by white-power bands can, as one member of the Colombian band Terror Brigade told a Greek interviewer, denote a brand of anti-communism popular among even non-European-descended supporters of right-wing politics: "Sympathy towards anticommunism makes these [non-white] people use these [Nazi] symbols."[150] Moreover, mestizo pro-white racists in Latin America are still willing to commit racial violence and to support racist social structures that contribute to the economic exploitation of their darker-skinned compatriots. They represent a particularly Latin American conception of racism and racial hierarchy, one that leaves the Latin American white-power music scene in a tenuous relationship with white-power music scenes elsewhere in the world, but which resonates deeply with the local histories of pro-white racism and European colonialism.

Even the most Nordic-centered European neo-Nazis today are often willing to forego their suspicions of white-power believers from Southern and Eastern Europe in order to combat the purportedly larger threats of Jewish world domination and non-white immigration into Europe. They are clearly less willing to accept pro-white racists whose appearances bear obvious physical traces of non-European ancestry. Latin American white-power musicians of "pure" European descent are welcome in international white-power music scenes, but rumors of mestizo ancestry can humiliate white-power musicians and estrange them from the rest of the international white-power music web. In contrast to musicians from Mediterranean and Eastern European white-power music scenes, then—many of whom have been successful in arguing that contemporary neo-Nazis need to expand their categories of privilege to include *all* groups of European descent and not just Northwestern Europeans—Latin American white-power musicians demonstrate the limits of the international white-power music web. Neo-Nazism has often proven to be a flexible ideology that can change to fit new socio-historical circumstances, but it is not an *endlessly* flexible ideology. As a belief system centered around racial hierarchy, it still clearly rests on the concept that brown-skinned individuals with even a few recent ancestors of non-European descent are not eligible for inclusion in the racial elite. The contrast between the systems of racial categorization that developed in colonial Latin America and in Nazi Germany reveal yet again the socially constructed nature of racial classification, making Latin American white-power music a particularly interesting lens for studying how different groups of white-power and neo-Nazi believers determine who does and does not, for them, belong in the category of "white." This obsession with policing a shifting boundary between white and non-white individuals is a common theme throughout white-power music and represents an important point of confluence among white-power music scenes in different parts of the world, even if white-power musicians in some areas define whiteness differently than those in other places do.

Australia

Settler colonialism in Australia has followed many of the same general trends as it has in the Americas. In particular, because Australia was colonized mainly by the British, the colonialism there resembled the forms of settler colonialism that developed among fellow Anglophone colonies in the United States and Canada. Europeans took much longer to colonize Australia than they did the Americas, first documenting the continent's existence in 1606 and only developing permanent colonies there beginning in the 1780s, when the British realized that they would need territory for a new colony following the United States' successful war for independence.[151] Due to mounting population pressures, internal displacement, and poverty-driven crime in Industrial Revolution–era Britain, the British government decided to employ its new Australian territory as a prison colony, exporting approximately 160,000 convicts from the British Isles between 1788 and 1868 and using them as cheap labor to build the colony's infrastructure.[152]

Hostilities developed between these British convict colonies and the indigenous Australian Aboriginal population as early as the 1790s, erupting initially over access to water and food sources in areas near the colonies.[153] As in the Americas and other European settler colonies, the indigenous Australians' lack of immunity to European diseases hastened the European takeover.[154] Yet also as in the Americas, disease cannot account for the entirety of the massive indigenous death toll. The Aboriginal population declined from about 750,000 when the first convict colony was founded in 1788 to only 31,000 in 1911—a population collapse of almost 96 percent—while the European settler population increased from virtually none to more than 3.8 million in the same period.[155] On the large island of Tasmania off the southern coast of Australia, British settlers had actually wiped out the full-blooded indigenous population *in its entirety* by 1876, allowing only a small group of mixed-race children of indigenous women and European men to survive and carry on the legacy of the island's indigenous population.[156] On the larger and less densely populated mainland, coordinated extermination was more difficult to orchestrate than on Tasmania, but massacres devastated the indigenous population nonetheless.[157]

As the direct killing of Australian Aborigines waned in the earliest years of the twentieth century, the Aborigines who had survived the massacres began to have their children removed from them and taken to government-sponsored residential schools similar to those that operated in the United

States and Canada during the same period.[158] This particularly applied to so-called half-caste, or mixed-race, children of Aboriginal women and European men.[159] Like in the United States and Canada, residential schools for indigenous children were intended to force indigenous populations to assimilate into white society, but also like in the United States and Canada, authorities at these schools often simply abused the children rather than teaching them valuable skills.[160] Some children with *living* indigenous parents were actually given away to white adoptive parents outright without their biological parents' consent.[161] The Australian government apologized to these so-called Stolen Generations in 2008, but the official government apology pointedly sidestepped the term genocide in order to avoid having to pay monetary reparations to the victims of its child removal policies, despite the fact that, as stated above, these policies stood in direct violation of a provision in the 1948 United Nations Genocide Convention.[162] Critics such as the genocide scholar Tony Barta have therefore suggested that the apology's real effect has been to stifle Aboriginal complaints of contemporary structural discrimination and to "bury" the country's history of genocide.[163]

The traumatic legacy of child removal policies and other forms of oppression clearly still affects Australian Aborigines today. An Australian Council of Social Service report found in 2006 that indigenous households in Australia had a median income that comprised only 65 percent of the median income for non-indigenous households, and as recently as 2009, the Australian government instituted new race-based laws that applied only to Aborigines, banning alcohol and hardcore pornography only in Aboriginal communities and restricting how Aboriginal welfare recipients but not welfare recipients of other races could spend their checks.[164]

Studies demonstrate that non-Aboriginal racial minority groups in Australia also experience discriminatory acts from the majority-white population today; in a March 2014 poll, in fact, 41 percent of recent immigrants to Australia from non-English-speaking countries reported having experienced discrimination in the past year alone, with official discrimination complaints on the rise.[165] The immigration of unwanted racial and religious others has long been a contentious issue in Australia; for example, the World War II–era Australian government instituted multiple measures specifically designed to limit Jewish immigration to the country when Nazi persecution created a flood of refugee applications.[166] The Australian government certainly does not limit contemporary immigration the same way it stemmed the influx of Jewish refugees during the war, but relaxed government immigration policies do not preclude resentment over non-white immigration to Australia from at least some sectors of the European-Australian population.

In this climate, an Australian white-power music scene has developed in recent decades. White-power and neo-Nazi believers represent only a tiny minority of the European-descended population in Australia, but they, like white-power musicians and fans elsewhere, respond to specific local histories of racism and racial privilege in their work. In Australia, this prejudice often manifests in statements denouncing Australian Aborigines, non-white immigrants, Jews, and other purported enemies of the white race. One example of anti-Aboriginal rhetoric in the white-power music community comes from a regular columnist for *Blood & Honour* magazine who calls himself "The Mad N.S. Biker," who wrote in 2000 to ridicule the land claims of the remaining indigenous Tasmanians under the heading "Joking Or What?" His column states, "It appears [. . .] that unlike the Tasman tiger, the Tasman Aborigines were not all extinguished after all. It appears that living descendants of the indigenous populace of this place have come forward to jump on the overloaded bandwagon for 'Land rights.' Apparently their forebears were on holiday at the time that the rest of the tribe were killed off, and have only just returned from the mainland!"[167] In other words, this *Blood & Honour* columnist is suggesting that Aboriginal Australians from the mainland who have no right to land in Tasmania have traveled to Tasmania to file unjust land claims that will place a heavy burden on already overtaxed white Tasmanians. This rhetoric minimizes and mocks the violence that the white settler population perpetrated against the indigenous Tasmanians, although, crucially, this author does not deny the genocide the way many white-power writers do. This piece dismisses the well-known fact that some mixed-race indigenous Tasmanians survived the nineteenth-century genocide, and that it is their descendants and not Aborigines from the mainland who are now filing claims to restore parcels of land to indigenous Tasmanian groups. The Mad N.S. Biker suggests instead that these indigenous land claims are fraudulent and that no real indigenous Tasmanians exist anymore. Such rhetoric draws on mainstream Australian discourse expressing suspicion of Aboriginal land claims, evoking some white Australians' resentment at being made to feel guilty for human rights abuses committed by past generations. Responding to this convergence of mainstream and white-power conversations about Aboriginal rights is one of the key ways in which Australian white-power musicians and fans shape Australian white-power music to their own group and personal experiences today, and pieces such as this one help to reinforce popular conceptions of Aboriginal Australians as drains on public resources and as unworthy recipients of hard-earned tax dollars.

This kind of structural and interpersonal racism toward Aborigines, immigrants, and other non-whites has made Australia a fertile area for white-power music since the late 1970s and early 1980s. White-power music developed there at approximately the same time it did in Europe, and as an English-speaking country, Australia provided a key international link for the early white-power oi! punk scene in Britain. One of the first Australian white-power bands to emerge was the Perth band the Quick & the Dead, featuring vocalist Andrew Baird (aka Andrew Bored), bassist Murray Holmes (a.k.a. Murray Ohms), guitarist Mark Oakley, and drummer Andy McPherson (a.k.a. Andy Priest). Members of the Quick & the Dead regrouped in 1985 to form another white-power band, White Noise—also known for a short time as Final Solution, a reference to the Third Reich's *Endlösung* or "final solution" policy of exterminating Jews—and Murray Holmes even joined the legendary Skrewdriver for several years while living in Britain, playing on Skrewdriver's *Hail the New Dawn* album.[168]

Other Australian bands, like Open Season, White Lightning, and the especially extremist Fortress, followed the Quick & the Dead and White Noise onto the Australian scene before the end of the 1980s.[169] In particular, Fortress—led by vocalist Scott McGuinness, who has also been involved in several other white-power bands, including Axis, Exxtrem, Raven's Wing, and Dissident, which was a collaboration with the guitarist from Billy Bartlett's Welsh band Celtic Warrior—has become an internationally popular white-power band. The Stormfront CD reviewer Ju-87 points out in a 2008 review of the 1991 White Noise album *The First Assault* that Fortress and other key Australian white-power bands of the 1990s and 2000s were heavily influenced by White Noise, writing that White Noise "sounds like a more unpolished version of Scott [McGuinness] and the boys. White Noise had certainly a big influence on Fortress . . . both musically and lyrically."[170] Rather than simply following the example of Skrewdriver and other seminal bands in the European white-power scene, then, Australian white-power musicians clearly developed their own scene, listening to and interacting with one another as well as with bands from Europe.

In the 1980s and early 1990s, White Noise, Fortress, and other early Australian bands generally recorded their albums through Rock-O-Rama Records and Rebelles Européens; before Rebelles Européens collapsed, it even had a short-lived partnership with the Australian record label White League. After Rock-O-Rama and Rebelles Européens closed their doors in the early 1990s, Australian white-power music fans founded a number of different home-grown record labels, including 9% Productions (a label name that refers to a belief among many white-power groups that only 9 percent of the world's population is white)—which is still in operation at the time of writing—as well as War Doctrine/White Noise Productions, Heathen Noise Productions, and Scythian Services, which all now appear to be defunct. Many Australian white-power musicians beginning in the mid-1990s also chose to market their work through US distributors such as Resistance Records. As in other countries, Australian white-power bands of the early 1980s played in the oi! punk style, but as the 1980s wore on, bands began to incorporate elements of hardcore punk and heavy metal as well. In recent years, the metal sound has especially dominated the Australian white-power music scene.[171]

In 1992, the Australian film companies Film Victoria and Village Roadshow released a mainstream feature film called *Romper Stomper*, a cautionary tale about racist skinheads in Melbourne. The film—starring a twenty-eight-year-old Russell Crowe in one of his earliest roles—has since become a favorite among white-power musicians and fans worldwide. For instance, Denis Gerasimov, lead singer of the prominent Russian neo-Nazi band Kolovrat, explained to a Hungarian interviewer in 2010 that *Romper Stomper*, however "questionable" its overall message of anti-violence might have been from the perspective of a devoted neo-Nazi, helped to kick-start the Russian white-power skinhead scene in the early 1990s: "the numbers of Skinheads grew tens of times bigger just in a year or so"; according to Gerasimov, this was at least partially a result of young Russians' enthusiasm for the movie, although it is important to note that *Romper Stomper*'s 1992 release date also coincides with the immediate post-communist period in Russia, meaning that much of the growth in white-power and neo-Nazi sentiment in Russia at the time stemmed from socioeconomic and socio-historical conditions, not just from the influence of one film.[172] At home in Melbourne, Australia, the film also had an impact on racist violence; for instance, four female skinheads attacked four Asian girls using clubs and a knife at a subway station in February 1994, chanting the phrase, "Romper stomper."[173]

Particularly interesting for white-power music fans is the fact that *Romper Stomper*'s soundtrack features several racist rock songs composed specifically for the film. For that reason, the album has actually appeared for sale through some white-power music distributors on occasion, including, for several years, Resistance Records. Despite the fact that the producers of the album were presumably not white-power believers, reviews of the soundtrack among white-power believers have been relatively positive, as is this 2008 comment from the Stormfront user Ju-87: "Romper Stomper. A movie we all love and hate at the same time I assume. The first half builds up quite some tension but it all ends in a dramatic anticlimax. . . . unsuprisingly. What else could you expect. This disc also contains the Oi! songs you hear in the movie. And although they were recorded by persons who were probably the complete opposite of the lyrical content, they are quite enjoyable. 'Pulling on the Boots,' 'Fuehrer, Fuehrer,' 'The Smack Song,' 'Fourth Reich Fighting Men.'"[174] Positive reviews like this one are especially interesting given the fact that *Romper Stomper*'s overall message is a warning about the dangers of involvement in white-power skinhead groups, not a glowing celebration of life in white-power organizations. At least some fans of white-power music seem to be able to overlook the cautionary nature of *Romper Stomper*'s plot and listen to the songs on its soundtrack for

pleasure without allowing the wider context of the film to sour their enjoy-
ment of the music. This film therefore represents one of the few crossovers
between English-language mainstream media and the international white-
power music market, one which, albeit inadvertently, seems to have bolstered
white-power music scenes both internationally and at home in Australia.

The late 1990s and early 2000s—which would have been peak years for
the international white-power music web even without taking *Romper Stomper*'s influence into consideration—saw several new Australian bands emerge,
including Ravenous, Blood Red Eagle, and the prolific, Hammerskin-affiliated
Deaths Head, founded in 1999 and named for the skull-and-crossbones *Totenkopf* insignia of Hitler's SS. Stormfront users like Ju-87 often praise the musical
talent of Deaths Head in particular, writing things like, "Right from the start
this band has released professional sounding albums; no amateuristic sound
or weak playing," and "Fortress were Australia's premier WP band before they
quit . . . and, more or less, handed over the torch to Deaths Head."[175] Under
the leadership of a vocalist who identifies himself only as Jesse, Deaths Head
has developed a loyal following among white-power music fans not only in
Australia, but also abroad. Band members, who have toured internationally
and been extraordinarily active in Australian white-power movements, actually moved from Brisbane to Melbourne to participate in Melbourne's thriving
white-power skinhead scene.[176] In fact, Jesse and other members of the band
were among the founding members of Melbourne's chapter of the Hammerskins.[177] Over the past decade, Deaths Head seems to have joined Fortress
as one of Australia's premier white-power music groups, nurturing younger
Australian white-power bands and performing at gigs both in Australia
and overseas.

As is the case among many white-power music scenes worldwide, Australian bands like Deaths Head can turn to local chapters of the Blood & Honour organization for help with concert organization, record distribution, and
advertising. Blood & Honour Australia has its headquarters in a small town
between Sydney and Melbourne, but reports that most of its supporters are
concentrated in the Melbourne area rather than in Sydney.[178] Blood & Honour Australia's house band is a Canberra group called Bail Up!—named for a
phrase used by Australian stagecoach robbers, meaning the same thing as "stick
'em up!" or "stand and deliver"—which, fronted by singer Damian Ovchynik,
has performed with a number of prominent Australian white-power bands
like Ravenous and Fortress, and has even toured in Europe.[179]

The Australian white-power music scene today is smaller than its cousins
in the United States and Britain, partially due to its geographic isolation from
other major centers of European-descended population and partially because
Australia's population is much smaller than that of the United States or Britain. However, the Australian scene has contributed several prominent bands

to the international white-power music web—most notably Fortress and Deaths Head—and markets through many of the same distribution channels as white-power musicians elsewhere. Like white-power music in the Americas, white-power music in Australia owes a heavy ideological debt not only to the hierarchical and purportedly primordial theories of race and nation that are common to white-power movements across the world, but also to the locally specific history of European settler colonialism outside the European continent. Australian white-power musicians adopt tropes common to white-power musicians from Europe and the Americas in order to discuss social issues that they feel are relevant to them as members of both transnational white-nationalist and local Australian nationalist circles. They modify racist ideologies from abroad to fit the specific rhetorical needs of pro-white racism in Australia. Their music scene is important not only because its size is significant relative to the country's population, but also because it demonstrates a key example of how individuals descended from European settler populations outside Europe can embrace, internalize, and update old racist concepts from Europe in order to give these ideas relevance for local and international audiences in the contemporary world.

The confluence of European settler-colonial ideology and racist ideologies from Europe, which features prevalently in the Australian case, actually functions as the defining characteristic linking together the three different white-power music scenes in this chapter. Unlike white-power musicians from Europe itself, white-power musicians from the Americas and Australia have had to negotiate what it means to adopt an identity based on European heritage and violently pro-European racism while living in extra-European locations. Their work responds to historical processes of genocide and European colonial exploitation that have been peripheral rather than central elements of white-power ideologies in Europe itself. In discussing locally specific ideas, white-power musicians from the Americas and Australia are doing what white-power musicians and fans from elsewhere in the world have also done: adapting broad racist narratives, ideologies, and tropes that are in some cases centuries or millennia old, and giving them new resonance for contemporary individuals in both locally specific and international contexts.

Whether or not white-power musicians and fans from Europe accept all of these new formulations of pro-white racism—and, as the example of backlash toward Latin American white-power bands with purportedly mestizo members demonstrates, in some cases they do not—these specifically settler-colonial understandings of white identity and white-power racism have helped to shape the ways in which the international white-power music web articulates concepts of race, nation, and collective memory. For white-power musicians and fans living in former European settler colonies, many of which have historically attracted immigrants from a wide range of European countries,

the concepts of white nationalism and pan-white solidarity are more pressing day-to-day concerns than they are in many parts of Europe. The speed of
contemporary population movement means, of course, that Europeans of differing national and ethnic backgrounds are now living side-by-side and interacting on a much greater scale than they did several hundred years ago, even
on the European continent. Nonetheless, places like contemporary Germany,
Greece, and Russia do not generally conceive of themselves as "melting pots"
or "mosaics" of European ethnic identities to the extent that settler societies
such as the United States, Canada, Argentina, Brazil, and Australia have been
doing for centuries. The influence of white-power believers in Europe's former
settler colonies, along with the increased pace of non-white migration into
previously European-controlled areas, has helped to persuade European white-
power music fans and practitioners to begin adopting pan-white racist ideologies and to downplay—albeit not to abandon completely—older concepts of
ultra-nationalism and national chauvinism.

6

Conclusion

Violent clashes and riots at gigs. Brutal assaults on left-wing activists, police officers, homosexuals, and members of ethnic minority groups. An attempted attack on the mayor of Athens by a member of the Greek Parliament. Convictions for possession and trafficking in illegal drugs and weapons. The publication of hit lists and bomb-making plans. A failed mail-bombing campaign. Dozens of church arsons, including the torching of a twelfth-century Norwegian national historic landmark. The financing of illegal arms transactions and weapons training. The attempted murder of a Swedish shop owner. The singing of racist songs during the murders of non-white immigrants. The release of a song betraying intimate knowledge of the violent deaths of nine workers in fast-food restaurants. The dismemberment, distribution, and likely cannibalism of a suicide victim's brain. The murders of classmates, former bandmates, homosexuals, and a Greek left-wing rapper. A string of bank robberies with potential links to a bombing that killed 168 people. The shooting of six worshippers at a Sikh temple. Terrorist attacks that killed seventy-seven people, many of them teenagers, at a left-wing summer camp. This is just *some* of the violent wreckage left behind by known fans and practitioners of white-power music.

Individuals associated with white-power music scenes in various countries have carved a swath of destruction and amassed a literal body count that, for a genre of music that many westerners have never even heard of, can sometimes seem staggering. Clearly, white-power music scenes can pose a direct physical danger to the societies around them. The violence associated with white-power music and white-power groups in general is worthy of attention from criminologists, psychologists, anthropologists, musicologists, and other scholars who want to understand why people join hate groups, listen to music that expresses violently racist sentiments, and occasionally commit spectacular acts of ideologically motivated violence.

The direct threat of physical violence from white-power musicians and their fans, however, is not the only reason why white-power music should matter to people who consider themselves to be non-racist and would never ordinarily listen to a Skrewdriver, Saga, or Johnny Rebel song for pleasure. While white-power music remains little-known among mainstream populations in some western countries, it is still a genre of music that has produced more than 1,000 bands and sustained itself in the face of concerted opposition from governments, law enforcement officials, and anti-racist activists for more than three decades.

Some of the most prominent acts in the white-power music web have influenced popular music beyond white-power circles. For example, anti-racist rock star Henry Rollins of the band Black Flag said in a 2002 interview that he respected Ian Stuart Donaldson's songwriting talent and actually still owned late-1970s and early-1980s Skrewdriver albums, despite the fact that he abhorred the political values that appeared on later Skrewdriver albums and stopped actually listening to the Skrewdriver LPs in his collection once Donaldson's neo-Nazism had become obvious.[1] The links between Skrewdriver and the world of mainstream popular music go deeper than just the grudging admiration of one anti-racist rock star, too. In the early 1980s, Skrewdriver played as an opening act for well-known British bands like Siouxsie and the Banshees, the Boomtown Rats, and even, on one occasion, in its pre-fame days, the multi-platinum post-punk band the Police.[2] Siouxsie and the Banshees was one of the purportedly non-racist British punk bands of the 1970s that had been most notorious for employing swastikas, Nazi uniforms, and other Third Reich imagery as a way of trying to shock and offend mainstream audiences. The fact that they occasionally performed on the same stage with the nascent Skrewdriver suggests that Donaldson almost certainly took the 1970s punk use of Nazi iconography as a source of inspiration.

Elsewhere, I have written at length about white-power music's complex relationship with the world of mainstream popular music, arguing that white-power music's ability to insult and upset many people who hear it does not automatically mean that it has no impact on or overlap with music, attitudes, and audiences beyond the world of organized hate groups.[3] White-power musicians have established an international web of concert promotion, record production and distribution, and online fan discussion, and a few dozen of the white-power music web's biggest "star" acts clearly maintain large, transnational fan bases. The near-total silence with which mainstream entertainment companies and news media outlets like MTV and *Rolling Stone* have treated white-power music—often failing to report on the genre even when white-power musicians commit egregious acts of mass violence—seems to represent a concerted effort to ignore white-power music rather than a legitimate reflection of the music's influence on non-racist popular music. This represents a significant missed opportunity on the part of music journalists and entertainment news outlets to stimulate public discussion on issues of race and racism. Because major entertainment news companies have the power to reach millions of readers and viewers, more effort to cover white-power music on their part might actually be able to change public perceptions of contemporary racism.

Of course, *Rolling Stone*, MTV, and other purveyors of mainstream pop-music journalism have reasons for overlooking white-power music. The grand narrative of popular music history that appears in most rock 'n' roll history textbooks and television documentaries suggests that rock 'n' roll and other forms of twentieth- and early-twenty-first-century popular music have helped to garner support for anti-racist and anti-war activism in many western countries, particularly in the United States, in the decades since the end of World War II.[4] Of course, this narrative is at least partially true. The development of rock 'n' roll in the US South in the 1950s brought European American and African American fans together in ways that seem to have weakened many white Southerners' resistance to racial integration over the next decade. Anti-war protest music from urban folk singers like Bob Dylan and Joan Baez clearly contributed to the increasing dissatisfaction with the violence of the Vietnam War among large sectors of the US populace in the 1960s and 1970s. Nonetheless, extrapolating from examples like these to construct a narrative in which *all* popular music serves pacifist and anti-racist purposes is erroneous at best and mendacious at worst.

Most westerners would likely prefer not to see photos of aggressive-looking skinheads waving swastika flags on the pages of the glossy rock 'n' roll history books on our coffee tables, and mainstream record companies would probably find themselves deluged with complaints if listeners opened CD box sets that celebrate rock 'n' roll history to find songs like Skrewdriver's "White Power" and Angry Aryans' "Nigger Loving Whore" alongside works by Elvis Presley and the Beatles. Ignoring white-power music does not, however, depict popular music history accurately. In itself, the clear historical connection between Britain's early neo-Nazi oi! punk scene and the confrontational but shallow use of Third Reich imagery among canonical 1970s punk bands like the Sex Pistols, the Ramones, and Siouxsie and the Banshees should be enough to demonstrate the futility of trying to draw a clear separation between socially acceptable and socially taboo references to racism and historical violence in popular music.

Cloistering white-power and neo-Nazi music away from other forms of popular music can also make racist music appear to be the dying relic of a past era, rather than what it really is: a relatively recent phenomenon that responds to current socio-historical pressures and continues to attract new fans and musicians by repackaging and updating pre-existing racist ideologies via contemporary popular culture. White-power fans and musicians in many countries often find themselves under serious pressure from political opponents and disapproving government officials, but their genre is by no means in its death throes, despite the fact that temporary setbacks like record label closures and the imprisonment of important musicians may seem to belie this fact. The fans and practitioners of the genre are not—as mainstream news accounts tend to suggest—uniformly crazy, uneducated, unintelligent, or evil individuals. People join white-power groups and adopt white-power beliefs for a wide variety of social and ideological reasons, and white-power music can fulfill a number of important functions in fans' lives, even as much of the music also urges fans to make choices that can endanger both themselves and others.

In fact, white-power musicians and fans are often expressing hard-line versions of racist attitudes that, in subtler forms, are still considered socially acceptable among mainstream European-descended populations in many places today. Spouting racial slurs in anger and physically attacking others on the basis of their perceived racial identities have become increasingly taboo types of social interactions among most European-descended populations over the course of the past century, but this does not mean that subtler forms of pro-white prejudice have ceased to exist. One of the reasons why white-power music has had staying power as a genre is that its ideologies stem from many of the same Enlightenment-derived philosophies that have justified the creation of widespread, pro-white racial disparities in wealth, education, criminal justice, and health care systems across the world over the past 500 years. Maintaining access to a disproportionate share of the world's resources is important to many people who—sometimes unknowingly—benefit from racial privilege.[5] Studies consistently show that regardless of an individual's financial status, job qualifications, or class background, public and private decision-makers still privilege people of European descent over almost all others when choosing whom to hire, arrest, incarcerate, educate, and medicate.[6] The majority of European-descended individuals will likely never listen to white-power music, support violent white-power racism, or willingly label themselves racists. Nevertheless, many of the subtly biased practices that European-descended populations across the western world continue to condone—such as racial profiling by police officers—fall on a spectrum of pro-white prejudice and discrimination that is rooted in centuries-old racist philosophies, and that includes, in one of its most extreme contemporary manifestations, white-power music.

Forms of systemic racism and oppression, of course, vary from country to country both within Europe and in its former settler colonies, but overall, white-power musicians from different countries are responding to similar pro-white racial hierarchies and histories when they write and perform racist music. Shared histories and interwoven racial formation processes among the white populations in most European and formerly European-controlled countries are some of the key reasons why the white-power music web has developed as a transnational phenomenon in recent decades, rather than remaining a disparate group of isolated ultra-nationalist music scenes with little international contact and little in common. Shared collective memories allow white-power believers to begin forging shared white-nationalist identities out of the ashes of various older, national-chauvinist identities, many of which used to stand in opposition to one another.

This increasing cooperation across national borders is a major reason why it is important to study white-power music as an international and transnational phenomenon, rather than focusing only on individual white-power music scenes in one or two countries, as the majority of the existing scholarly literature on white-power music tends to do. If the trajectory of the international white-power music web to date is any indication, these transnational connections among white-power musicians and fans will likely become increasingly important as communication technologies improve and international collaboration becomes ever more logistically practical. Cross-border interactions among white-power musicians and fans should matter to scholars, on one level, because this type of cooperation indicates that the violence associated with white-power music scenes has the power to spread to new locations and populations. Even more than that, international collaboration among white-power musicians is an important area for further study because it demonstrates the ease with which new racist groups can update and adapt old racist ideologies, making long-held ideas seem relevant to new groups of people while continuing to reinforce existing hierarchies and systems of oppression. If readers are interested in trying to effect any measure of systemic racial and ethnic equality in the near future, then it is crucial to examine how systems of *in*equality manage to reproduce themselves over and over, despite the fact that the societies around them are constantly changing. The transnational nature of the white-power music web presents a particularly interesting lens through which to conduct this type of research. By examining this music further and understanding better what it means to its fans and practitioners, perhaps we can find ways to make tolerant and inclusive ideologies seem more appealing for individuals in various countries who might otherwise choose to view racial, sexual, and political others as existential threats.

The central focus of this book has been to demonstrate that white-power music is a transnational phenomenon rather than a group of discrete local scenes. This web connects white-power believers from across the world in ways that should matter to *everyone* and not just to anti-racist activists or to victims of racist violence. White-power musicians' multifaceted ideas about

whiteness, government, media, anti-Semitism, territory, and violence interact with mainstream discourse to create a body of racist music that draws not
only on concepts that have existed in western thought for centuries, but also
on current trends in popular culture that link white-power music to groups
and concepts far beyond the reaches of the contemporary extremist fringe.
These connections between past and present, which couple white-power ideology both with hot-button issues and with venerated philosophical traditions, are crucial in building a future for racist beliefs.

While white-power music may appear to many people as an "extremist"
phenomenon beyond the realm of reputable society, dismissing white-power
musicians and fans as old-fashioned, deranged, or monstrous simply allows
damaging and widespread forms of racism to flourish unabated in the mainstream. Most westerners would prefer not to examine the ways in which racist and ultra-nationalist ideologies influence our own viewpoints and personal
privileges. This process involves a painful reckoning, and—at least for those
of us lucky enough to have been on the receiving end of this deep-rooted system of racial privilege—a realization that we have not earned and might not
deserve to keep all of the wealth and opportunities that we possess. It is simply
easier not to face this reality, and so most of us choose to ignore it. However,
for the billions of people who work at underpaid jobs in former European
colonies with struggling economies, as well as for the millions who live as
undervalued or second-class citizens within the borders of wealthy first-world
countries, these racial inequalities are more difficult to ignore. If the legacy
of white-power music has anything to teach us, it is that addressing racism
as an isolated, individualized phenomenon will do nothing to stop its spread
or curb its destructive power. Only when we acknowledge that racism is not
something limited to outspoken bigots, racist terrorists, and tattooed neo-
Nazis in Skrewdriver T-shirts who sing songs to celebrate gas chambers and
swastikas will we be able to deal with the actual threat that white-power music
represents—that is, the threat that we will fail to ameliorate the racial tensions
rife in our world, and will instead pass the legacy of racial oppression on to
future generations.

Notes

Chapter 1 What Is White-Power Music?

1 Paul Jackson, "'The Hooked-Cross, the Symbol of Re-Awakening Life': The Memory of Ian Stuart Donaldson," in *White Power Music: Scenes of Extreme-Right Cultural Resistance*, ed. Anton Shekhovtsov and Paul Jackson (Ilford: Searchlight, 2012), 85, 89.

2 Jackson, "The Hooked-Cross," 92.

3 Christian Dornbusch and Jan Raabe, "'White-Power'-Music in Germany: Development—Dimensions—Trends" (presentation at the workshop White-Power Music: Germany in the World, Göttingen, Germany, June 4, 2012).

4 "Extremism in America: William Pierce," Anti-Defamation League of B'nai B'rith, accessed May 9, 2014, http://archive.adl.org/learn/ext_us/pierce.html?LEARN _Cat=Extremism&LEARN_SubCat=Extremism_in_America&xpicked=2& item=wp.

5 Stefan Rheinbay, "Ensnaring Young People with Right-Wing Music," *Deutsche Welle*, April 26, 2013, accessed August 22, 2015, http://www.dw.com/en/ensnaring -young-people-with-right-wing-music/a-16774494.

6 Svolska, October 4, 2013 (5:53 AM), comment on MirkoS, "Ian Stuart Donaldson," *Stormfront*, February 22, 2011 (7:34 AM), https://www.stormfront.org/forum/ t781833/; New Sons Of The Black Sun, July 15, 2014 (4:23 PM), comment on skoal-lio, "Is White Power Music dead? What happened . . . ?," *Stormfront*, July 5, 2014 (9:49 PM), https://www.stormfront.org/forum/t1050805/.

7 Pete Simi and Robert Futrell, *American Swastika: Inside the White Power Movement's Hidden Spaces of Hate* (New York: Rowman & Littlefield, 2010), 2.

8 Robert Futrell, Pete Simi, and Simon Gottschalk, "Understanding Music in Movements: The White Power Music Scene," *Sociological Quarterly* 47 (2006), 276.

9 Henning Flad, "Trotz Verbot nicht Tot," in *RechtsRock: Bestandsaufnahme und Gegenstrategien*, ed. Christian Dornbusch and Jan Raabe (Münster: Unrast, 2002), 91.

10 Myriam V. Thoma et al., "The Effects of Music on the Human Stress Response," *PLoS One* 8.8 (2013), 1; Valorie N. Salimpoor et al., "Anatomically Distinct Dopamine Release during Anticipation and Experience of Peak Emotion to Music," *Nature Neuroscience* 14 (2011), 257.

11 Alice Speri, "Half of America Thinks We Live in a Post-Racial Society—The Other Half, Not So Much," *Vice News*, December 9, 2014, accessed August 28, 2015,

https://news.vice.com/article/half-of-america-thinks-we-live-in-a-post-racial
-society-the-other-half-not-so-much.

12 Betty A. Dobratz and Stephanie L. Shanks-Meile, *"White Power, White Pride!": The White Separatist Movement in the United States* (New York: Macmillan, 1997), 2.

Chapter 2   The History of White-Power Music in Britain

1 Matthew Rebhorn, *Pioneer Performances: Staging the Frontier* (New York: Oxford University Press, 2011), 72; Anton Shekhovtsov, "Introduction," in *White-Power Music: Scenes of Extreme-Right Cultural Resistance*, ed. Anton Shekhovtsov and Paul Jackson (Ilford: Searchlight, 2012), 1.

2 Ian Stuart, "Interview in *Terminal,"* in *White Riot: Punk Rock and the Politics of Race*, ed. Stephen Duncombe and Maxwell Tremblay (New York: Verso, 2011), 131.

3 Ibid., 133.

4 "Diamond in the Dust: The Ian Stuart Biography," Combat 18, accessed August 24, 2015, http://www.skrewdriver.com/Ian_Stuart_Diamond_In_The_Dust.html.

5 "A Tribute to Ian Stuart," Combat 18, accessed August 24, 2015, http://www.skrewdriver.net/stuart.html.

6 "Diamond in the Dust."

7 Paul Jackson, "'The Hooked-Cross, the Symbol of Re-Awakening Life': The Memory of Ian Stuart Donaldson," in *White Power Music: Scenes of Extreme-Right Cultural Resistance*, ed. Anton Shekhovtsov and Paul Jackson (Ilford: Searchlight, 2012), 90

8 Nick Lowles and Steve Silver, "From Skinhead to Bonehead—The Roots of Skinhead Culture," in *White Noise: Inside the International Nazi Skinhead Scene*, ed. Nick Lowles and Steve Silver (Ilford: Searchlight, 1998), 5–6; Steve Silver, "Blood and Honour 1987–1992," in *White Noise: Inside the International Nazi Skinhead Scene*, ed. Nick Lowles and Steve Silver (Ilford: Searchlight, 1998), 17.

9 Timothy S. Brown, "Subcultures, Pop Music and Politics: Skinheads and 'Nazi Rock' in England and Germany," *Journal of Social History* 38:1 (2004), 158, 161.

10 Christian Dornbusch and Jan Raabe, "20 Jahre RechtsRock: Vom Skinhead-Rock zur Alltagskultur," in *RechtsRock: Bestandsaufnahme und Gegenstrategien*, ed. Christian Dornbusch and Jan Raabe (Münster: Unrast, 2002), 20.

11 John M. Cotter, "Sounds of Hate: White Power Rock and Roll and the Neo-Nazi Skinhead Subculture," *Terrorism and Political Violence* 11:2 (1999), 116.

12 Dornbusch and Raabe, "20 Jahre RechtsRock," 20–21.

13 Devin Burghart, "Beyond Boots and Braces: The White Power Skinhead Music Scene in the United States," in *Soundtracks to the White Revolution: White Supremacist Assaults on Youth Music Subcultures*, ed. Devin Burghart (Chicago: Center for New Community, 1999), 27; Lowles and Silver, "From Skinhead to Bonehead," 1–2; Brown, "Subcultures," 162; Cotter, "Sounds of Hate," 116.

14 Cotter, "Sounds of Hate," 116.

15 Lowles and Silver, "From Skinhead to Bonehead," 3.

16 Brown, "Subcultures," 159.

17 Gerd Baumann, *Contesting Culture: Discourses of Identity in Multi-Ethnic London* (Cambridge: Cambridge University Press, 1996), 59.

18 "Race Riot Strikes London," *Associated Press*, July 5, 1981, accessed August 16, 2015, https://news.google.com/newspapers?nid=932&dat=19810705&id=t1YLAAAAIBAJ&sjid=qVIDAAAAIBAJ&pg=6426,404910&hl=en.

19 Lowles and Silver, "From Skinhead to Bonehead," 4; "Race Riot."

20 Lowles and Silver, "From Skinhead to Bonehead," 4.

21 "London Branch: Original R.A.C," *Blood & Honour* 20 (2000), accessed October 6, 2015, http://www.bloodandhonourworldwide.co.uk/magazine/issue20/issue20p3.html.

22 Cotter, "Sounds of Hate," 119.

23 Lowles and Silver, "From Skinhead to Bonehead," 6–7.

24 Ibid., 10.

25 Cotter, "Sounds of Hate," 119.

26 Silver, "Blood and Honour," 10, 18.

27 Ibid., 15–16.

28 Heléne Lööw, "White-Power Rock 'n' Roll: A Growing Industry," in *Nation and Race: The Developing Euro-American Racist Subculture*, ed. Jeffrey Kaplan and Tore Bjørgo (Boston: Northeastern University Press, 1998), 139; Silver, "Blood and Honour," 12.

29 Silver, "Blood and Honour," 13.

30 Klaus Farin, "'Rechts-Rock,'" in *Rechtsextremismus in Deutschland: Voraussetzungen, Zusammenhänge, Wirkungen*, ed. Wolfgang Benz (Frankfurt am Main: Fischer Taschenbuch Verlag, 1994), 142.

31 Silver, "Blood and Honour," 19.

32 Ibid., 9; "Ian Stuart Donaldson and a Legacy of Hate," Channel 4 News, September 24, 2013, accessed May 6, 2014, http://www.channel4.com/news/ian-stuart-donaldson-a-legacy-of-hate.

33 Stephen E. Atkins, *Encyclopedia of Modern Worldwide Extremists and Extremist Groups* (Westport, CT: Greenwood, 2004) 80; Silver, "Blood and Honour," 22–24.

34 Silver, "Blood and Honour," 24.

35 For one website featuring stills of Crane's porn films, see Skinmarvin, "Nicky Crane Porn," May 17 and June 29, 2011, accessed July 23, 2013, http://www.skinmarvin.co.uk/content/?s=nicky+crane (viewer discretion strongly advised).

36 "Diamond in the Dust."

37 Johann Hari, "Sleeping with the Enemy," *The Guardian*, December 12, 1990, accessed July 23, 2013, http://www.guardian.co.uk/world/2002/dec/13/gayrights.thefarright; Richard Plant, *The Pink Triangle: The Nazi War against Homosexuals* (New York: Henry Holt and Company, 1986), 61–62.

38 Mark S. Hamm, *In Bad Company: America's Terrorist Underground* (Boston: Northeastern University Press, 2002), 169, 171, 173, 183.

39 "The Violent Storm Memorial," *Blood & Honour Worldwide*, accessed July 26, 2013. http://www.bloodandhonourworldwide.co.uk/history/violentstorm.html.

40 Silver, "Blood and Honour," 25.

41 "The Violent Storm Memorial" [capital letters in the original].

42 "Celtic Warrior," *Resistance* 12 (2000), 10; Mark Honigsbaum, "Straw Urged to Stop Secret Skinhead Gig in Wales," *The Independent*, August 3, 1997, accessed August 14, 2015, http://www.independent.co.uk/news/straw-urged-to-stop-secret-skinhead-gig-in-wales-1243460.html.

43 "So, What About 'the Battle of Waterloo 1992'?," *Kriegsberichter*, 1995, accessed June 1, 2014, https:// www.youtube.com/watch?v=RO-VQlvgPvQ.

44 Silver, "Blood and Honour," 26–27.

45 Nick Lowles, "ISD—The Money Machine 1992–1998," in *White Noise: Inside the International Nazi Skinhead Scene*, ed. Nick Lowles and Steve Silver (Ilford: Searchlight, 1998), 28–29.

46 For details of the Rostock attack, see Walter Wüllenweber, "Das Feuerschein aus Rostock," in *Un-Heil über Deutschland: Fremdenhaß und Neofaschismus nach der Wiedervereinigung*, ed. Manfred Leier (Hamburg: Grunder + Jahr, 1993), 21–31.

47 "A White Farewell to No Remorse: 1986–1996 a Legend Put to Rest," *Resistance* 8 (1997), 10–13.

48 Scott Stoneking, November 5, 2007 (3:21 P.M.), comment on pyccka82, "CD Reviews," *Stormfront*, April 16, 2007 (9:50 PM), https://www.stormfront.org/forum/t198817-20/.

49 Joe Stroud, "'And for Those of You that Hate Metal . . .': The Softer Side of Extreme Right Music" (presentation at the workshop White-Power Music: Germany in the World, Göttingen, Germany, June 4, 2012); Silver, "Blood and Honour," 28–30; Nick Lowles, "Die Internationale des Hasses," in *RechtsRock: Bestandsaufnahme und Gegenstrategien*, ed. Christian Dornbusch and Jan Raabe (Münster: Unrast, 2002), 236.

50 "Diamonds in the Dust."

51 "Ian Stuart Donaldson."

52 Jackson, "'The Hooked-Cross," 89.

53 "Diamonds in the Dust."

54 "Blood and Honour East Midlands Progress Report—June 2000," *Blood & Honour* 19 (2000), accessed October 6, 2015, http://www.bloodandhonourworldwide.co.uk/magazine/issue19/issue19p07,14.html.

55 Michael Simkin, director, *Nazi Hate Rock: A Donal MacIntyre Investigation* (Demand DVD, 2009).

56 "Ian Stuart: A Personal Veiw" [*sic*], *Blood & Honour* 20 (2000), accessed October 6, 2015, http://www.bloodandhonourworldwide.co.uk/magazine/issue20/issue20p4.html.

57 MirkoS, February 22, 2011 (7:50 AM), comment on MirkoS, "Ian Stuart Donaldson," February 22, 2011 (7:34 AM), https://www.stormfront.org/forum/t781833/.

58 Jackson, "The Hooked-Cross," 85–86.

59 Lowles, "ISD," 30–31, 35.

60 Honigsbaum, "Straw Urged."

61 Lowles, "Die Internationale," 236.

62 Ibid.

63 Lowles, "ISD," 37, 39, 47.

64 "The Future," *Blood & Honour* 17 (1999), accessed October 6, 2015, http://www.bloodandhonourworldwide.co.uk/magazine/issue17/page12.htm; "The Harley Column of the Mad N.S. Biker," *Blood & Honour* 19 (2000), 22–23.

65 "So, What About."

66 Ibid.

67 "Editorial: What Are We?," *Blood & Honour* 42 (2009), 3.

68 Ed Winchester, "Warlord in Finland 4.12.99," *Blood & Honour* 18 (2000), accessed October 6, 2015, http://www.bloodandhonourworldwide.co.uk/magazine/issue18/issue18p23,32a.html.

69 "Legion of St. George: Skinhead Resistance 2000," *Blood & Honour* 18 (2000), accessed October 6, 2015, http://www.bloodandhonourworldwide.co.uk/magazine/issue18/issue18p16,17,18.html.

70 "Reich Force," *Blood & Honour* 20 (2000), accessed October 6, 2015, http://www.bloodandhonourworldwide.co.uk/magazine/issue20/issue20p15.html.

71 Anton Shekhovtsov, "Introduction," in *White-Power Music: Scenes of Extreme-Right*

Cultural Resistance, ed. Anton Shekhovtsov and Paul Jackson (Ilford: Searchlight, 2012), 4.
72 Stroud, "And for Those."
73 Alexander Gray, "Conflict Besets Blood and Honour Rivals," *Searchlight*, July 8, 2012, accessed September 28, 2015, http://www.searchlightmagazine.com/archive/conflict-besets-blood-and-honour-rivals.

Chapter 3   The History of White-Power Music in Continental Western Europe

1 Timothy S. Brown, "Subcultures, Pop Music and Politics: Skinheads and 'Nazi Rock' in England and Germany," *Journal of Social History* 38:1 (2004), 161; Steve Silver, "Blood and Honour 1987–1992," in *White Noise: Inside the International Nazi Skinhead Scene*, ed. Nick Lowles and Steve Silver (Ilford: Searchlight, 1998), 13.
2 Christian Dornbusch and Jan Raabe, "20 Jahre RechtsRock: Vom Skinhead-Rock zur Alltagskultur," in *RechtsRock: Bestandsaufnahme und Gegenstrategien*, ed. Christian Dornbusch and Jan Raabe (Münster: Unrast, 2002), 28.
3 Eike Wunderlich, "German White Power—A Programme for Cultural Hegemony," in *White Noise: Inside the International Nazi Skinhead Scene*, ed. Nick Lowles and Steve Silver (Ilford: Searchlight, 1998), 49–50; Nick Lowles and Steve Silver, "From Skinhead to Bonehead—The Roots of Skinhead Culture," in *White Noise*, 7; Brown, "Subcultures," 163; Dornbusch and Raabe, "20 Jahre RechtsRock," 26–27.
4 Dornbusch and Raabe, "20 Jahre RechtsRock," 27.
5 Wunderlich, "German White Power," 50; Brown, "Subcultures," 164.
6 Dornbusch and Raabe, "20 Jahre RechtsRock," 26.
7 Ibid., 30–31.
8 Ibid., 42.
9 Jacob Grimm and Wilhelm Grimm [The Brothers Grimm], "The Bremen Town-Musicians," in *Grimm's Complete Fairy Tales*, trans. Margaret Hunt (San Diego: Canterbury Classics, 2011 [1819]), 99–101.
10 Dornbusch and Raabe, "20 Jahre RechtsRock," 42; Michael Weiss, "Deutschland im September," in *Rechtsrock: Bestandsaufnahme und Gegenstrategien*, ed. Christian Dornbusch and Jan Raabe (Münster: Unrast Verlag, 2002), 66.
11 Simone Rafael, "Warum Tragen Rechtsextreme Palästinenser-Tücher?," *Netz-Gegen-Nazis*, April 9, 2009, accessed August 20, 2015, http://www.netz-gegen-nazis.de/artikel/warum-tragen-rechtsextreme-palaestinenser-tuecher.
12 Hannah Cleaver, "German Nazis' Dress Code Angers British Firm," *The Telegraph*, February 22, 2001, accessed August 19, 2015, http://www.telegraph.co.uk/news/worldnews/europe/1323701/German-Nazis-dress-code-angers-British-firm.html.
13 "Thor Steinar," accessed August 19, 2015, https://www.thorsteinar.de/; Samantha Payne, "Is Thor Steinar Hollister for Neo Nazis? London Jews' Anger at Shop," *International Business Times*, April 25, 2014, accessed August 20, 2015, http://www.ibtimes.co.uk/neo-nazi-clothes-shop-opens-yards-uk-chief-rabbi-office-locals-protest-1446126.
14 Amy Beth Cooter, "Neo-Nazi Normalization: The Skinhead Movement and Integration into Normative Structures," *Sociological Inquiry* 76:2 (2006), 145.
15 Thomas Rogers, "Heil Hipster: The Young Neo-Nazis Trying to Put a Stylish Face on Hate," *Rolling Stone*, June 23, 2014, accessed August 20, 2015, http://www.rollingstone.com/culture/news/heil-hipster-the-young-neo-nazis-trying-to-put-a-stylish-face-on-hate-20140623.

16 Dornbusch and Raabe, "20 Jahre RechtsRock," 31.

17 Ibid., 37.

18 Henning Flad, "Trotz Verbot nicht Tot," in *RechtsRock: Bestandsaufnahme und Gegenstrategien*, ed. Christian Dornbusch and Jan Raabe (Münster: Unrast, 2002), 98.

19 Klaus Farin, "Reaktionäre Rebellen: Die Geschichte einer Provokation," in *Rock von Rechts II: Milieus, Hintergründe und Materialien*, ed. Dieter Baacke, Klaus Farin, and Jürgen Lauffer (Bielefeld: Vorstand der Gesellschaft für Medienpädagogik und Kommunikationskultur in der Bundesrepublik Deutschland [GMK] e.V., 2000), 19–20.

20 Klaus Farin, "'Rechts-Rock,'" in *Rechtsextremismus in Deutschland: Voraussetzungen, Zusammenhänge, Wirkungen*, ed. Wolfgang Benz (Frankfurt am Main: Fischer Taschenbuch Verlag, 1994), 145.

21 "Stones May Drop Controversial Band," *BBC*, June 2, 2003, accessed September 25, 2015, http://news.bbc.co.uk/2/hi/entertainment/2956018.stm.

22 Ju-87, July 1, 2005 (6:10 AM), comment on pyccka82, "CD Reviews," *Stormfront*, April 16, 2005 (9:50 PM), https://www.stormfront.org/forum/t198817-2/?s= 2117de657b50e2945392ad84fd5d9901.

23 Mary Fulbrook, *A History of Germany, 1918–2008: The Divided Nation*, 3rd ed. (Oxford: Blackwell, 2009), 280.

24 Michael Schmidt, *Der Untergang des alten Dresden in der Bombennacht vom 13./14. Februar 1945./The Destruction of Dresden in the Night of 13–14 February 1945* (Dresden: Sonnenblumen-Verlag, 2010), 55.

25 Fulbrook, *A History of Germany*, 280, 288.

26 Klaudia Prevezanos, "Turkish Guest Workers Transformed German Society," *Deutsche Welle*, October 30, 2011, accessed May 26, 2014, http://www.dw.de/turkish -guest-workers-transformed-german-society/a-15489210.

27 Julia Mahncke, "Asylum Policy Debate Intensifies in Germany," *Deutsche Welle*, July 13, 2013, accessed July 24, 2013, http://www.dw.de/asylum-policy-debate -intensifies-in-germany/a-16949134.

28 Stephen Kinzer, "A Wave of Attacks on Foreigners Stirs Shock in Germany," *New York Times*, October 1, 1991, accessed July 25, 2013, http://www.nytimes.com/1991/ 10/01/world/a-wave-of-attacks-on-foreigners-stirs-shock-in-germany.html.

29 Christian Dornbusch and Jan Raabe, "Rechtsrock fürs Vaterland," in *Braune Kameradschaften: Die neuen Netzwerke der militanten Neonazis*, ed. Andrea Röpke and Andreas Speit (Berlin: Ch. Links Verlag, 2004), 71.

30 Chiara Pierobon, "*Rechtsrock*: White Power Music in Germany," in *White Power Music: Scenes of Extreme-Right Cultural Resistance*, ed. Anton Shekhovtsov and Paul Jackson (Ilford: Searchlight, 2012), 12.

31 Dornbusch and Raabe, "20 Jahre RechtsRock," 41; Weiss, "Deutschland im September," 51.

32 Farin, "'Rechts-Rock,'" 149–150; Dornbusch and Raabe, "20 Jahre RechtsRock," 38.

33 Farin, "'Rechts-Rock,'" 150; Dornbusch and Raabe, "20 Jahre RechtsRock," 39.

34 Norman Birnbaum, "How Germany's Surveillance Scandals Echo Our Own," *The Nation*, August 14, 2015, accessed September 26, 2015, http://www.thenation.com/ article/how-germanys-surveillance-scandals-echo-our-own/.

35 Farin, "Reaktionäre Rebellen," 27; Karrie Jacobs, "Germany Stomps Skinhead Music," *Rolling Stone* 669 (November 11, 1993), 18; Dornbusch and Raabe, "20 Jahre RechtsRock," 39.

36 Irwin Suall et al., *The Skinhead International: A Worldwide Survey of Neo-Nazi Skinheads* (New York: Anti-Defamation League of B'nai B'rith, 1995), 38.
37 Farin, "'Rechts-Rock,'" 143.
38 Suall et al., *The Skinhead International*, 38.
39 Farin, "'Rechts-Rock,'" 143.
40 Ju-87, February 9, 2008 (4:41 AM), comment on pyccka82, "CD Reviews," April 16, 2005 (9:50 PM), *Stormfront*, https://www.stormfront.org/forum/t198817-21/.
41 Dornbusch and Raabe, "20 Jahre RechtsRock," 39, 41.
42 Nick Lowles, "Die Internationale des Hasses," in *RechtsRock: Bestandsaufnahme und Gegenstrategien*, ed. Christian Dornbusch and Jan Raabe (Münster: Unrast, 2002), 235.
43 Flad, "Trotz Verbot nicht Tot," 114.
44 Dornbusch and Raabe, "20 Jahre RechtsRock," 40; Weiss, "Deutschland im September," 68.
45 Dornbusch and Raabe, "20 Jahre RechtsRock," 44; Weiss, "Deutschland im September," 61.
46 Weiss, "Deutschland im September," 61.
47 Farin, "'Rechts-Rock,'" 143; Suall et al., *The Skinhead International*, 38; Dornbusch and Raabe, "20 Jahre RechtsRock," 36.
48 Dornbusch and Raabe, "20 Jahre RechtsRock," 40.
49 Dornbusch and Raabe, "Rechtsrock fürs Vaterland," 71.
50 Weiss, "Deutschland im September," 70.
51 *Encyclopaedia Metallum: The Metal Archives*, accessed November 3, 2012, http://www.metal-archives.com/.
52 Dornbusch and Raabe, "20 Jahre RechtsRock," 36.
53 "Blood & Honour Scene News," *Blood & Honour* 41 (2009); "Blood & Honour Scene News," *Blood & Honour* 42 (2009), accessed October 6, 2015, http://www.bloodandhonourworldwide.co.uk/magazine/issue42/issue42p_26.html; "Blood & Honour Scene News," *Blood & Honour* 43 (2010), accessed October 6, 2015, http://www.bloodandhonourworldwide.co.uk/magazine/issue43/issue43p_26.html; "News from the Frontline," *Blood & Honour* 43 (2010), accessed October 6, 2015, http://www.bloodandhonourworldwide.co.uk/magazine/issue43/issue43p_31.html.
54 Ju-87, March 9, 2006 (8:07 AM), comment on pyccka82, "CD Reviews," April 16, 2005 (9:50 PM), *Stormfront*, https://www.stormfront.org/forum/t198817-8/.
55 Ju-87, June 17, 2005 (6:07 AM), comment on pyccka82, "CD Reviews," April 16, 2005 (9:50 PM), *Stormfront*, https://www.stormfront.org/forum/t198817-2/?s=2117de657b50e2945392ad84fd5d9901.
56 Pierobon, *"Rechtsrock,"* 9; Dornbusch and Raabe, "Rechtsrock fürs Vaterland," 74.
57 "Banned but Marching On," *Blood & Honour* 20 (2000), accessed October 6, 2015, http://www.bloodandhonourworldwide.co.uk/magazine/issue20/issue20p18.html.
58 Pierobon, *"Rechtsrock,"* 17.
59 Ibid., 17, 20.
60 "D.S.T.," *Blood & Honour* 24 (2002), accessed October 6, 2015, http://www.bloodandhonourworldwide.co.uk/magazine/issue24/issue24p11.html.
61 "Appeal—The Rennicke Family in Misery," *Blood & Honour* 23 (2001), October 6, 2015, http://www.bloodandhonourworldwide.co.uk/magazine/issue23/issue23%20rennicke%20appeal.html; "Rechtsextreme Liedermacher und

Balladensänger—Zum Beispiel Frank Rennicke," *Informations- und Dokumentationszentrum für Antirassismusarbeit in Nordrhein-Westfalen,* accessed May 27, 2014, http://www.ida-nrw.de/hintergrundwissen/musik/liedermacher/liedermacher.html.

62 "Appeal."

63 Anton Maegerle and Holger Kulick, "Ein völkischer Bundespräsident?," *Bundeszentrale für politische Bildung,* April 10, 2009, accessed May 27, 2014, http://www.bpb.de/politik/extremismus/rechtsextremismus/41235/ein-voelkischer-bundespraesident; "Rechtsextreme Liedermacher."

64 Maegerle and Kulick, "Ein völkischer Bundespräsident?"

65 Hauke Friederichs, "Singender Neonazi will Bundespräsident werden," *Die Zeit,* June 7, 2010, accessed May 27, 2014, http://www.zeit.de/politik/deutschland/2010-06/rennicke-npd; Maegerle and Kulick, "Ein völkischer Bundespräsident?"

66 Pierobon, "*Rechtsrock,*" 9–10; Bundesgerichtshof, *Urteil des 3. Strafsenats vom 10.3.2005—3 StR 233/04* (March 10, 2005).

67 Dornbusch and Raabe, "Rechtsrock fürs Vaterland," 76.

68 Heike Kleffner, "Alberto Adriano—der Tod eines Vaters," *Der Tagesspiegel,* September 15, 2010, accessed May 22, 2014, http://www.tagesspiegel.de/politik/rechtsextremismus/opfer-rechter-gewalt-alberto-adriano-der-tod-eines-vaters/1934726.html.

69 Dornbusch and Jan, "Rechtsrock fürs Vaterland," 75.

70 Ibid., 80.

71 Pierobon, "*Rechtsrock,*" 14–15.

72 "Sleipnir," *Blood & Honour* 23 (2001), accessed October 6, 2015, http://www.bloodandhonourworldwide.co.uk/magazine/issue23/issue23%20sleipnir.html.

73 Bundesamt für Verfassungsschutz, *Verfassungsschutzbericht 2010* (Berlin: Bundesamt für Verfassungsschutz, 2011), 55.

74 Pierobon, "*Rechtsrock,*" 15.

75 "S.E.K.," *Blood & Honour* 19 (2000), 16–17.

76 Christian Dornbusch and Jan Raabe, "'White-Power'-Music in Germany: Development—Dimensions—Trends" (presentation at the workshop White-Power Music: Germany in the World, Göttingen, Germany, June 4, 2012); "n'Socialist Soundsystem: Nationale Rapmusik," accessed May 6, 2014, http://eneseess.befehlston.com/?page_id=2.

77 Benjamin Cunningham, "The Far Right's New Face," *Prague Post* 21:10 (March 7, 2012), A1.

78 "Report on Extremism and Manifestations of Racism and Xenophobia on the Territory of the Czech Republic in 2011" (Prague: Czech Ministry of Interior, Security Policy Department, 2012), accessed August 22, 2015, retrieved from http://www.mvcr.cz/mvcren/article/documents-on-the-fight-against-extremism.aspx.

79 Rob Cameron, "Hardbass—We Will Bring Heil Hitler to Your Home," *Český Rozhlas,* August 16, 2011, accessed November 3, 2013, http://www.radio.cz/en/section/curraffrs/hardbass-we-will-bring-heil-hitler-to-your-home; "14 Words," *Hate on Display Hate Symbols Database,* Anti-Defamation League of B'nai B'rith, accessed September 5, 2015, http://www.adl.org/combating-hate/hate-on-display/c/14-words.html#.VesYCck4xyw.

80 Miroslav Mareš, "Trans-National Cooperation of Right-Wing Extremists in East-Central Europe," *The Daily.SK,* October 30, 2012, accessed August 22, 2015, http://www.thedaily.sk/right-wing-extremism-in-central-and-eastern-europe/.

81 Stefan Rheinbay, "Rechte Szene: Rumpelrock und Wummerbass," *Deutsche Welle*, April 30, 2013, accessed June 30, 2015, http://www.dw.com/de/rechte-szene -rumpelrock-und-wummerbass/a-16756812.

82 "Haftbefehl gegen Beate Z. Erlassen," *Hamburger Abendblatt*, November 14, 2011, accessed November 3, 2013, http://www.abendblatt.de/politik/deutschland/ article2092181/Haftbefehl-gegen-Beate-Z-erlassen.html.

83 Ibid.

84 Weiss, "Deutschland im September," 81.

85 Ibid., 60, 81.

86 Julia Jüttner and Hendrik Ternieden, "'Döner-Killer-Lied':Rechtsrocker Bekommt Bewährungsstrafe," *Der Spiegel*, October 15, 2012, accessed May 6, 2014, http://www .spiegel.de/panorama/justiz/volksverhetzung-daniel-giese-zu-bewaehrungsstrafe -verurteilt-a-861296.html.

87 "Volksverhetzung in Liedtext: Richter Bestätigen Urteil gegen Rechtsrocker," *Spiegel Online*, March 27, 2014, accessed October 4, 2015, http://www.spiegel .de/panorama/justiz/daniel-giese-olg-oldenburg-bestaetigt-urteil-wegen -volksverhetzung-a-961112.html.

88 Ibid.

89 Debórah Dwork and Robert Jan van Pelt, *Holocaust: A History* (New York: W.W. Norton, 2002), 327–328.

90 David Lagerlöf, "The Rise and Fall of White Power Music in Sweden," *White Power Music: Scenes of Extreme-Right Cultural Resistance*, ed. Anton Shekhovtsov and Paul Jackson (Ilford: Searchlight, 2012), 36.

91 Jonas Hellentin, "Ragnarock Records," *Expo Idag*, April 16, 2003, accessed December 1, 2013, http://expo.se/2003/ragnarock-records_220.html.

92 Stieg Larsson, "Racism Incorporated—White Power Music in Sweden," *White Noise: Inside the International Nazi Skinhead Scene*, ed. Nick Lowles and Steve Silver (Ilford: Searchlight, 1998), 60.

93 Ibid., 58, 60, 62.

94 Ken Neptune, "EMI Sweden Drops Ultima Thule; Neo-Nazism Taints Successful Rockers," *Billboard* 105:49 (December 4, 1993), 42; Lagerlöf, "Rise and Fall," 37–38; Lowles, "Die Internationale," 240–241.

95 Larsson, "Racism Incorporated," 60; Lagerlöf, "Rise and Fall," 37; Anton Shekhovtsov, "European Far-Right Music and Its Enemies," *Analysing Fascist Discourse: European Fascism in Talk and Text*, ed. Ruth Wodak and John E. Richardson (London: Routledge, 2013), 280.

96 Benjamin Teitelbaum, *Lions of the North: Sounds of the New Nordic Racial Nationalism*, pre-publication draft (Oxford: Oxford University Press, forthcoming), 1; Teitelbaum, email message to author, June 2, 2014; Shekhovtsov, "European Far-Right Music," 280; Larsson, "Racism Incorporated," 60; Ugo Corte and Bob Edwards, "White Power Music and the Mobilization of Racist Social Movements," *Music & Arts in Action* 1:1 (2008), 14–15.

97 "Ultima Thule Calls It Quits after 30 Years of Music," *Label 56*, May 27, 2012, accessed June 9, 2014, http://www.label56.com/2012/05/ultima-thule-calls-it-quits -after-30-years-of-music/.

98 Lowles, "Die Internationale," 241.

99 Ibid.; Larsson, "Racism Incorporated," 61.

100 Larsson, "Racism Incorporated," 61.

101 Lagerlöf, "Rise and Fall," 38.

102 Ibid.; Larsson, "Racism Incorporated," 63.
103 Lagerlöf, "Rise and Fall," 39.
104 Ibid.
105 Larsson, "Racism Incorporated," 62.
106 Ibid.
107 Ibid.; "Midgård Söner's Vocalist 'Nitton' SHARPens His Anti-Racist Argument," *Resistance* 8 (1996), 6.
108 Sundquist quoted in Nick Lowles and Steve Silver, "Turning Down the Sound of Hate," *White Noise: Inside the International Nazi Skinhead Scene*, ed. Nick Lowles and Steve Silver (Ilford: Searchlight, 1998), 85 [ellipses in the original].
109 Larsson, "Racism Incorporated," 63.
110 Lagerlöf, "Rise and Fall," 35.
111 Larsson, "Racism Incorporated," 64.
112 Lagerlöf, "Rise and Fall," 41.
113 Ibid.
114 *Nazi Hate Rock: A Donal MacIntyre Investigation*, directed by Michael Simkin (London: Channel 5, 2009), DVD.
115 Ibid.
116 Lagerlöf, "Rise and Fall," 40; Cliff Southwell, "'White Pride World Wide'?: The Internet and the Global Marketing of White Power Rock," in *White Noise: Inside the International Nazi Skinhead Scene*, ed. Nick Lowles and Steve Silver (Ilford: Searchlight, 1998), 79.
117 *Nazi Hate Rock.*
118 Teitelbaum, email messages to the author, June 2, 2014 and June 4, 2014.
119 John Murdoch, "Saga Speaks . . . ," *Resistance* 13 (2000), 10.
120 Ibid.
121 Ju-87, December 10, 2007 (9:34 AM), comment on pyccka82, "CD Reviews," April 16, 2005 (9:50 PM), *Stormfront*, https://www.stormfront.org/forum/t198817-20/.
122 Ibid.
123 Murdoch, "Saga Speaks . . . ," 11.
124 *Nazi Hate Rock.*
125 Anders Behring Breivik (as Andrew Berwick), *2083: A European Declaration of Independence* (self-published, 2011), 847.
126 Saga, "Official Statement," *This is Saga*, July 27, 2011, accessed August 18, 2015, http://www.thisissaga.com/news-20112711-newsite.html.
127 David T. Zabecki, "Milorg," *World War II in Europe: An Encyclopedia*, ed. David T. Zabecki (New York: Routledge, 1999), 704.
128 Peter Davies, *Dangerous Liaisons: Collaboration and World War Two* (New York: Routledge, 2004), 90; Martin Hughes, "Vidkun Quisling," *The Nazi Collaborators* (MG Entertainment, 2010); Samuel Abrahamsen, *Norway's Response to the Holocaust: A Historical Perspective* (New York: Holocaust Library, 1991), 148; Jan Petter Myklebust and Bernt Hagtvet, "Regional Contrasts in the Membership Base of the Nasjonal Samling: A Study of the Political Ecology of Norwegian Fascism 1933–1945," *Who Were the Fascists?*, ed. Stein Ugelvik Larsen, Bernt Hagtvet, and Jan Petter Myklebust (Oslo: Universitetsvorlaget, 1980), 621–650.
129 Helen Pidd, "Andres Behring Breivik Spent Years Training and Plotting for Massacre," *The Guardian*, August 24, 2012, accessed September 4, 2013, http://www.theguardian.com/world/2012/aug/24/anders-behring-breivik-profile-oslo.

130 "Racism in Norway," *The Local: Sweden's News in English*, July 22, 2013, accessed September 4, 2013, http://www.thelocal.se/49200/20130722/.

131 Jens Ryndgren and Patrick Ruth, "Voting for the Radical Right in Swedish Munici-palities: Social Marginality and Ethnic Competition?," *Scandinavian Political Studies* 34:3 (2011), 202, 204; Amy Lifland, "Right Wing Rising: Eurozone Crisis and Nationalism," *Harvard International Review* 34:3 (2013), 9.

132 Justin Massa, "Unholy Alliance: The National Socialist Black Metal Underground," *Soundtracks to the White Revolution: White Supremacist Assaults on Youth Music Subcultures*, ed. Devin Burghart (Chicago: Center for New Community, 1999), 55; S. Johansen, "Between Hitler and Satan: Norwegian Black Metal as a Spearhead for Racial Hatred," *Soundtracks to the White Revolution: White Supremacist Assaults on Youth Music Subcultures*, ed. Devin Burghart (Chicago: Center for New Community, 1999), 65; Johannes Lohmann and Hans Wanders, "Evolas Jünger und Odins Krieger: Extrem rechte Ideologien in der Dark-Wave- und Black-Metal-Szene," *RechtsRock: Bestandsaufnahme und Gegenstrategien*, ed. Christian Dornbusch and Jan Raabe (Münster: Unrast, 2002), 297.

133 Nicholas Goodrick-Clarke, *Black Sun: Aryan Cults, Esoteric Nazism and the Politics of Identity* (New York: New York University Press, 2002), 204.

134 Ibid., 203.

135 Mattias Gardell, *Gods of the Blood: The Pagan Revival and White Separatism* (Durham, NC: Duke University Press, 2003), 305.

136 Mutilation, June 14, 2005 (11:56 PM), comment on pyccka82, "CD Reviews," April 16, 2005 (9:50 PM), *Stormfront*, https://www.stormfront.org/forum/t198817 -2/?s=2117de657b50e2945392ad84fd5d9901.

137 Otsdr, December 11, 2007 (4:57 PM), comment on pyccka82, "CD Reviews," April 16, 2005 (9:50 PM), *Stormfront*, https://www.stormfront.org/forum/t198817 -20/.

138 Mutilation, July 3, 2005 (11:06 PM), comment on pyccka82, "CD Reviews," April 16, 2005 (9:50 PM), *Stormfront*, https://www.stormfront.org/forum/t198817-3/.

139 Michael Moynihan, "The Lords of Black Metal: Scandinavian Satanists Go Berserk," Burzum.com, accessed September 22, 2013, http://www.burzum.com/ burzum/library/articles/high_society/ [reader discretion strongly advised].

140 Enrico Ahlig, "Marduk-Gitarrist besitzt Leichenteile von Dead: Hirn und Knochen an einem sicheren Ort," *Metal Hammer*, June 5, 2012, accessed September 22, 2013, http://www.metal-hammer.de/news/meldungen/article299447/marduk-gitarrist -besitzt-leichenteile-von-dead.html.

141 Nicholas Goodrick-Clarke, *Black Sun*, 205.

142 Michael Moynihan and Didrik Søderlind, *Lords of Chaos: The Bloody Rise of the Satanic Metal Underground*, rev. ed. (Port Townsend, WA: Feral House, 2003), 111.

143 Ibid., 145.

144 Ibid., 92–93, 149.

145 Ibid., 148.

146 Varg Víkernes, "A Burzum Story: Part II—Euronymous," *Burzum.org: Official Varg Vikernes' Website*, December 2004, accessed September 22, 2013, http://www .burzum.org/eng/library/a_burzum_story02.shtml.

147 Ibid.

148 Philip Sherburne, "Burzum's Varg Vikernes, Neo-Nazi, Arrested in France on Terrorism Suspicions," *Spin*, July 16, 2013, accessed May 26, 2014, http://www.spin .com/articles/burzum-varg-vikernes-neo-nazi-arrested-terrorism/.

149 "'Neo-Nazi' Musician Vikernes in French Terror Arrest," *BBC News Europe*, July 16, 2013, accessed September 22, 2013, http://www.bbc.co.uk/news/world-europe -23327165.

150 "Man Linked to Norwegian Mass Killer Breivik Arrested in France," *Reuters*, July 16, 2013, accessed September 22, 2013, http://www.reuters.com/article/2013/ 07/16/us-france-norway-breivik-idUSBRE96F0FY20130716.

151 Varg Vikernes, "A Burzum Story: Part VII—The Nazi Ghost," *Burzum.org: Official Varg Vikernes' Website*, July 2005, accessed September 22, 2013, http://www.burzum .org/eng/library/a_burzum_story07.shtml.

152 Kyle McGovern, "Varg Vikernes' Lawyer Needs More Time to Defend Neo-Nazi in 'Racial Hatred' Trial," *Spin*, October 18, 2013, accessed November 1, 2013, http:// www.spin.com/articles/varg-vikernes-neo-nazi-racial-hatred-trial-delay-2014 -burzum/; "Norwegian Neo-Nazi Released from Custody," *UPI Top News* (July 19, 2013).

153 Sean Michaels, "Kristian 'Varg' Vikernes Guilty of Inciting Racial Hatred, French Court Rules," *The Guardian*, July 9, 2014, accessed August 4, 2014, http://www .theguardian.com/music/2014/jul/09/kristian-varg-vikernes-guilty-inciting-racial -hatred; Dan Reilly, "Burzum's Varg Vikernes Found Guilty of 'Inciting Racial Hatred,'" *Spin*, July 10, 2014, accessed August 4, 2014, http://www.spin.com/ articles/varg-vikernes-guilty-inciting-racial-hatred/.

154 Krieger Germaniens14, September 21, 2008 (1:52 PM), comment on pyccka82, "CD Reviews," April 16, 2005 (9:50 PM), *Stormfront*, https://www.stormfront.org/ forum/t198817-23/.

155 Weiss, "Deutschland im September," 61; Lohmann and Wanders, "Evolas Jünger," 301.

156 Lowles, "Die Internationale," 257.

157 Gardell, *Gods of the Blood*, 317.

158 Massa, "Unholy Alliance," 52.

159 Bob Moore, "The Rescue of Jews from Nazi Persecution: A Western European Per-spective," *Journal of Genocide Research* 5:2 (2003), 299; Christopher Tyerman, *God's War: A New History of the Crusades* (Cambridge, MA: Belknap Press of Harvard University Press, 2009), 100.

160 Roger Cohen, "French Church Issues Apology to Jews on War," *New York Times*, October 1, 1997, accessed August 18, 2015, http://www.nytimes.com/1997/10/01/ world/french-church-issues-apology-to-jews-on-war.html.

161 Ibid.

162 "Paris Marks Algerian Protest 'Massacre,'" *BBC News*, October 17, 2001, accessed December 1, 2013, http://news.bbc.co.uk/2/hi/world/monitoring/media_reports/ 1604970.stm.

163 Claire Suddath, "Who Are Gypsies, and Why Is France Deporting Them?," *Time World*, August 26, 2010, accessed September 25, 2013, http://content.time.com/ time/world/article/0,8599,2013917,00.html.

164 Kim Willsher, "France's Deportation of Roma Shown to be Illegal in Leaked Memo, Say Critics," *The Guardian*, September 13, 2010, accessed September 25, 2013, http://www.theguardian.com/world/2010/sep/13/france-deportation-roma-illegal -memo.

165 Steven Erlanger, "Has the 'Burqa Ban' Worked in France?," *International Herald Tribune*, September 2, 2012, accessed September 24, 2013, http://rendezvous.blogs .nytimes.com/2012/09/02/has-the-burqa-ban-worked-in-france/?_r=0.

166 Catherine Mayer et al., "The March to the Far Right," *Time International* South Pacific Edition 174:5 (August 10, 2009), accessed October 6, 2015, http://content .time.com/time/magazine/article/0,9171,1913651,00.html.

167 Angelique Chrisafis, "France's Burqa Ban: Women are 'Effectively under House Arrest,'" *The Guardian*, September 19, 2011, accessed September 25, 2013, http:// www.theguardian.com/world/2011/sep/19/battle-for-the-burqa.

168 Adam Nossiter and Liz Alderman, "After Paris Attacks, a Darker Mood Toward Islam Emerges in France," *New York Times*, November 16, 2015, accessed November 22, 2015, http://www.nytimes.com/2015/11/17/world/europe/after-paris -attacks-a-darker-mood-toward-islam-emerges-in-france.html?_r=0.

169 James Shields, *The Extreme Right in France: From Pétain to Le Pen* (New York: Routledge, 2007), 229.

170 Cas Mudde, *Populist Radical Right Parties in Europe* (Cambridge: Cambridge University Press, 2007), 41.

171 Edward G. DeClair, *Politics on the Fringe: The People, Policies and Organization of the French National Front* (Durham, NC: Duke University Press, 1999), 115; Shields, *The Extreme Right*, 272; Lifland, "Right Wing Rising," 10.

172 Bruno Waterfield, "Jean-Marie Le Pen Repeats Holocaust Comments in European Parliament," *The Telegraph*, March 25, 2009, accessed May 26, 2014, http://www .telegraph.co.uk/news/worldnews/europe/france/5050338/Jean-Marie-Le-Pen -repeats-Holocaust-comments-in-European-Parliament.html; Mayer et al, "The March to the Far Right."

173 Dornbusch and Raabe, "20 Jahre RechtsRock," 25.

174 Nicolas Lebourg and Dominique Sistach, "The Role of Underground Music in the Renewal of the French Radical Right-Wing," in *White Power Music: Scenes of Extreme-Right Cultural Resistance*, ed. Anton Shekhovtsov and Paul Jackson (Ilford: Searchlight, 2012), 25.

175 Ibid.

176 Lowles, "Die Internationale," 259.

177 Ju-87, July 6, 2006 (10:34 AM), comment on pyccka82, "CD Reviews," April 16, 2005 (9:50 PM), *Stormfront*, https://www.stormfront.org/forum/t198817-11/.

178 Lebourg and Sistach, "The Role," 26 & 32.

179 Ibid., 25, 26; Lowles, "Die Internationale," 238.

180 Gardell, *Gods of the Blood*, 85.

181 Silver, "Blood and Honour," 12–13.

182 Ibid., 13.

183 "Blood & Honour Midgard Expands," *Blood & Honour* 22 (2001), accessed October 6, 2015, http://www.bloodandhonourworldwide.co.uk/magazine/issue22/ issue22p15.html.

184 Lowles, "Die Internationale," 238.

185 Ian Westwell, *Condor Legion: The Wehrmacht's Training Ground* (Birmingham, UK: Ian Allen Publishing, 2004), 23; Sebastian Balfour and Paul Preston, *Spain and the Great Powers in the Twentieth Century* (New York: Routledge, 2009), 172.

186 Chris Ealham and Michael Richards, *The Splintering of Spain: Cultural History and the Spanish Civil War, 1936–1939* (Cambridge: Cambridge University Press, 2005), 2–3.

187 C. U. Lipschitz, *Franco, Spain, the Jews, and the Holocaust* (New York: Ktav Publishing House, 1984), 8.

188 Haim Avni, *Spain, the Jews, and Franco*, trans. Emanuel Shimoni (Philadelphia:

Jewish Publication Society of America, 1982 [1974]), 50; Bernd Rother, *Spanien und der Holocaust* (Tübingen: Max Niemeyer Verlag, 2001), 130–132.

189 Bernard Spolsky, *Language Policy* (Cambridge: Cambridge University Press, 2004), 197.

190 Manuela Caiani and Linda Parenti, "The Spanish Extreme Right and the Internet," *Análise Social* 46:201 (2011), 721.

191 Marcial, June 29, 2014 (10:43 AM), comment on guest, "European Mediterranean Folk Music [Greek, Dalmatian (South Croatian) & Italian etc . . .]," *Stormfront*, June 26, 2014 (7:28 PM), https://www.stormfront.org/forum/t1049172/#post12197457.

192 Silver, "Blood and Honour," 25; "The Violent Storm Memorial," *Blood & Honour Worldwide*, accessed July 26, 2013, http://www.bloodandhonourworldwide.co.uk/history/violentstorm.html; Carlos Caballero Jurado and Ramiro Bujeiro, *Blue Division Soldier 1941–1945: Spanish Volunteer on the Eastern Front* (Essex: Osprey Publishing, 2009), 34.

193 "Encontre Neonazi a Alacant Organitzat per l'Associació Ultra Alfonso X," *Antifeixistes*, August 5, 2009, accessed July 27, 2013, http://www.antifeixistes.org/3334_encontre-neonazi-alacant-organitzat-lassociacio-ultra-alfonso.htm.

194 "Patria," *Blood & Honour* 23 (2001), accessed October 6, 2014, http://www.bloodandhonourworldwide.co.uk/magazine/issue23/issue23%20patria.html; Lowles, "Die Internationale," 244; "Iberos Saiti," accessed November 1, 2011, http://www.oocities.org/sunsetstrip/performance/1378/iberos.htm.

195 Lowles, "Die Internationale," 244.

196 "News from the Frontline."

197 Lowles, "Die Internationale," 244.

198 Ibid.

199 "Patria."

200 Lowles, "Die Internationale," 237.

201 Ibid., 244.

202 "News from the Frontline."

203 Lowles, "Die Internationale," 244.

204 Ju-87, February 17, 2007 (7:53 AM), comment on pyccka82, "CD Reviews," April 16, 2005 (9:50 PM), *Stormfront*, https://www.stormfront.org/forum/t198817-15/.

205 Ann Thomas Wilkins, "Augustus, Mussolini, and the Parallel Imagery of Empire," *Donatello among the Blackshirts: History and Modernity in the Visual Culture of Fascist Italy*, ed. Claudia Lazzaro and Roger J. Crum (Ithaca, NY: Cornell University Press, 2005), 53.

206 Jozo Tomasevich, *War and Revolution in Yugoslavia, 1941–1945: Occupation and Collaboration* (Stanford: Stanford University Press, 2001), 131; Giancarlo Cresciani, "A Clash of Civilizations?: The Slovene and Italian Minorities and the Problem of Trieste from Borovnica to Bonegilla," *Italian Historical Society Journal* 12:2 (2004), 4; Davide Rodogno, *Fascism's European Empire: Italian Occupation during the Second World War* (Cambridge: Cambridge University Press, 2006), 106; Owen Pearson, *Albania in the Twentieth Century: A History*, vol. 3 (New York: I. B. Taurus Publishers, 2004), 389; John F. L. Ross, *Neutrality and International Sanctions: Sweden, Switzerland and Collective Security* (Santa Barbara: Praeger, 1989), 91; John Wright, *A History of Libya* (New York: Columbia University Press, 2012), 165; MacGregor Knox, *Mussolini Unleashed 1939–1941: Politics and Strategy in Fascist Italy's Last War* (Cambridge: Cambridge University Press, 1982), 38.

207 Aaron Gillette, *Racial Theories in Fascist Italy* (New York: Routledge, 2002), 51–52.

208 *Constitution of the Italian Republic,* Senate of the Republic, official translation, 1947, accessed November 2, 2013, http://www.senato.it/documenti/repository/ istituzione/costituzione_inglese.pdf, 41.
209 Richard J. Evans, "A New Threat for a New Era," *New Statesman* 141:5112 (July 2, 2012), 30.
210 Mayer et al., "The March to the Far Right."
211 K. Biswas, "Eyes to the Far Right," *New Internationalist* 443 (June 2011), 17.
212 Lowles, "Die Internationale," 245.
213 Dornbusch and Raabe, "20 Jahre RechtsRock," 25; Lowles, "Die Internationale," 245–246.
214 Silver, "Blood and Honour," 25; Lowles, "Die Internationale," 246.
215 Lowles, "Die Internationale," 247.
216 "Veneto Front Show the Way!," *Blood & Honour* 20 (2000), accessed October 6, 2015, http://www.bloodandhonourworldwide.co.uk/magazine/issue20/issue20p10 .html; Lowles, "Die Internationale," 246.
217 Ibid.
218 "Veneto Front Report," *Blood & Honour* 23 (2001), accessed October 4, 2015, http://www.bloodandhonourworldwide.co.uk/magazine/issue23/issue23 %20veneto%20front%20report.html.
219 Lowles, "Die Internationale," 246–247.
220 Ibid., 247.
221 "Gesta Bellica," *Blood & Honour* 19 (2000), accessed October 6, 2015, http://www .bloodandhonourworldwide.co.uk/magazine/issue19/issue19p34,35.html.
222 *Nazi Hate Rock.*

Chapter 4   The History of White-Power Music in Eastern Europe

1 Roger Boyes, "Germans Dance to Neo-Nazi Tune of Racial Hatred," *The Times* (October 30, 1997), 14; Rafał Pankowski, "Nazi Music in Poland," in *White Noise: Inside the International Nazi Skinhead Scene,* ed. Nick Lowles and Steve Silver (Ilford: Searchlight, 1998), 66; Miroslav Mareš and Josef Smolík, "White Power Music and Interconnected Issues in the Czech Republic, 1999–2011," *White Power Music: Scenes of Extreme-Right Cultural Resistance,* ed. Anton Shekhovtsov and Paul Jackson (Ilford: Searchlight, 2012), 72–73.
2 Debórah Dwork and Robert Jan van Pelt, *Holocaust: A History* (New York: W.W. Norton, 2002), 379.
3 Bohdan Vitvitsky, "Slavs and Jews: Consistent and Inconsistent Perspectives on the Holocaust," in *A Mosaic of Victims: Non-Jews Persecuted and Murdered by the Nazis,* ed. Michael Berenbaum (New York: New York University Press, 1990), 104.
4 Norman Davies, *God's Playground: A History of Poland, Vol. 2: 1795 to the Present,* rev. 2nd ed. (New York: Columbia University Press, 2005), 329–330.
5 "Kolovrat Interview 2010," *Revolt NS,* November 9, 2010, accessed November 5, 2013, http://revoltns.blogspot.com/2010/11/kolovrat-interview-2010.html.
6 Norman Polmar and Thomas B. Allen, *World War II: The Encyclopedia of the War Years: 1941–1945* (New York: Random House, 1996), 831.
7 James V. Wertsch, "National Narratives and the Conservative Nature of Collective Memory," *Neohelicon* 34:2 (2007), 23.
8 *The Jewish Peril: Protocols of the Learned Elders of Zion* (London: The Britons, 1920; reprinted by Elibron Classics, 2005).

9 Dwork and van Pelt, *Holocaust*, 46-48.
10 Orlando Figes, *The Whisperers: Private Life in Stalin's Russia* (New York: Picador USA, 2007), 493.
11 Jonathan Brent and Vladimir Naumov, *Stalin's Last Crime: The Plot Against the Jewish Doctors, 1948-1953* (New York: Harper Perennial, 2004), 328.
12 John M. Cotter, "Sounds of Hate: White Power Rock and Roll and the Neo-Nazi Skinhead Subculture," *Terrorism and Political Violence* 11:2 (1999), 275.
13 "Vandal," *Blood & Honour* 22 (2001), accessed October 7, 2015, http://www.bloodandhonourworldwide.co.uk/magazine/issue22/issue22p22,23a.html.
14 Anne Applebaum, *Gulag: A History*, 1st ed. (New York: Doubleday, 2003), 437-438.
15 J. Otto Pohl, "Stalin's Genocide Against the 'Repressed Peoples,'" *Journal of Genocide Research* 2:2 (2000), 267.
16 Eric J. Schmaltz and Samuel D. Sinner, "'You Will Die under Ruins and Snow': The Soviet Repression of Russian Germans as a Case Study of Successful Genocide," *Journal of Genocide Research* 4:3 (2002), 335-336.
17 Tom Parfitt, "Billionaires Boom as Putin Puts Oligarchs at No. 2 in Global Rich List," *The Guardian*, February 18, 2008, accessed December 2, 2013, http://www.theguardian.com/world/2008/feb/19/russia.
18 John B. Dunlop, *Russia Confronts Chechnya: Roots of a Separatist Conflict* (Cambridge: Cambridge University Press, 1998), 169; Valery Tishkov, *Chechnya: Life in a War-Torn Society* (Berkeley: University of California Press, 2004), 127-128.
19 Bruno S. Sergi, *Misinterpreting Modern Russia: Western Views of Putin and his Presidency* (New York: Continuum International Publishing Group, 2009), 60-62.
20 Martin Laryš and Miroslav Mareš, "Right-Wing Extremist Violence in the Russian Federation," *Europe-Asia Studies* 63:1 (2011), 133.
21 John B. Dunlop, "The Moscow Bombings of September 1999 (full text): Examinations of Russian Terrorist Attacks at the Onset of Vladimir Putin's Rule," *The Stanford Post-Soviet Post*, February 20, 2013, accessed August 19, 2015, http://postsovietpost.stanford.edu/node/161.
22 "Vandal."
23 Artyom Liss, "Neo-Nazi Skinheads Jailed in Russia for Racist Killings," *BBC News*, February 25, 2013, accessed November 5, 2013, http://news.bbc.co.uk/2/hi/8537861.stm.; Richard Arnold, "Visions of Hate: Explaining Neo-Nazi Violence in the Russian Federation," *Problems of Post-Communism* 57:2 (2010), 38.
24 Laryš and Mareš, "Right-Wing Extremist Violence," 138.
25 Ibid., 137.
26 Ibid., 148.
27 Arnold, "Visions of Hate," 37.
28 Vladimir Shlapentokh, "The Hatred of Others: The Kremlin's Powerful but Risky Weapon," *World Affairs* 169:3 (2007), 134, 135.
29 Ibid., 135.
30 Laryš and Mareš, "Right-Wing Extremist Violence," 133.
31 Ibid., 134.
32 Arnold, "Visions of Hate," 43.
33 Laryš and Mareš, "Right-Wing Extremist Violence," 150.
34 Liss, "Neo-Nazi Skinheads."
35 Alec Luhn, "Russian Anti-Gay Law Prompts Rise in Homophobic Violence," *The Guardian*, September 1, 2013, accessed November 5, 2013, http://www.theguardian.com/world/2013/sep/01/russia-rise-homophobic-violence.

36 Jaymi McCann, "Russian Neo-Nazis Torture Gay Teenager they Tricked into Meeting them as Part of Online Scam," *Daily Mail*, July 27, 2013, accessed November 5, 2013, http://www.dailymail.co.uk/news/article-2379967/Russian-neo-Nazis -torture-gay-teenager-tricked-meeting-online-scam.html.

37 Kyle McGovern, "Pussy Riot Protest Footage Scrubbed from Russian Internet," *Spin*, January 31, 2013, accessed September 27, 2015, http://www.spin.com/2013/ 01/pussy-riot-putin-protest-footage-banned-russia-internet/; Miriam Elder, "Pussy Riot Sentenced to Two Years in Prison Colony over Anti-Putin Protest," *The Guardian*, August 17, 2012, accessed September 27, 2015, www.theguardian.com/music/ 2012/aug/17/pussy-riot-sentenced-prison-putin?newsfeed=true.

38 "Kolovrat Interview 2010."

39 Ibid.

40 "Kolovrat Interview," *Hail the New Dawn R.A.C. Skinhead Webzine*, October 26, 2012, accessed May 26, 2014, http://hailthenewdawn.blogspot.com/2012/10/ kolovrat-interview.html; "Kolovrat Interview 2010."

41 "Kolovrat Interview 2010."

42 Ibid.

43 Ibid.

44 "Blood & Honour Scene News," *Blood & Honour* 44 (2010), accessed October 7, 2015, http://www.bloodandhonourworldwide.co.uk/magazine/issue44/issue44p _26.html.

45 Jan Velinger, "Court Acquits Member of Russian Skinhead Band of Nazi Propagation Charges," *Radio Praha*, October 19, 2004, accessed May 26, 2014, http:// radio.cz/en/section/news/court-acquits-member-of-russian-skinhead-band-of -neo-nazi-propagation-charges; "Prague Court Drops Neo-Nazi Singer's Acquittal," *Israel National News*, December 25, 2004, accessed May 26, 2014, http://www .israelnationalnews.com/News/Flash.aspx/74152; "Czech—Arrest of a Russian Neo-Nazi in Prague," *The Coordination Forum for Countering Antisemitism*, February 4, 2004, accessed May 26, 2014, http://antisemitism.org.il/article/53824/czech -%E2%80%93-arrest-russian-neo-nazi-prague.

46 Pavla Horáková, "Acquittal of Russian Skinhead Singer Overturned," *Radio Praha*, December 16, 2004, accessed May 26, 2014, http://www.radio.cz/en/section/ news/acquittal-of-russian-skinhead-singer-overturned.

47 "Kolovrat Interview 2010."

48 Ibid.

49 "Vandal"; "Kolovrat Interview 2010."

50 Branikald, December 7, 2008 (1:02 PM), comment on pyccka82, "CD Reviews," April 16, 2005 (9:50 PM), *Stormfront*, https://www.stormfront.org/forum/t198817 -25/.

51 Stephen D. Shenfield, *Russian Fascism: Traditions, Tendencies, Movements* (Armonk, NY: M. E. Sharpe, 2001), 278.

52 Anna Arutunyan, "Sobyanin Registers to Run for Moscow Mayor," *The Moscow News*, June 17, 2013, accessed November 6, 2013, http://themoscownews.com/ politics/20130617/191618046-print/Sobyanin-registers-to-run-for-Moscow -mayor.html; "Number of Khimki Mayoral Hopefuls up to 15," *The Moscow Times*, August 31, 2012, accessed November 6, 2013, http://www.themoscowtimes.com/ news/article/number-of-khimki-mayoral-hopefuls-up-to-15/467445.html; Jacek Hugo-Bader, *White Fever: A Journey to the Frozen Heart of Siberia*, trans. Antonia Lloyd-Jones (London: Portobello Books, 2009), 73–74.

53 *Encyclopaedia Metallum: The Metal Archives*, accessed November 3, 2012, http://www.metal-archives.com/.

54 "Russian Thrash Metal Legend's Song Banned as Extremist," *Russian Legal Information Agency*, September 27, 2013, accessed November 6, 2013, http://rapsinews.com/news/20130927/268980454.html.

55 Hugo-Bader, *White Fever*, 75.

56 "Russian Thrash Metal."

57 "Kolovrat Interview 2010."

58 "Sokyra Peruna Interview," *Revolt NS*, October 16, 2010, accessed November 7, 2013, http://revoltns.blogspot.com/2010/10/sokyra-peruna-interview.html.

59 Marta Baziuk, "Behind Ukraine's Protest Are Memories of Moscow's Famine," *The Globe and Mail*, December 11, 2013, accessed May 7, 2014, http://www.theglobeandmail.com/globe-debate/behind-ukraines-protest-are-memories-of-moscows-famine/article15868147/.

60 Harriet Alexander, "Ukraine Revolution: Tuesday February 25 as it Happened," *The Daily Telegraph*, February 25, 2014, accessed May 7, 2014, http://www.telegraph.co.uk/news/worldnews/europe/ukraine/10659755/Ukraine-revolution-live.html; Somini Sengupta, "Russia Vetoes U.N. Resolution on Crimea," *New York Times*, March 15, 2014, accessed May 7, 2014, http://www.nytimes.com/2014/03/16/world/europe/russia-vetoes-un-resolution-on-crimea.html?_r=0.

61 "Crimea Votes to Secede: Ukraine's Amputation," *The Economist*, March 17, 2014, accessed May 7, 2014, http://www.economist.com/blogs/easternapproaches/2014/03/crimea-votes-secede.

62 Louis Charbonneau, "U.N. Will Treat Crimea as Part of Ukraine, not Russia: U.S.," *Reuters*, April 2, 2014, accessed May 7, 2014, http://www.reuters.com/article/2014/04/02/us-ukraine-crisis-un-idUSBREA311TD20140402.

63 Luke Harding and Shaun Walker, "Ukraine's President Fears Russia Could Invade after Crimea Referendum," *The Guardian*, March 15, 2014, accessed May 26, 2014, http://www.theguardian.com/world/2014/mar/15/ukraine-russia-invade-crimea-referendum.

64 Poison, May 5, 2014 (11:50 PM), comment on Nikolay88, "Война в Украине. На чьей вы стороне? War in Ukraine. What party you support?," *Stormfront*, May 4, 2014, https://www.stormfront.org/forum/t1039382/.

65 White Army, May 6, 2014 (12:09 AM), comment on Nikolay88, "Война в Украине. На чьей вы стороне? War in Ukraine. What party you support?," *Stormfront*, May 4, 2014, https://www.stormfront.org/forum/t1039382/.

66 Poison May 6, 2014 (7:28 AM), comment on Nikolay88, "Война в Украине. На чьей вы стороне? War in Ukraine. What party you support?," *Stormfront*, May 4, 2014, https://www.stormfront.org/forum/t1039382/.

67 "Interview with Nokturnal Mortum," *Firegoat.com*, November 1, 2001, accessed November 6, 2013, http://www.firegoat.com/eng/?id=3&d=16.

68 "Pagan of Ukraine: Interview with Sokyra Peruna," *Resistance* 25 (Winter 2005), 25.

69 Krieger Germaniens14, August 17, 2008 (2:44 PM), comment on pyccka82, "CD Reviews," April 16, 2005 (9:50 PM), *Stormfront*, https://www.stormfront.org/forum/t198817-23/.

70 StormBeforeCalm, September 15, 2008 (8:42 PM), comment on pyccka82, "CD Reviews," April 16, 2005 (9:50 PM), *Stormfront*, https://www.stormfront.org/forum/t198817-23/.

71 Krieger Germaniens14, August 17, 2008 (2:44 PM), comment on pyccka82,

"CD Reviews," April 16, 2005 (9:50 PM), *Stormfront*, https://www.stormfront.org/forum/t198817-23/.

72 Thomas Land, "Disappointed Eastern Europe Confronts its Neo-Nazis," *Contemporary Review* 291:1694 (2009), 284.

73 *Encyclopaedia Metallum*.

74 Ibid.

75 Romme115, March 14, 2014 (12:40 PM), comment on VasiliofMurmansk, "Who owns Belarus and Ukraine?," January 22, 2014 (7:39 PM), https://www.stormfront.org/forum/t1019226/#post11963452.

76 Shlapentokh, "The Hatred of Others," 134; Laryš and Mareš, "Right-Wing Extremist Violence," 136; Marlène Laruelle, "The Ideological Shift on the Russian Radical Right: From Demonizing the West to Fear of Migrants," *Problems of Post-Communism* 57:6 (2010), 23.

77 "Interview with Nokturnal Mortum."

78 Norman Davies, *God's Playground*, 297 & 320; Lucy S. Dawidowicz, *The War Against the Jews: 1933-1945* (New York: Bantam, 1986), 112.

79 Dawidowicz, *The War*, 111-112.

80 Norman Davies, *God's Playground*, 330, 332; Jan Tomasz Gross, *Fear: Anti-Semitism in Poland after Auschwitz* (Westminster, MD: Random House, 2006), 5.

81 Davies, *God's Playground*, 334-335; Gross, *Fear*, 9-10.

82 Wojciech Materski and Tomasz Szarota, *Polska 1939-1945. Straty Osobowe i Ofiary Represji pod Dwiema Okupacjami* (Warsaw: Institute of National Remembrance, 2009), 29-30, 32; Davies, *God's Playground*, 366.

83 Megan G. Swindal, "Ideology and Social Position in Poland: The Determinants of Voting for the Right, 1991-2005," *Social Science Quarterly* 92:1 (March 2011), 190; Norman Davies, *God's Playground*, 129.

84 Bonnie G. Smith, *Europe in the Contemporary World 1900 to the Present: A Narrative History with Documents* (Boston: Bedford/St. Martin's, 2007), 632.

85 Ibid., 634-635.

86 Gross, *Fear*, 260.

87 Nick Lowles, "Die Internationale des Hasses," in *RechtsRock: Bestandsaufnahme und Gegenstrategien*, ed. Christian Dornbusch and Jan Raabe (Münster: Unrast, 2002), 234.

88 Michael Weiss, "Deutschland im September," in *Rechtsrock: Bestandsaufnahme und Gegenstrategien*, ed. Christian Dornbusch and Jan Raabe (Münster: Unrast Verlag, 2002), 80.

89 PatrykNOP, September 15, 2007 (8.48 AM), comment on CelticaPL, "Polish thread," *Stormfront*, March 4, 2006 (6:05 AM), https://www.stormfront.org/forum/t275274-89/#post4602976.

90 Henning Flad, "Trotz Verbot nicht Tot," in *RechtsRock: Bestandsaufnahme und Gegenstrategien*, ed. Christian Dornbusch and Jan Raabe (Münster: Unrast, 2002), 104.

91 Falangist, October 22, 2011 (11:26 AM), comment on *revision*, "WWII German soldiers reburied in Poland," *Stormfront*, October 21, 2011 (1:43 PM), https://www.stormfront.org/forum/t840059-3/#post9671464.

92 "Polish Musical Resistance: History of the Polish Musical Resistance Scene," *Blood & Honour* 44 (2010), 9; "S.E.K.," *Blood & Honour* 19 (2000), accessed October 7, 2015, http://www.bloodandhonourworldwide.co.uk/magazine/issue19/issue19p16,17a.html.

93 Pankowski, "Nazi Music in Poland," 65.

94 Ibid.

95 Hugh Trevor-Roper, *From Counter-Reformation to Glorious Revolution* (Chicago: University of Chicago Press, 1992), 51.

96 Dawidowicz, *The War*, 395–397; Gross, *Fear*, 28.

97 Gross, *Fear*, 258.

98 T. David Curp, *A Clean Sweep? The Politics of Ethnic Cleansing in Western Poland, 1945–1960* (Rochester, NY: University of Rochester Press, 2006), 3; Gross, *Fear*, 4–5.

99 Lowles, "Die Internationale," 251.

100 Ibid., 252.

101 "Polish Musical Resistance."

102 Lowles, "Die Internationale," 252.

103 Pankowski, "Nazi Music in Poland," 66–67.

104 Ibid., 67.

105 Pankowski, "Nazi Music in Poland," 67–68; "Polish Musical Resistance"; Lowles, "Die Internationale," 253.

106 Pankowski, "Nazi Music in Poland," 68–69; Lowles, "Die Internationale," 252–253.

107 "Polish Musical Resistance."

108 Ibid.

109 Pankowski, "Nazi Music in Poland," 69.

110 "Polish Musical Resistance."

111 Pankowski, "Nazi Music in Poland," 69.

112 Ibid.

113 "White Devils," *Blood & Honour* 44 (2010), accessed October 7, 2015, http://www .bloodandhonourworldwide.co.uk/magazine/issue44/issue44p_10.html.

114 Weiss, "Deutschland im September," 83.

115 Misha Glenny, *The Balkans: Nationalism, War, and the Great Powers, 1804–1999* (New York: Penguin Books, 1999), 465, 477, 536–540; Stevan K. Pavlowitch, *A History of the Balkans: 1804–1999* (London and New York: Longman, 1999), 309.

116 Smith, *Europe*, 392–393.

117 Glenny, *The Balkans*, 620–622.

118 "George Papadopoulos; Led Military Junta in Greece," *Los Angeles Times*, June 28, 1999, accessed December 3, 2013, http://articles.latimes.com/1999/jun/28/news/ mn-50904.

119 Glenny, *The Balkans*, 620–622.

120 "George Papadopoulos."

121 Smith, *Europe*, 684.

122 William Spindler, "Number of Refugees and Migrants Arriving in Greece Soars 750 Per Cent over 2014," *United Nations High Commissioner for Refugees*, August 7, 2015, accessed September 27, 2015, http://www.unhcr.org/55c4d1fc2.html.

123 Yiannis Baboulias, "The EU's Woeful Response to the Refugee Crisis has Revived Golden Dawn," *The Guardian*, September 21, 2015, accessed September 27, 2015, http://www.theguardian.com/commentisfree/2015/sep/21/eu-refugee-crisis -golden-dawn-greek-neo-nazi-europe; Sarah Burke, "Golden Dawn Doubles Vote Share on Greek Island of Kos," *NBC News*, Associated Press and Reuters, September 21, 2015, accessed September 27, 2015, http://www. nbcnews.com/storyline/ europes-border-crisis/golden-dawn-doubles-vote-share-greek-island-kos-n430776.

124 Sofia Tipaldou, "Rock for the Motherland: White Power Music Scene in Greece,"

White Power Music: Scenes of Extreme-Right Cultural Resistance, ed. Anton Shek-hovtsov and Paul Jackson (Ilford: Searchlight, 2012), 47, 49.

125 Ibid., 49.

126 "Naer Mataron," *Black MetalTR English*, April 3, 2009, accessed December 3, 2013, http://blackmetaltr.forumotion.com/t16-blackmetaltr-naer-mataron.

127 Tipaldou, "Rock," 49.

128 Ibid., 51.

129 Ju-87, May 2, 2005 (6:53 AM), comment on pyccka82, "CD Reviews," April 16, 2005 (9:50 PM), *Stormfront*, https://www.stormfront.org/forum/t198817/.

130 *Skinhouse Hellas*, accessed August 4, 2014, http://www.skinhouse.gr/.

131 Tipaldou, "Rock," 52–53.

132 Manfred Ertel, "'Like 1930s Germany': Greek Far Right Gains Support," *Finweek*, trans. Ella Ornstein (May 2, 2013), 20.

133 "Stosstrupp," *Blood & Honour* 22 (2001), accessed October 7, 2015, http://www.bloodandhonourworldwide.co.uk/magazine/issue22/issue22p16,17.html.

134 James Bone, "Neo-Nazi MP 'Hit Girl' after Greek Food Bank Clash," *The Times* (May 3, 2013), 24.

135 "Far-Right Golden Dawn MP Giorgos Germenis Hits 12-Year-Old Girl in Attack on Athens Mayor Giorgos Kaminis over Greek-Only Food Handout," *The Independent*, May 2, 2013, accessed November 28, 2013, http://www.independent.co.uk/news/world/europe/farright-golden-dawn-mp-giorgos-germenis-hits-12yearold-girl-in-attack-on-athens-mayor-giorgos-kaminis-over-greekonly-food-handout-8600980.html.

136 "Two Golden Dawn MPs Imprisoned in Greece," *Al-Jazeera*, January 12, 2014, accessed August 22, 2015, http://www.aljazeera.com/news/europe/2014/01/two-golden-dawn-mps-imprisoned-greece-2014112316757959.html.

137 Bonnie Malkin, ed., "Two More Golden Dawn MPs Jailed in Greece," *The Telegraph*, January 12, 2014, accessed August 22, 2015, http://www.telegraph.co.uk/news/worldnews/europe/greece/10566498/Two-more-Golden-Dawn-MPs-jailed-in-Greece.html.

138 "Jailed Greek Lawmakers Appear in Parliament," *Daily Mail*, Associated Press, May 7, 2014, accessed August 22, 2015, http://www.dailymail.co.uk/wires/ap/article-2622314/Jailed-Greek-lawmakers-appear-Parliament.html.

139 Niki Kitsantonis, "Trial Postponed for Greek Neo-Fascist Golden Dawn Party Members," *New York Times*, April 20, 2015, accessed August 22, 2015, http://www.nytimes.com/2015/04/21/world/europe/golden-dawn-trial-greece.html?_r=0.

140 propagandistis, September 28, 2013 (3:05 AM), comment on Therion, "Greece's Golden Dawn leader Nikos Mihaloliakos arrested," *Stormfront*, September 28, 2013 (2:41 AM), https://www.stormfront.org/forum/t996347/.

141 AmericanRobin, September 28, 2013 (3:08 AM), comment on Therion, "Greece's Golden Dawn leader Nikos Mihaloliakos arrested," *Stormfront*, September 28, 2013 (2:41 AM), https://www.stormfront.org/forum/t996347/.

Chapter 5   The History of White-Power Music outside Europe

1 See, for example, Noel Ignatiev, *How the Irish Became White* (New York: Routledge, 1995); and Thomas Guglielmo, *White on Arrival: Italians, Race, Color, and Power in Chicago, 1890–1945* (London: Oxford University Press, 2003).

2 David E. Stannard, *American Holocaust: Columbus and the Conquest of the New World* (Oxford: Oxford University Press, 1992), x.

3 Frank Schumacher, "Colonization through Education: A Comparative Exploration of Ideologies, Practices, and Cultural Memories of 'Aboriginal Schools' in the United States and Canada," *Zeitschrift für Kanada-Studien* 2 (2006), 99–102, 107; United Nations, *Convention on the Prevention and Punishment of the Crime of Genocide* (Paris: United Nations, 1948); Tony Barta, "Sorry, and not Sorry, in Australia: How the Apology to the Stolen Generations Buried a History of Genocide," *Journal of Genocide Research* 10:2 (2008), 201–214.

4 Michelle Sarche and Paul Spicer, "Poverty and Health Disparities for American Indian and Alaska Native Children: Current Knowledge and Future Prospects," *Annals of the New York Academy of Sciences* 1136 (2008), accessed October 7, 2015, http://www.ncbi.nlm.nih.gov/pmc/articles/PMC2567901/, 2 & 5.

5 "An Overview of Aboriginal Health in Canada," National Collaborating Centre for Aboriginal Health, 2013, accessed August 20, 2015, http://www.nccah -ccnsa.ca/Publications/Lists/Publications/Attachments/101/abororiginal_health _web.pdf, 4.

6 Joe R. Feagin, *The White Racial Frame: Centuries of Racial Framing and Counter Framing*, 1st ed. (New York: Routledge, 2010), 46.

7 Robert A. Divine et al., *The American Story*, 5th ed., combined volume (Upper Saddle River, NJ: Pearson & Penguin Academics, 2013), 88–90.

8 James L. Roark et al., *Understanding the American Promise: A Brief History* (New York: Bedford St. Martin's, 2011), 125.

9 Ibid., 341.

10 Douglas A. Blackmon, *Slavery by Another Name: The Re-Enslavement of Black Americans from the Civil War to World War II* (New York: Anchor Books, 2009), 226–227; Jennifer D. Keene, Saul Cornell, and Edward T. O'Donnell, *Visions of America: A History of the United States*, 2nd ed., combined volume (Boston: Pearson, 2013), 422, 432–433.

11 Feagin, *White Racial Frame*, 210.

12 Valerie Strauss, "From Ferguson to Baltimore: The Consequences of Government-Sponsored Segregation," *Washington Post*, May 3, 2015, accessed August 20, 2015, http://www.washingtonpost.com/blogs/answer-sheet/wp/2015/05/03/from -ferguson-to-baltimore-the-consequences-of-government-sponsored-segregation/.

13 Ralph Ellis, Ben Brumfield, and Meridith Edwards, "S.C. Governor Signs Bill to Remove Confederate Flag from Capitol Grounds," *CNN*, July 10, 2015, accessed August 26, 2015, http://www.cnn.com/2015/07/09/us/south-carolina-confederate -battle-flag/.

14 Ibid.

15 "Reactions to Racism Not as Strong as We Think, Study Finds," *CBC News*, January 8, 2009, accessed April 5, 2014, http://www.cbc.ca/news/technology/reactions -to-racism-not-as-strong-as-we-think-study-finds-1.858913. (In the interest of full disclosure, I was among the research subjects who participated in this study.)

16 Keene, Cornell, and O'Donnell, *Visions of America*, 505–506 & 624; Canadian Race Relations Foundation, "Legalized Racism," accessed April 6, 2014, http:// www.crr.ca/divers-files/en/pub/faSh/ePubFaShLegRac.pdf, 1–2.

17 Suzanne Goldenberg, "Islamophobia Worse in America Now than after 9/11, Survey Finds," *The Guardian*, March 9, 2006, accessed May 26, 2014, http://www .theguardian.com/world/2006/mar/10/usa.religion.

18 John Geddes, "Canadian Anti-Muslim Sentiment is Rising, Disturbing New Poll Reveals," *Maclean's*, October 3, 2013, accessed May 5, 2014, http://www.macleans.ca/politics/land-of-intolerance/.

19 Jonathan J. Cooper, "Ariz. Immigration Law Target of Protest," *NBC News*, April 26, 2010, accessed August 20, 2015, http://www.nbcnews.com/id/36768649/#.VdZ70ck4xyw; Jens Manuel Krogstad and Mark Hugo Lopez, "Hispanic Population Reaches Record 55 Million, but Growth has Cooled," *Pew Research Center*, June 25, 2015, accessed August 20, 2015, http://www.pewresearch.org/fact-tank/2015/06/25/u-s-hispanic-population-growth-surge-cools/.

20 Mattias Gardell, *Gods of the Blood: The Pagan Revival and White Separatism* (Durham, NC: Duke University Press, 2003), 339–340; *Nazi Hate Rock: A Donal MacIntyre Investigation*, directed by Michael Simkin, (London: Channel 5, 2009), DVD.

21 Gardell, *Gods of the Blood*, 47; *Metapedia*, accessed July 31, 2013, www.metapedia.org.

22 Jessica S. Henry, "Beyond Free Speech: Novel Approaches to Hate on the Internet in the United States," *Information & Communications Technology Law* 18:2 (2009), 237.

23 Ju-87, January 25, 2006 (5:55 PM), comment on pyccka82, "CD Reviews," April 16, 2005 (9:50 PM), *Stormfront*, https://www.stormfront.org/forum/t198817-7/.

24 Beth A. Messner et al., "The Hardest Hate: A Sociological Analysis of Country Hate Music," *Popular Music and Society* 30:4 (2007), 516.

25 Michael Wade, "Johnny Rebel and the Cajun Roots of Right-Wing Rock," *Popular Music and Society* 30:4 (October 2007), 496; Nick Pittman, "Johnny Rebel Speaks," *Gambit*, June 10, 2003, accessed August 23, 2015, http://www.bestofneworleans.com/gambit/johnny-rebel-speaks/Content?oid=1241588.

26 Wade, "Johnny Rebel," 501.

27 Ibid., 496.

28 Pittman, "Johnny Rebel Speaks."

29 Ibid.

30 Ibid.

31 Fiddler, June 6, 2008 (8:54 PM), comment on portuguesevisigoth, "Johnny rebel," *Stormfront*, March 7, 2008 (6:03 PM), https://www.stormfront.org/forum/t467297-2/.

32 Wade, "Johnny Rebel," 494.

33 Pittman, "Johnny Rebel Speaks."

34 Ibid.

35 Jovina74, December 11, 2014 (7:30 AM), comment on UlsterScot12, "19 year old girl burned alive in Mississippi," *Stormfront*, December 8, 2014 (5:31 PM), https://www.stormfront.org/forum/t1077502-48/#post12531850.

36 IIII SWP IIII, March 31, 2008 (12:29 AM), comment on portuguesevisigoth, *Stormfront*, March 7, 2008 (6:03 PM), https://www.stormfront.org/forum/t467297/.

37 Nick Lowles, "Die Internationale des Hasses," in *RechtsRock: Bestandsaufnahme und Gegenstrategien*, ed. Christian Dornbusch and Jan Raabe (Münster: Unrast, 2002), 255.

38 Leonard Zeskind, "A Bad Moon Rising—White Power Skins in America," *White Noise: Inside the International Nazi Skinhead Scene*, ed. Nick Lowles and Steve Silver (Ilford: Searchlight, 1998), 70–71.

39 Ibid., 74.

40 "Geraldo Rivera's Nose Broken in Scuffle on his Talk Show," *New York Times*, November 4, 1988, accessed May 26, 2014, http://www.nytimes.com/1988/11/04/ nyregion/geraldo-rivera-s-nose-broken-in-scuffle-on-his-talk-show.html.

41 Robb London, "Sending a $12.5 Million Message to a Hate Group," *New York Times*, October 26, 1990, accessed July 26, 2013, http://www.nytimes.com/1990/10/ 26/news/sending-a-12.5-million-message-to-a-hate-group.html.

42 Zeskind, "A Bad Moon Rising," 74.

43 Ibid., 74–75.

44 "Educator Alert! Hate Music Label Targets Schools," *Anti-Defamation League of B'nai B'rith*, November 8, 2004, accessed July 29, 2013, http://archive.adl.org/ education/neo_nazi_music.asp.

45 "Bound for Glory," *Blood & Honour* 19 (2000), 25.

46 Ju-87, April 30, 2005 (9:40 AM), comment on pyccka82, "CD Reviews," April 16, 2005 (9:50 PM), *Stormfront*, https://www.stormfront.org/forum/t198817/.

47 Zeskind, "A Bad Moon Rising," 75.

48 Gardell, *Gods of the Blood*, 86.

49 Hawthorne, George Eric [George Burdi], "Music of the White Resistance," *White Riot: Punk Rock and the Politics of Race*, ed. Stephen Duncombe and Maxwell Tremblay (New York: Verso, 2011), 138.

50 "National Alliance's Resistance Magazine Loses its Printer," *Southern Poverty Law Center Intelligence Report* 121 (2006), accessed October 7, 2015, https://www .splcenter.org/fighting-hate/intelligence-report/2006/national-alliances-resistance -magazine-loses-its-printer; Heléne Lööw, "White-Power Rock'n'Roll: A Growing Industry," in *Nation and Race: The Developing Euro-American Racist Subculture*, ed. Jeffrey Kaplan and Tore Bjørgo (Boston: Northeastern University Press, 1998), 138; Steve Silver, "Blood and Honour 1987–1992," in *White Noise: Inside the International Nazi Skinhead Scene*, ed. Nick Lowles and Steve Silver (Ilford: Searchlight, 1998), 19.

51 Cliff Southwell, "'White Pride World Wide'?: The Internet and the Global Marketing of White Power Rock," in *White Noise: Inside the International Nazi Skinhead Scene*, ed. Nick Lowles and Steve Silver (Ilford: Searchlight, 1998), 78.

52 *Nazi Hate Rock*.

53 Zeskind, "A Bad Moon Rising," 76.

54 Southwell, "'White Pride World Wide'?," 80.

55 Ibid.; Nicholas Goodrick-Clarke, *Black Sun: Aryan Cults, Esoteric Nazism and the Politics of Identity* (New York: New York University Press, 2002), 211.

56 "'Inside Hate Rock': George Burdi," *USA Today*, January 21, 2005, accessed May 26, 2014, http://usatoday30.usatoday.com/community/chat/2002-02-18-burdi.htm.

57 Ju-87, January 16, 2008 (10:54 AM), comment on pyccka82, "CD Reviews," April 16, 2005 (9:50 PM), *Stormfront*, https://www.stormfront.org/forum/t198817-20/.

58 Ju-87, April 30, 2005 (8:31 AM), comment on pyccka82, "CD Reviews," April 16, 2005 (9:50 PM), *Stormfront*, https://www.stormfront.org/forum/t198817/.

59 ISA, March 13, 2005 (4:27 AM), "What Was The First WN Band You Listened To?," *Stormfront*, https://www.stormfront.org/forum/t191011/.

60 madmark88, January 28, 2012 (2:11 AM), "YOUR TOP 10 WHITE POWER BANDS," *Stormfront*, https://www.stormfront.org/forum/t862818/.

61 "Deafening Hate: Deafening Hate: The Revival of Resistance Records," Anti-Defamation League of B'nai B'rith, 2000, accessed November 3, 2013, http:// archive.adl.org/resistance%20records/print.asp.

62 Ibid.; Weiss, "Deutschland im September," in *Rechtsrock: Bestandsaufnahme und Gegenstrategien*, ed. Christian Dornbusch and Jan Raabe (Münster: Unrast Verlag, 2002), 71.

63 William L. Pierce, "Message from the Publisher," *Resistance* 10 (Winter 2000), 3.

64 Ibid.; Gardell, *Gods of the Blood*, 316; *Metapedia*.

65 Erich Gliebe, "Editorial," *Resistance* 13 (Fall 2000), 2.

66 Robert Futrell, Pete Simi, and Simon Gottschalk, "Understanding Music in Movements: The White Power Music Scene," *The Sociological Quarterly* 47 (2006), 283; "Erich Gliebe," Southern Poverty Law Center, accessed September 17, 2012, http://www.splcenter.org/get-informed/intelligence-files/profiles/erich-gliebe; "Shaun Walker," Southern Poverty Law Center, accessed May 26, 2014, http://www .splcenter.org/get-informed/intelligence-files/profiles/shaun-walker.

67 "National Alliance's Resistance."

68 Ju-87, April 3, 2006 (6:59 AM), comment on pyccka82, "CD Reviews," April 16, 2005 (9:50 PM), *Stormfront*, https://www.stormfront.org/forum/t198817-9/.

69 "Neo-Nazi Group Run by North Royalton Man has Withered, Says Southern Poverty Law Center," *United Skinheads*, July 23, 2012, accessed April 6, 2014, http:// www.unitedskins.net/index.php/tag/resistance-records/.

70 Odessa14, January 31, 2014 (12:25 PM), comment on WhiteMarine1488, "Resistance Records died," *Stormfront*, January 28, 2014 (10:56 PM), http://www.stormfront .org/forum/t1020483/; Ian Moone [username], February 8, 2014 (9:08 AM), comment on WhiteMarine1488, "Resistance Records died," *Stormfront*, January 28,2014 (10:56 PM), http://www.stormfront.org/forum/t1020483/.

71 Resistance Records, accessed February 15, 2016, http://www.resistance.com/site/.

72 "Tri-State Terror: The Music that Hurts Your Feelings," *Blood & Honour* 19 (2000), accessed October 7, 2015, http://www.bloodandhonourworldwide.co.uk/ magazine/issue19/issue19p03.html.

73 Ibid.; *Metapedia*.

74 Weiss, "Deutschland im September," 55.

75 "Tri-State Terror: The Music that Hurts Your Feelings."

76 Heidi Beirich and Mark Potok, "'40 to Watch: Leaders of the Radical Right," *Southern Poverty Law Center Intelligence Report* 111 (2003), accessed July 29, 2013, http:// www.splcenter.org/get-informed/intelligence-report/browse-all-issues/2003/fall/ 40-to-watch?page=0,5.

77 Jeff Horwich, "Top 'White Power' Music Label Prospers from Twin Cities Home Base," *Minnesota Public Radio*, May 13, 2004, accessed July 29, 2013, http://news .minnesota.publicradio.org/features/2004/05/13_horwichj_panzerfaust/.

78 Jeff Horwich, "Racist Sampler CDs Headed for the 'Schoolyard,'" *Minnesota Public Radio*, September 29, 2004, accessed July 29, 2013, http://news.minnesota .publicradio.org/features/2004/09/29_horwichj_panzerfaust/; "Educator Alert!"; "Panzerfaust Collapses amid Aryan Purity Debate," *Southern Poverty Law Center Intelligence Report* 117 (Spring 2005), accessed July 29, 2013, http://www.splcenter.org/ get-informed/intelligence-report/browse-all-issues/2005/spring/white-power-music.

79 "Educator Alert!"

80 Horwich, "Top 'White Power'" (parenthetical expression in the original).

81 "Panzerfaust Collapses."

82 Ibid.; "Panzerfaust Apparently Out of Business," Anti-Defamation League of B'nai B'rith, March 1, 2005, accessed July 29, 2013, http://archive.adl.org/extremism/ panzerfaust_records.asp.

83 Odessa14, July 15, 2014 (3:58 P.M.), comment on skoallio, "Is White Power Music dead? What happened. . . . ?," *Stormfront*, July 5, 2014 (9:49 PM), https://www.stormfront.org/forum/t1050805/.

84 DomesticTerror, January 2, 2015 (2:36 AM), comment on skoallio, "Is White Power Music dead? What happened. . . . ?," *Stormfront*, July 5, 2014 (9:49 PM), https://www.stormfront.org/forum/t1050805-3/.

85 Ju-87, April 26, 2008 (8:06 AM), comment on pyccka82, "CD Reviews," April 16, 2005 (9:50 PM), *Stormfront*, https://www.stormfront.org/forum/t198817-22/.

86 Lowles, "Die Internationale," 256.

87 "April Gaede," Southern Poverty Law Center, accessed April 6, 2014, http://www.splcenter.org/get-informed/intelligence-files/profiles/april-gaede.

88 "Double Vision with Prussian Blue: Interview with Lynx and Lamb Gaede," *Resistance* 22 (Winter 2004), 12.

89 "Neo-Nazi Girl Band Reinvent themselves as Liberal 'Healers' with Medicinal Marijuana Cards," *The Daily Mail*, July 19, 2011, accessed May 1, 2014, http://www.dailymail.co.uk/news/article-2016296/Were-healers-Prussian-Blue-twins-say-Neo-Nazi-pop-group-phase-plan-push-legalisation-marijuana.html.

90 "Double Vision," 13.

91 *Nazi Pop Twins*, directed by James Quinn (IMG Media, 2007); Louis Theroux, *Louis and the Nazis*, directed by Stuart Cobb (BBC, 2003); "Teen People Magazine Neglects to Mention Neo-Nazism in Profile of Singers Lynx and Lamb Gaede," *Southern Poverty Law Center Intelligence Report* 120 (2005); Aaron Gell, "Minor Threat," *GQ*, March 2006, accessed May 26, 2014, http://www.gq.com/entertainment/music/200602/prussia-blue-hitler.

92 Juju Chang, Cameron Brock, and Jim Dubreuil, "Teen Twins Lamb and Lynx Gaede Deny Neo-Nazi Past, Say 'It Was a Job,'" *Good Morning America*, July 21, 2011, accessed May 26, 2014, http://abcnews.go.com/US/teen-twins-lamb-lynx-gaede-deny-neo-nazi/story?id=14124412.

93 Ibid.; "Double Vision," 14; Nick Enoch, "'Marijuana Changed Us from Nazis to Peace-Loving Hippies': Twin Sisters who Sparked Outrage with Pop Band Named after Gas Used on Jews Claim They've Grown Up," *Daily Mail*, June 27, 2012, accessed May 29, 2014, http://www.dailymail.co.uk/news/article-2165342/Prussian-Blue-twins-Lynx-Lamb-Marijuana-changed-Nazis-peace-loving-hippies.html.

94 David Daugherty [username], "Fragment of the Future Review," August 4, 2005 (3:38 AM), comment on pyccka82, "CD Reviews," *Stormfront*, April 16, 2005 (9:50 PM), https://www.stormfront.org/forum/t198817-3/.

95 WhiteMansBurden82, December 3, 2014 (12:33 AM), comment on Tremley, "Halle Berry takes ex to Court because he is making their daughter look too White," *Stormfront*, November 25, 2014 (7:11 PM), https://www.stormfront.org/forum/t1075407-4/#post12516199.

96 Dr. Ford [username], December 3, 2014 (1:16 AM), comment on Tremley, "Halle Berry takes ex to Court because he is making their daughter look too White," *Stormfront*, November 25, 2014 (7:11 PM), https://www.stormfront.org/forum/t1075407-4/#post12516199.

97 Mazombo, July 1, 2015 (4:02 AM), comment on skoallio, "Is White Power Music dead? What happened. . . . ?," *Stormfront*, July 5, 2014 (9:49 PM), https://www.stormfront.org/forum/t1101530/; laptop, January 28, 2015 (12:30 AM), comment on skoallio, "Is White Power Music dead? What happened. . . . ?," *Stormfront*, July 5, 2014 (9:49 PM), https://www.stormfront.org/forum/t1050805-3/.

98 Branikald, October 18, 2008 (3:13 AM), comment on pyccka82, "CD Reviews," *Stormfront*, April 16, 2005 (9:50 PM), https://www.stormfront.org/forum/ t198817-24/.

99 John Lunsford, "Nazis, Noise and Nihilism: Infiltrating the Experimental Music Scene," *Soundtracks to the White Revolution: White Supremacist Assaults on Youth Music Subcultures*, ed. Devin Burghart (Chicago: Center for New Community, 1999), 75.

100 Lowles, "Die Internationale," 256.

101 Lunsford, "Nazis," 79.

102 Joe Heim, "Wade Michael Page was Steeped in Neo-Nazi 'Hate Music' Movement," *Washington Post,* August 7, 2012, accessed May 26, 2014, http://www .washingtonpost.com/lifestyle/style/wade-michael-page-was-steeped-in-neo-nazi -hate-music-movement/2012/08/07/b879451e-dfe8-11e1-a19c-fcfa365396c8_story .html; Heidi Beirich and Mark Potok, "Alleged Sikh Temple Shooter Former Member of Skinhead Band," Southern Poverty Law Center, August 6, 2012, accessed May 26, 2014, http://www.splcenter.org/get-informed/news/alleged-sikh-temple -shooter-former-member-of-skinhead-band.

103 Steven Yaccino, Michael Schwirtz, and Marc Santora, "Gunman Kills 6 at a Sikh Temple Near Milwaukee," *New York Times*, August 5, 2012, accessed November 3, 2013, http://www.nytimes.com/2012/08/06/us/shooting-reported-at-temple-in -wisconsin.html.

104 Anton Shekhovtsov, "Introduction," in *White-Power Music: Scenes of Extreme-Right Cultural Resistance*, ed. Anton Shekhovtsov and Paul Jackson (Ilford: Searchlight, 2012), 5; Ryan Lenz, "Neo-Nazi Killer Wade Michael Page was Member of Hammerskin Nation," *Southern Poverty Law Center Hatewatch*, August 8, 2012, accessed July 18, 2015, http://www.splcenter.org/blog/2012/08/08/neo-nazi-killer -wade-page-was-member-of-hammerskin-nation/.

105 Ju-87, May 14, 2005 (12:58 P.M.), comment on pyccka82, "CD Reviews," April 16, 2005 (9:50 P.M.), *Stormfront*, https://www.stormfront.org/forum/t198817/.

106 Mark S. Hamm, *In Bad Company: America's Terrorist Underground* (Boston: Northeastern University Press, 2002), 144–145, 173–174, 177, 242; Ambrose Evans-Pritchard, "America's 'Aryan' Hard Men Take Lead from IRA," *London Sunday Telegraph*, December 8, 1996, accessed August 21, 2015, http://web.archive.org/ web/20050308065313/ http://www.telegraph.co.uk/htmlContent.jhtml?html=/ archive/1996/12/08/wamby08.html.

107 Andrew V. Pestano, "20 Years Since Oklahoma City Bombing; Worst Act of Domestic Terrorism," *United Press International (UPI)*, April 19, 2015, accessed August 21, 2015, http://www.upi.com/Top_News/US/2015/04/19/20-years-since -Oklahoma-City-bombing-worst-act-of-domestic-terrorism/4771429452092/.

108 Hamm, *In Bad Company*, 244, 296–297.

109 Ibid., 294–295.

110 Scott Stedeford, "Official Letter," *Scottstedeford.com*, 2015, accessed August 21, 2015, http://www.scottstedeford.com/wp-content/uploads/2014/05/Scott-Anthony -Stedeford-Official-letter.pdf.

111 Reebee Garofalo, *Rockin' Out: Popular Music in the USA* (Needham Heights, MA: Allyn & Bacon, 1997), 145.

112 Michael A. McDonnell and A. Dirk Moses, "Raphael Lemkin as Historian of Genocide in the Americas," *Journal of Genocide Research* 7:4 (2005), 502–505.

113 See, for example, Christopher Powell, *Barbaric Civilization: A Critical Sociology of Genocide* (Montreal: McGill-Queen's University Press, 2011), 194–198.

114 "Race and Poverty in Latin America: Addressing the Development Needs of African Descendants," *UN Chronicle*, September 2007, accessed April 22, 2014, http://unchronicle.un.org/article/race-and-poverty-latin-america-addressing-development-needs-african-descendants/.

115 "Inequality in Latin America & the Caribbean: Breaking with History?," *The World Bank*, October 7, 2003, accessed April 22, 2014, http://web.worldbank.org.

116 Jeronimo Montero, *Neoliberal Fashion: The Political Economy of Sweatshops in Europe and Latin America* (PhD dissertation, Durham University, UK, 2011), accessed May 27, 2014, http://etheses.dur.ac.uk/3205/1/Montero._PhD_THESIS_FINAL.pdf#?. 105.

117 Goodrick-Clarke, *Black Sun*, 173.

118 Edward Paulino, "Open Wounds from the Past: Repercussions of the 1937 Haitian Massacre" (presentation at Kean University, Union, NJ, April 10, 2014).

119 Gitta Sereny, *Into That Darkness: An Examination of Conscience* (New York: Vintage Books, 1983 [1974]), 357; Allan Hall, "Secret Files Reveal 9,000 Nazi War Criminals Fled to South America after WWII," *Daily Mail*, March 19, 2012, accessed April 21, 2014, http://www.dailymail.co.uk/news/article-2117093/Secret-files-reveal-9-000-Nazi-war-criminals-fled-South-America-WWII.html; Georg Bönisch and Klaus Wiegrefe, "From Nazi Criminal to Postwar Spy: German Intelligence Hired Klaus Barbie as Agent," *Der Spiegel*, January 20, 2011, accessed April 30, 2014, http://www.spiegel.de/international/germany/from-nazi-criminal-to-postwar-spy-german-intelligence-hired-klaus-barbie-as-agent-a-740393.html.

120 Nicholas Goodrick-Clarke, *Black Sun*, 174–175, 177.

121 Ibid., 180–182.

122 Ibid., 184.

123 For example, see Mark Jonathan Rogers, *The SS-Ahnenerbe and the 1938/39 German-Tibet Expedition* (Ann Arbor, MI: UMI Dissertation Services, 2002).

124 Nicholas Goodrick-Clarke, *Black Sun*, 191.

125 Serrano quoted in Irwin Suall et al., *The Skinhead International: A Worldwide Survey of Neo-Nazi Skinheads* (New York: Anti-Defamation League of B'nai B'rith, 1995), 24.

126 galazoaimatos-hellas, November 9, 2014 (9:30 AM), comment on galazoaimatos-hellas, "LATIN AMERICA RAC & W.P. MUSIC !," *Stormfront*, December 28, 2013 (9:09 AM), https://www.stormfront.org/forum/t1014007-4/.

127 Suall et al., *The Skinhead International*, 10.

128 "Gig in Argentina," *NS Revolt*, June 11, 2010, accessed April 16, 2014, http://revoltns.blogspot.com/2010/06/gig-in-argentina.html.

129 Ibid.; "ISD Memorial Argentina," *NS Revolt*, September 21, 2011, accessed April 16, 2014, http://revoltns.blogspot.com/2011/09/isd-memorial-aregentina.html.

130 "ISD Memorial Argentina;" "Gig in Argentina."

131 Sereny, *Into That Darkness*, 40; Suall et al., *The Skinhead International*, 17.

132 Suall et al., *The Skinhead International*, 17–18.

133 Ibid., 18.

134 Ibid., 17–18.

135 "R.A.C. Encyclopedia—Part 7," *Revolt NS*, January 31, 2012, accessed April 20, 2014, http://revoltns.blogspot.com/2012/01/rac-encyclopedia-part-7.html.

136 Ibid.

137 "D.A.," *Blood & Honour* 19 (2000), 6.

138 "ISD Memorial Argentina 2010," *Blood & Honour*, accessed April 16, 2014, http://28magallanes.blogspot.com/p/foro.html.

139 Suall et al., *The Skinhead International*, 24.

140 Ibid.

141 "Banda," *Blood & Honour*, accessed April 16, 2014, http://28magallanes.blogspot.com/p/banda_30.html.

142 "South América Skinheads," accessed April 16, 2014, http://www.oocities.org/sunsetstrip/performance/1378/southamerica.htm; "ISD Memorial Argentina"; galazoaimatos-hellas, November 9, 2014 (9:29 AM), comment on galazoaimatos-hellas, "LATIN AMERICA RAC & W.P. MUSIC !," *Stormfront*, December 28, 2013 (9:09 AM), https://www.stormfront.org/forum/t1014007-4/.

143 'South América Skinheads;' Suall et al., *The Skinhead International*, 25; galazoaimatos-hellas, February 8, 2007 (9:27 AM), "huetramannaland—interview," *Stormfront*, http://www.stormfront.org/forum/t362674/.

144 "R.A.C. Encyclopedia"; galazoaimatos-hellas, December 4, 2010 (10:16 AM), "SOUTHERN WARRIORS Interview," *Stormfront*, http://www.stormfront.org/forum/t761799/.

145 galazoaimatos-hellas January 6, 2014 (3:38 PM), comment on galazoaimatos-hellas, "LATIN AMERICA RAC & W.P. MUSIC !," *Stormfront*, December 28, 2013 (9:09 AM), http://www.stormfront.org/forum/t1014007/.

146 galazoaimatos-hellas January 19, 2014 (3:43 PM), comment on galazoaimatos-hellas, "LATIN AMERICA RAC & W.P. MUSIC !," *Stormfront*, December 28, 2013 (9:09 AM), http://www.stormfront.org/forum/t1014007-2/.

147 "Racial Discrimination and Miscegenation: The Experience in Brazil," *UN Chronicle* 44:3 (2007), accessed May 27, 2014, http://unchronicle.un.org/article/racial-discrimination-and-miscegenation-experience-brazil/.

148 Ibid.; Paulino, "Open Wounds."

149 Paulino, "Open Wounds."

150 galazoaimatos-hellas, May 14, 2015 (4:18 PM), comment on galazoaimatos-hellas, "LATIN AMERICA RAC & W.P. MUSIC !," *Stormfront*, December 28, 2013 (9:09 AM), https://www.stormfront.org/forum/t1014007-6/#post12811692.

151 James Henderson, *Sent Forth a Dove: Discovery of the Duyfken* (Perth: University of Western Australia Press, 1999), 35; Norbert Finzsch, "'The Aborigines . . . were Never Annihilated, and still they are Becoming Extinct': Settler Imperialism and Genocide in Nineteenth-Century America and Australia," in *Empire, Colony, Genocide: Conquest, Occupation, and Subaltern Resistance in World History*, ed. A. Dirk Moses (New York: Berghahn Books, 2008), 254–255; Jan Kociumbas, "Genocide and Modernity in Colonial Australia, 1788–1850," in *Genocide and Settler Society: Frontier Violence and Stolen Indigenous Children in Australian History*, ed. A. Dirk Moses (New York: Berghahn Books, 2004), 79.

152 Suemedha Sood, "Australia's Penal Colony Roots," *BBC*, January 26, 2012, accessed May 5, 2014, http://www.bbc.com/travel/blog/20120126-travelwise-australias-penal-colony-roots.

153 Finzsch, "'The Aborigines,'" 254.

154 Kociumbas, "Genocide and Modernity," 80–83.

155 A. Dirk Moses, "Genocide and Settler Society in Australian History," in *Genocide and Settler Society: Frontier Violence and Stolen Indigenous Children in Australian History*, ed. A. Dirk Moses (New York: Berghahn Books, 2004), 18.

156 Henry Reynolds, "Genocide in Tasmania?," in *Genocide and Settler Society: Frontier*

Violence and Stolen Indigenous Children in Australian History, ed. A. Dirk Moses (New York: Berghahn Books, 2004), 129.

157 Colin Tatz, "Genocide in Australia," *Journal of Genocide Research* 1:3 (1999), 324–325.

158 Robert Manne, "Aboriginal Child Removal and the Question of Genocide, 1900–1940," in *Genocide and Settler Society: Frontier Violence and Stolen Indigenous Children in Australian History*, ed. A. Dirk Moses (New York: Berghahn Books, 2004), 220.

159 Ibid.

160 Tatz, "Genocide in Australia," 334–335.

161 Ibid., 331, 334.

162 Barta, "Sorry," 201, 208–211.

163 Ibid.

164 "Poverty Report: October 2011 Update," *Australian Council of Social Service*, 2011 [2006], accessed May 5, 2014, http://acoss.org.au/images/uploads/ACOSS _Poverty_October_2011.pdf; "UN Accuses Australia of 'Entrenched Racism' towards Aborigines," *The Guardian*, August 27, 2009, accessed May 5, 2014, http:// www.theguardian.com/world/2009/aug/27/aborigines-un-racism-australia.

165 Tom Minear, "Australians are Racist and Unfriendly, Say Migrants," *Herald Sun*, March 25, 2014, accessed May 5, 2014, http://www.news.com.au/national/ australians-are-racist-and-unfriendly-say-migrants/story-fncynjr2-1226862883355.

166 Paul R. Bartrop, "The Holocaust, the Aborigines, and the Bureaucracy of Destruction: An Australian Dimension of Genocide," *Journal of Genocide Research* 3:1 (2001), 80.

167 "The Harley Column of the Mad N.S. Biker," *Blood & Honour* 19 (2000), 22–23.

168 "A Brief History of Neo-Nazi Music in Australia," *Slackbastard*, December 2, 2010, accessed July 30, 2013, http://slackbastard.anarchobase.com/?p=22224.

169 Ibid.

170 Ju-87, February 3, 2008 (9:04 AM), comment on pyccka82, "CD Reviews," April 16, 2005 (9:50 PM), *Stormfront*, https://www.stormfront.org/forum/t198817-21/.

171 "A Brief History."

172 "Kolovrat Interview 2010," *Revolt NS*, November 9, 2010, accessed November 5, 2013, http://revoltns.blogspot.com/2010/11/kolovrat-interview-2010.html.

173 Suall et al., *The Skinhead International*, 11.

174 Ju-87, January 21, 2008 (1:16 PM), comment on pyccka82, "CD Reviews," April 16, 2005 (9:50 PM), *Stormfront*, https://www.stormfront.org/forum/t198817-21/.

175 Ju-87, June 28, 2005 (9:39 AM), comment on pyccka82, "CD Reviews," April 16, 2005 (9:50 PM), *Stormfront*, https://www.stormfront.org/forum/t198817-2/?s= 2117de657b50e2945392ad84fd5d9901; Ju-87, February 3, 2008 (8:29 AM), comment on pyccka82, "CD Reviews," April 16, 2005 (9:50 PM), *Stormfront*, https://www .stormfront.org/forum/t198817-21/.

176 "Deaths Head," *Blood & Honour* 24 (2002), accessed October 7, 2015, http://www .bloodandhonourworldwide.co.uk/magazine/issue24/issue24p18.html.

177 Ibid.

178 "Blood & Honour Australia: The Independent Voice of Rock Against Communism," *Blood & Honour* 21 (2001), 14; "Bail Up!," *Blood & Honour* 23 (2001), accessed October 7, 2015, http://www.bloodandhonourworldwide.co.uk/ magazine/issue23/issue23%20bail%20up!.html.

179 Ibid.

Chapter 6 Conclusion

1 Larry Hochberg, "Henry Rollins: Walking on Dry Land," *VH1 News*, January 29, 2002, accessed January 7, 2014, http://www.mtv.com/news/articles/1452005/henry-rollins-walking-on-dry-land.jhtml.

2 "Diamond in the Dust: The Ian Stuart Biography," Combat 18, accessed August 24, 2015, http://www.skrewdriver.com/Ian_Stuart_Diamond_In_The_Dust.html.

3 Kirsten Dyck, "The (Un)Popularity of White-Power Music," in *Music at the Extremes: Essays on Sounds outside the Mainstream*, ed. Scott Wilson (Jefferson, NC: McFarland, 2015), 157–177.

4 See, for example, the description of Skrewdriver in Al Spicer, "Skrewdriver," *The Rough Guide to Punk* (New York: Rough Guides, 2006), 292.

5 Joe R. Feagin, *The White Racial Frame: Centuries of Racial Framing and Counter Framing*, 1st ed. (New York: Routledge, 2010), 109–110, 130–131.

6 Ibid., viii–ix, 144–145, 210; Michelle Alexander, *The New Jim Crow: Mass Incarceration in the Age of Colorblindness* (New York: New Press, 2012), 124–125, 182–183, 236–238.

Select Bibliography

Baacke, Dieter, Klaus Farin, and Jürgen Lauffer, eds. *Rock von Rechts II: Milieus, Hintergründe und Materialien.* Bielefeld: Vorstand der Gesellschaft für Medienpädagogik und Kommunikationskultur in der Bundesrepublik Deutschland (GMK) e.V., 2000.

Brown, Timothy S. "Subcultures, Pop Music and Politics: Skinheads and 'Nazi Rock' in England and Germany." *Journal of Social History* 38:1 (2004). 157–178.

Burghart, Devin, ed. *Soundtracks to the White Revolution: White Supremacist Assaults on Youth Music Subcultures.* Chicago: Center for New Community, 1999. 23–40.

Corte, Ugo, and Bob Edwards. "White Power Music and the Mobilization of Racist Social Movements." *Music & Arts in Action* 1:1 (2008). 4–20.

Cotter, John M. "Sounds of Hate: White Power Rock and Roll and the Neo-Nazi Skinhead Subculture." *Terrorism and Political Violence* 11:2 (1999). 111–140.

Dobratz, Betty A., and Stephanie L. Shanks-Meile. *"White Power, White Pride!": The White Separatist Movement in the United States.* New York: Macmillan, 1997.

Dornbusch, Christian, and Jan Raabe, eds. *RechtsRock: Bestandsaufnahme und Gegenstrategien.* Münster: Unrast, 2002. 19–50.

———. "Rechtsrock fürs Vaterland." *Braune Kameradschaften: Die neuen Netzwerke der militanten Neonazis,* ed. Andrea Röpke and Andreas Speit. Berlin: Ch. Links Verlag, 2004. 67–85.

———. "'White-Power'-Music in Germany: Development—Dimensions—Trends." *White-Power Music: Germany in the World.* Göttingen, Germany, June 4, 2012.

Farin, Klaus. "'Rechts-Rock.'" *Rechtsextremismus in Deutschland: Voraussetzungen, Zusammenhänge, Wirkungen,* ed. Wolfgang Benz. Frankfurt am Main: Fischer Taschenbuch Verlag, 1994. 137–153.

Futrell, Robert, Pete Simi, and Simon Gottschalk. "Understanding Music in Movements: The White Power Music Scene." *Sociological Quarterly* 47 (2006). 275–304.

Gardell, Mattias. *Gods of the Blood: The Pagan Revival and White Separatism.* Durham, NC: Duke University Press, 2003.

Goodrick-Clarke, Nicholas. *Black Sun: Aryan Cults, Esoteric Nazism and the Politics of Identity.* New York: New York University Press, 2002.

Hamm, Mark S. *In Bad Company: America's Terrorist Underground.* Boston: Northeastern University Press, 2002.

Laryš, Martin, and Miroslav Mareš. "Right-Wing Extremist Violence in the Russian Federation." *Europe-Asia Studies* 63:1 (2011). 129–154.

Lööw, Heléne. "White-Power Rock'n'Roll: A Growing Industry." *Nation and Race: The Developing Euro-American Racist Subculture.* Ed. Jeffrey Kaplan and Tore Bjørgo. Boston: Northeastern University Press, 1998. 126–143.

Lowles, Nick, and Steve Silver, eds. *White Noise: Inside the International Nazi Skinhead Scene.* Ilford: Searchlight, 1998.

Messner, Beth A., et al. "The Hardest Hate: A Sociological Analysis of Country Hate Music." *Popular Music and Society* 30:4 (2007). 513–531.

Moynihan, Michael, and Didrik Søderlind. *Lords of Chaos: The Bloody Rise of the Satanic Metal Underground.* Rev. ed. Port Townsend, WA: Feral House, 2003.

Nazi Hate Rock: A Donal MacIntyre Investigation. Directed by Michael Simkin. Channel 5, 2009.

Nazi Pop Twins. Directed by James Quinn. IMG Media, 2007.

Romper Stomper. Directed by Geoffrey Wright. Film Victoria, 1992.

Shekhovtsov, Anton. "European Far-Right Music and Its Enemies." *Analysing Fascist Discourse: European Fascism in Talk and Text.* Ed. Ruth Wodak and John E. Richardson. London: Routledge, 2013. 277–296.

Shekhovtsov, Anton, and Paul Jackson, eds. *White-Power Music: Scenes of Extreme-Right Cultural Resistance.* Ilford: Searchlight, 2012.

Simi, Pete, and Robert Futrell. *American Swastika: Inside the White Power Movement's Hidden Spaces of Hate.* New York: Rowman & Littlefield, 2010.

Stroud, Joe. "'And for Those of You that Hate Metal . . .': The Softer Side of Extreme Right Music." *White-Power Music: Germany in the World.* Göttingen, Germany, June 4, 2012.

Suall, Irwin, et al. *The Skinhead International: A Worldwide Survey of Neo-Nazi Skinheads.* New York: Anti-Defamation League of B'nai B'rith, 1995.

Teitelbaum, Benjamin. *Lions of the North: Sounds of the New Nordic Radical Nationalism.* Pre-publication draft. Oxford: Oxford University Press, forthcoming.

Theroux, Louis. *Louis and the Nazis.* Directed by Stuart Cobb. BBC, 2003.

Wade, Michael. "Johnny Rebel and the Cajun Roots of Right-Wing Rock." *Popular Music and Society.* 30:4 (October 2007). 493–512.

Select Recordings Cited

Absurd. *Asgardsrei*. IG Farben Produktion/No Colours Records, 1999.

Angry Aryans. *Racially Motivated Violence*. Tri-State Terror Records, 1998.

———. "Nigger Loving Whore." *Old School Hate*. Resistance Records, 2001.

Böhse Onkelz. "Türken Raus." *Demotape*. Self-released, 1981.

———. *Der Nette Mann*. Rock-O-Rama Records, 1984.

Bound for Glory. "46 Years Hell." *Last Act of Defiance*. B.F.G. Productions, 1999.

Brigada Totenkopf. *Avanzando*. Rata-Ta-Ta-Tá Records, 2006.

Brutal Attack. *Steel Rolling On*. Rock-O-Rama, 1990.

———. "Always Near." *White Pride, White Passion*. Nordland Records, 1998.

Burzum. *Burzum*. Deathlike Silence Productions, 1992.

———. *Aske*. Deathlike Silence Productions, 1993.

———. *Filosofem*. Misanthropy Records/Cymophane Productions, 1996.

Celtic Warrior. "White Reich." *Live! French-British-Italian-Friendship*. ISD Records, 1995.

———. *The Legend Lives On*. Independent Voice Records, 1997.

———. *Invader*. Pühses Liste, 1998.

Code of Violence. *Purge*. Hate Records, 1998.

Cotzbrocken. *Jedem das Seine* . . . Rock-O-Rama Records, 1990 [1981].

D.I.V. "Mein Kampf." *Mein Kampf*. Moroz Records, 1992.

———. "Rap Monkey." *Ночь Длинных Ножей*. JetNoise Records, 1995.

Donaldson, Ian Stuart. *No Turning Back*. Rock-O-Rama Records, 1989.

———. *Slay the Beast*. Rock-O-Rama Records, 1990.

———. *Patriot*. Rock-O-Rama Records, 1991.

Dub Buk. *Иду На Вы!* Eastside Records, 2002.

———. *Місяць Помсти*. Eastside Records, 2003 [1999].

Genocide Lolita. "Holocaust Erotica." *Fuck Equality*. Open Wound, 2005.

———. "Gulag Mentality." *Targets of Opportunity*. White Power Electronics/Third Position Recordings, 2007.

———. "I Want to Kill the President." *Targets of Opportunity*. White Power Electronics/ Third Position Recordings, 2007.

Gestapo SS. *Vinlandic Stormtroopers*. Clawhammer Records, 2002.

Gigi und die Braunen Stadtmusikanten. "Döner-Killer." *Adolf Hitler Lebt!* PC Records, 2010.

———. "Geschwür am After." *Adolf Hitler Lebt!* PC Records, 2010.

Graveland. *In the Glare of Burning Churches.* Witching Hour Productions, 1993.

Griffin. *Thunderclap.* Panzerfaust Records, 2002.

Huetramannaland. *Land of the White Gods.* Production information unavailable.

Ian Stuart and Rough Justice. *Justice for the Cottbus Six.* Rock-O-Rama Records, 1992.

Ian Stuart & Stigger. *Patriotic Ballads.* Rock-O-Rama Records, 1991.

———. *Patriotic Ballads II—Our Time Will Come.* Rock-O-Rama Records, 1992.

Kill Baby, Kill! *A Prophet Returns.* Halal Records, 2009.

The Klansmen. *Rebel with a Cause.* Klan Records, 1989.

———. *Rock 'n' Roll Patriots.* Rock-O-Rama Records, 1989.

———. *Fetch the Rope.* Klan Records, 1991.

Kolovrat. "Арийский Реванш." *Национальная Революция.* Kolovrat NS, 1998.

———. "88 RAC'n'Roll Band." *Кровь Патриотов.* Kolovrat NS, 1999.

———. "Косовский Фронт." *Рок Кованых Сапог.* Kolovrat NS, 2000.

———. "Наш Символ—Свастика." *Пробивая Молотом Дорогу к Победе.* Kolovrat NS, 2003.

Korroziya Metalla. *1.966.* Moroz Records, 1995.

———. "Бей Чертей." *Он Не Любил Учителей.* Eyepiece, 1999.

Kraftschlag. "Festung Europa." *Festung Europa.* Funny Sounds Records, 1997.

Landser. "Polacken Tango." *Rock gegen Oben.* Rebell Records, 1997.

———. "88 Rock'n'Roll Band." *Das Kleine Album.* Reich Records, 2000.

Legion of St. George. "White Preservation Society." *Shadows of the Empire.* Movement Records, 1998.

———. *In Defence of the Realm.* Movement Records, 1999.

Mayhem. *Dawn of the Black Hearts.* Live bootleg album. Warmaster Records, 1995.

No Remorse. *Barbecue in Rostock.* ISD Records, 1996.

———. *Oi! Monkey.* ISD Records, 2005.

Noie Werte. *Kraft für Deutschland.* Rebelles Européens, 1991.

Nokturnal Mortum. *Weltanschauung.* Self-released demo, 2003.

Nordic Thunder. *Final Stand.* Tri-State Terror Records, 1994.

Owens, Eric. *Folk the System!* Phoenix, 1994.

———. *Res Gestae.* Nordland Records, 1998.

Prussian Blue. *Fragment of the Future.* Resistance Records, 2004.

———. *The Path We Chose.* Self-released, 2005.

RaHoWa. *Declaration of War.* Resistance Records, 1992.

———. *Cult of the Holy War.* Resistance Records, 1995.

Rebel, Johnny. *Lookin' for a Handout/Kajun Klu Klux Klan.* Reb Rebel Records, 1966.

———. *Nigger Hatin' Me/Who Likes a Nigger.* Reb Rebel Records, 1966.

———. *Nigger, Nigger/Move Them Niggers North.* Reb Rebel Records, 1968.

———. *For Segregationists Only.* Reb Rebel Records, 1971.

———. "Fuck You, Osama Bin Laden! (Infidel Anthem)." Aggwood, 2002.

———. *It's the Attitude, Stupid!* Try It Man, 2006.

Rockanoi! "Camarada Rudolph Hess." Production information unavailable.

———. "One in a Million." Production information unavailable.

———. "Someone Like You Will Never Be Forgotten." Production information unavailable.

Saga. *My Tribute to Skrewdriver, Volume 1.* Midgård Records, 2000.

———. *My Tribute to Skrewdriver, Volume 2.* Midgård Records, 2000.

———. *My Tribute to Skrewdriver, Volume 3.* Midgård Records, 2002.

———. *On My Own.* Midgård Records, 2007.

———. "Goodbye David Lane." *On My Own.* Midgård Records, 2007.

———. *Weapons of Choice.* Midgård Records, 2014.

Skrewdriver. *All Skrewed Up.* Chiswick Records, 1977.

———. *White Power / Smash the IRA / Shove the Dove.* Single. White Noise Records, 1983.

———. "Europe Awake." *Hail the New Dawn.* Rock-O-Rama Records, 1984.

———. "Free My Land." *Hail the New Dawn.* Rock-O-Rama Records, 1984.

———. *Hail the New Dawn.* Rock-O-Rama Records, 1984.

———. *Blood & Honour.* Rock-O-Rama Records, 1985.

———. *White Rider.* Rock-O-Rama Records, 1987.

———. *After the Fire.* Rock-O-Rama Records, 1988.

———. *Warlord.* Rock-O-Rama Records, 1989.

———. *The Strong Survive.* Rock-O-Rama Records, 1990.

———. *Live and Kicking.* Rock-o-Rama Records, 1991.

———. *Freedom What Freedom.* Rock-O-Rama Records, 1992.

———. *Hail Victory.* ISD Records, 1994.

———. *Live at Waterloo.* ISD Records / White Terror Records, 1995.

Staatsfeind. "60 Sekunden für Ian Stuart." *Widersand.* Pühses Liste, 1997.

Stahlgewitter. *Das Eiserne Gebet.* Self-released, 1996.

Ultima Thule. *Hurra för Nordens Länder.* EP. Rock-O-Rama Records, 1990.

———. *Havets Vargar.* EP. Rebelles Européens, 1991.

———. *Live at Kuggnäs 2012.* Ultima Thule Records, 2012.

———. *30-Åriga Kriget.* Ultima Thule Records, 2012.

Vaginal Jesus. *Affirmative Apartheid.* Tri-State Terror Records, 2000.

Various Artists. *Strength Thru Oi!* Decca Records, 1981.

———. *A Tribute to Ian Stuart and the Glory of Skrewdriver: The Flame that Never Dies.* Resistance Records, 1996.

———. *Anpassung ist Feigheit: Lieder aus dem Untergrund.* Blood & Honour Deutschland, 2004.

———. *Project Schoolyard USA.* Panzerfaust Records, 2004.

———. *Tribute to Skrewdriver, Volume 1.* MolokoPlus Versand, 2004.

———. *Tribute to Skrewdriver, Volume 2.* MolokoPlus Versand, 2005.

Violent Storm. *Celtic Warrior.* ISD Records, 1995.

Volkolak. *Слава Яриле.* Othal Productions, 2004.

White Diamond. *The Reaper.* Rock-O-Rama Records, 1991.

———. *The Power & the Glory.* Glory Discs, 1992.

Index

Rock Against Communism (RAC), 19, 25,
40, 50, 55, 83–84, 135
Rock Against Racism, 19
Rockanoi!, 133
Rock Identitaire Français, 67
Rock mot Kommunismen, 51
Rock Nord, 43
Rock'n'Roll Rebels, 99
Rock-O-Rama Records, 21–22, 34–35,
42–43, 51, 113, 140
Rockwell, George Lincoln, 109
Roma and Sinti, hostility towards, 64, 78,
91, 97
Rommel Skins, 73
Romper Stomper, 141–142
Rupe Tarpea Produzioni, 74
Russia: and colonialism, 9, 88, 127; con-
flict with Ukraine, 80, 87–89, 92, 98; in
WWII, 78–80; racism in, 1, 9, 78–83,
87, 91–92, 97, 103, 115, 130, 144; Soviet
era, 77–81, 83, 86–88, 92–93, 97–98;
white-power music in, 7, 70, 77–78,
83–87, 89–92, 94–95, 97, 101–102,
122, 141
Russian National Socialist Party, 80
Russkoye Natsional'noye Edinstvo, 83

Saccara (band), 36, 48
Saga (musician), 28, 54–55, 121, 146
Salut, 96
Sangre Joven, 70
São Paulo Reich, 133
Sargent, Paul "Charlie," 24, 29
Schilf, Marcel, 29, 43
Schutzstaffel (band), 134
Schwarze Front, 66
Scythian Services, 140
Sedition (band), 116
Selbstmord, 96
Septembre Noir, 66
Seraw, Mulageta, 112
Serrano, Miguel, 128–130, 133–134
settler colonialism. *See* colonialism
Sham '69, 17
Shit-Town Streetbulls (S.T.S.), 85
Shturm, 84–85
Sieg '88, 133
Skin Army, 73
skinhead movement: anti-racism and

non-racism in, 15–18; first-wave, 13, 15–17;
in Australia, 141–142; in France, 65–67;
in Germany, 36–40, 42; in Greece, 99; in
Italy, 73–74; in Latin America, 129–133;
in Poland, 94–96; in Russia, 81, 84, 92,
141; in Spain, 70–71; in the United States
and Canada, 111–112, 116–117; normaliza-
tion, 38, 54; second-wave, 13, 15–21, 31–32,
37–38, 53, 76, 147; violence, 17–18, 24,
30, 32
Skinhouse Hellas, 100
Skinkorps, 65
Skrewdriver: influence, 4, 10, 13, 28, 31, 36,
46, 94, 114, 130–131, 146, 150; music,
14–15, 18–23, 25, 44, 51, 112, 118, 140,
146–147; tributes to, 27–28, 54
Skullhead, 20–21, 23
Skull Records, 43
Sleep Chamber, 123
Sleipnir, 46, 100
Smith, Gary, 29
Snix, 65
Sociedad Violenta, 135
Sokyra Peruna, 10, 87, 89
Solidarność movement, 93
Southall riot (Hambrough Tavern), 18–21
Southern Warriors, 133–134
Southrise, 99
Soviet Union. *See* Russia
Spain: and colonialism, 127; racism in, 50,
68–70; white-power music in, 23, 35,
70–72, 75, 131
Spreegeschwader, 44
Springstoifel, 36
Squadron, 10, 20, 29–30
Staatsfeind, 26
Stahlgewitter, 37, 44, 48
Stahlhelm Records, 119
Stedeford, Scott, 23, 123–124
Steelcap, 116
Steelcapped Strength, 52
Stonehammer, 117
Störkraft, 39–40, 42–43
Storm (band), 52
Storm (magazine), 50
Stormfront (internet forum), 4, 10, 24, 28,
39, 42, 44, 54, 57–58, 61, 66, 68, 72, 85,
88–91, 94, 100–102, 109, 111–112, 114, 116,
118–119, 121–122, 124, 134–135, 140–142

About the Author

KIRSTEN DYCK earned an honours BFA in music (2005) and an MA in ethnomusicology (2008) from York University in Toronto, Canada, followed by a PhD in American Studies (2012) from Washington State University in Pullman, Washington. She has received an Auschwitz Jewish Center Fellowship (2011), a Fulbright Study/Research Grant to Germany (2011–2012), and a US Holocaust Memorial Museum Visiting Research Fellowship (2014). She teaches for the Department of History and the Department of Writing, Rhetoric, & Technical Communication at James Madison University in Harrisonburg, Virginia, as well as for James Madison University's International Study Center.

Printed in the United States
By Bookmasters